Ferenczi on Freud's Couch

This fascinating book assesses Sándor Ferenczi's role in the history of psychoanalysis, examining his personal analysis with Freud, the father of the discipline.

The book delves into archival material to shed light on issues around transference between Freud and Ferenczi, as well as Ferenczi's own development as "the first analyst." It offers a unique deciphering of the transmission of psychoanalysis, distinguishing between self-analysis, personal analysis and training analysis, including a discussion on the duration and end of treatment, subjects rarely discussed in contemporary circles.

This book is an important read for practising clinicians and scholars alike.

Yves Lugrin is a practising psychoanalyst in Paris, France. He is an Associate Member of the *Société de psychanalyse freudienne* (SPF). His research interests include the treatment of psychoses, as well as the relation of psychoanalysis to literature and writing. His interest in Freudian correspondence has led him to question the place held by Sándor Ferenczi and his work in the history of psychoanalysis.

Ferenczi on Freud's Couch

A Finished Analysis?

Yves Lugrin

Translated by Agnès Jacob

Routledge
Taylor & Francis Group

LONDON AND NEW YORK

First published 2021
by Routledge
2 Park Square, Milton Park, Abingdon, Oxon OX14 4RN

and by Routledge
52 Vanderbilt Avenue, New York, NY 10017

Routledge is an imprint of the Taylor & Francis Group, an informa business

Published in French by CampagnePremière 2017

© 2021 Yves Lugrin

Translated by Agnès Jacob

The right of Yves Lugrin to be identified as author of this work has been asserted by him in accordance with sections 77 and 78 of the Copyright, Designs and Patents Act 1988.

British Library Cataloguing-in-Publication Data
A catalogue record for this book is available from the British Library

Library of Congress Cataloging-in-Publication Data
Names: Lugrin, Yves, author.
Title: Ferenczi on Freud's couch : a finished analysis? / Lugrin, Yves.
Description: Abingdon, Oxon ; New York, NY : Routledge, 2021. |
    Includes bibliographical references and index.
Identifiers: LCCN 2020052917 (print) | LCCN 2020052918 (ebook) |
    ISBN 9780367444990 (pbk) | ISBN 9780367722531 (hbk) |
    ISBN 9781003154044 (ebk)
Subjects: LCSH: Ferenczi, Sándor, 1873–1933. | Freud, Sigmund,
    1856–1939. | Psychoanalysts. | Psychoanalysis.
Classification: LCC BF109.F47 L4234 2021 (print) | LCC BF109.F47
    (ebook) | DDC 150.19/52—dc23
LC record available at https://lccn.loc.gov/2020052917
LC ebook record available at https://lccn.loc.gov/2020052918

ISBN: 978-0-367-72253-1 (hbk)
ISBN: 978-0-367-44499-0 (pbk)
ISBN: 978-1-003-15404-4 (ebk)

Typeset in Times New Roman
by Apex CoVantage, LLC

Contents

Preface

An unprecedented analytic adventure

> The best analyst is a cured patient. Otherwise the student must be made ill, then cured and made aware.
>
> S. Ferenczi, *The Clinical Diary*, June 3, 1932 entry, under the heading: "No special didactic analysis."

The friendship and collaboration that started in 1908 and developed over a quarter of a century between Sigmund Freud (1856–1939), the father of psychoanalysis, and Sándor Ferenczi (1873–1933), his "paladin and secret grand vizier," have aroused the interest of many analysts in France and elsewhere for a number of decades. However, it seems that the numerous and diverse works dedicated to the life and writings of Ferenczi have said little about the important personal experience of his analysis with Freud. Indeed, in the autumn of 1914, and then in early summer and again the fall of 1916, Ferenczi went to Vienna to have three segments of analysis, each lasting two or three weeks, with two or three sessions conducted each day. Shortly after the last segment, Freud put an end to any prospect of continuing this analysis, which he considered "finished," although not "terminated." Ferenczi was prevented from making decisions that should have been his; Freud was clearly eager to transform his analysand into what he was before – an associate fighting for their common cause.

These three segments of analysis are part of a therapeutic process that started with a request for analysis made by Ferenczi on December 26, 1912, and ended, according to him, in May 1922. Indeed, in 1923 Freud praised him as the most accomplished of his pupils, as an analyst who had become, thanks to his personal analysis and its consequences, "a master and teacher of psychoanalysis." Extending over a period of about ten years, this experience of undergoing analysis constituted, for Ferenczi, a stage in an even longer trajectory, since it was preceded by five years of active participation in the newly constituted Freudian circle (1908–1913), and followed by a period of ten years (1923–1933) during which he wrote his most original and subversive texts.

Why is it that Freud never recounted the story of this analysis we consider unprecedented, although he remained haunted by it? Why is it that, four years after Ferenczi's death, when he referred to it, it was tersely and with justified unease? Indeed, in 1937 he made this analysis the subject of his article "Analysis Terminable and Interminable," without mentioning the name of his eminent analysand:

> A certain man, who had himself been a most successful practitioner of analysis, came to the conclusion that his relations with men as well as with women – the men who were his rivals and the woman whom he loved – were not free from neurotic inhibitions, and he therefore had himself analysed and by an analyst whom he believed to be more expert than himself.

In 1937, Freud still considered this analysis to have been a success: "This critical exploration of his own personality was entirely successful. He married the woman whom he loved and became the friend and teacher of the men whom he had regarded as rivals."

But, Freud goes on to say, after a time the success of the analysis proved not to be lasting. The patient seems to have relapsed and to have experienced, once again, the torments that had driven him to ask, as it was very unusual to do at the time, for in-depth personal analysis. This is Freud's major argument in his attempt to prove that even a very successful analysis can never be said to be terminated, because long-term sustainability of these good results cannot be guaranteed. This means that someone who has become a recognised analyst can, alas, never be certain of remaining one. In Ferenczi's case, Freud admits, the friendship between the analysand and his former analyst lasted several years following the analysis, before becoming troubled; it deteriorated, according to Freud, "for no demonstrable external reason," given that the analysand blamed his analyst "for having neglected to complete the analysis" by not taking into account negative transference. Ferenczi's detractors in Freud's inner circle even tried to convince him that these belated reproaches were signs of mental illness.

However, in the second part of his text Freud calls upon Ferenczi in person, and has a posthumous conversation with him. Freud knows better than anyone that Ferenczi was the first and only one to have attempted to formulate a doctrine applying to becoming and remaining an analyst, to be evaluated in the light of an in-depth personal analysis of the whole personality. Contrary to Freud, and even in opposition to him, Ferenczi was convinced that personal analysis leads to permanent gains and a clear termination of the analysis. This termination could be achieved thanks to re-establishing in the therapy and through transference a pre-traumatic relationship. According to Ferenczi, the traumatolytic function of analysis is equivalent to healing, and he considers this function to be compatible with Freud's objective of accepting castration.

By effecting this split of the figure of Ferenczi into his analysand and the brilliant analyst Freud continues to see in him, the latter avoids looking at the possible relation between Ferenczi's ultimate positions on the end of analysis, and his own analysis with its lasting transferential residues.

The evolution and nature of the disagreements between Ferenczi and Freud concerning this major question of the end of analysis of a future analyst are well known. Therefore, our focus will be the reconstruction of the missing element in the story, that which relates to what this unusual analysis was, or might have been like, since the analysand "had himself been a most successful practitioner of analysis," even before undergoing analysis. And after the experience of transference and the couch, what changes were produced in the experienced analyst Ferenczi already was?

For instance, what is to be made of Freud's allegations? Why does he remain silent about the crucial and most painful symptom that led Ferenczi to the couch? Freud must have known that aside from the difficulties Ferenczi experienced in his romantic and passionate relations with women, and his conflicts with colleagues, his close association with Freud himself made him suffer as much, if not more, given their master-pupil relationship in which Ferenczi could not find the space of "reciprocity" he so ardently desired.

Was the analysis, in fact, "entirely successful," as Freud asserted? What did Ferenczi himself think? Once the analysis was over, did his relation to his former analyst really remain "unclouded"? In the early 1930s, when trouble arose between them, was it really "for no external reason"? And what are we to think of Freud's assertion that "every happy relation between analyst and analysand, during and after analysis, was not to be regarded as transference"?

Because neither Ferenczi nor Freud recorded an explicit account of this analysis, we must rely on the many references and allusions to it in their extensive *Correspondence*,[1] and in Ferenczi's work. Although our elaboration remains fictional, what we can deduce about the context, the risks and the unfolding of this long and exceptional therapy invites us to broaden our perspective beyond Freud's contentions.

We believe that Ferenczi's experience with personal analysis, between the end of 1912 and May 1922, was a decisive event in his long involvement with psychoanalysis, constituting a clear pivotal point. During the analysis, his friendship with Freud was caught up in the transference, and afterwards was no longer what it had been; the relation of work and friendship left between them was neither the recent transferential one, nor the previous friendship. In 1922, Ferenczi was happy with the benefits he drew from his analysis, but also saw its limits and failings, for which he did not blame his analyst explicitly. He knew that the stumbling blocks encountered in his analysis constituted a field of enquiry that he intended to make the focus of his research. These stumbling blocks would become an opening. Ferenczi came away from his analysis with mixed feelings about its results, uncertain about his role in his collaboration with Freud, but with a wealth of crucial questions he was eager to explore. Thus, in the early 1920s, Ferenczi did not importune Freud with any recriminations.

It was only in the 1930s that he started to reproach Freud severely. When, in 1937, Freud said that these belated grievances were made "for no demonstrable external reason," he had forgotten the difficulties Ferenczi encountered between

1924 and 1930 in his attempts to be heard and to demonstrate the value of his innovative work. His subversive views concerning the analyst's activity in his practice, the end of analysis and the analyst's training, as well as his support of lay analysis, antagonised some of his colleagues and caused painful disappointments. In 1937, Freud seems to have forgotten how much Ferenczi suffered, after the analysis and quite alone, as a result of his desperate desire to maintain a radical analytic standard that would make no concessions to the requirements of an institutionalised organisation of the analytic movement. Under cover of his complaint about the insufficient consideration given to the covert presence of negative transference in the analysis, was Ferenczi not submitting a more serious grievance: his conclusion that Freud refused to acknowledge the things that Ferenczi was desperately trying to convey after his analysis, through his research?

In 1932, Freud admitted to a third party that he did not understand "Confusion of the Tongues between the Adults and the Child," the paper Ferenczi intended to present at the Wiesbaden Congress. He did not refuse his consent to the presentation of the paper, but asked Ferenczi to postpone it. He felt that Ferenczi needed more time, just as he himself needed to take time when ideas different than his own left him momentarily speechless. When Ferenczi died in the spring of 1933, the two men had not reconciled.

In 1937, Freud was still haunted by the fact that Ferenczi had blamed him, in the early 1930s, for not allowing him to complete his analysis. Wounded by this reproach, Freud's conclusion was not that the treatment failed, but simply that the beneficial effects of a past analysis become unreliable with the passing of time. This conclusion led him to make the sensible suggestion that analysts should have a segment of personal analysis every five years.

Still, based on Ferenczi's analytic path, of which his personal analysis was an inherent part, might it not be possible to arrive at a conclusion vastly different from Freud's? Above all, could the examination of this analysis with Freud make it possible to propose a different interpretation of the transferential complaint that resurfaced for Ferenczi about ten years after the analysis ended, and for Freud four years after the death of the one he called his "bitter pill"?

Will our research lead us, as we suspect, to the paradoxical conclusion that a return to previous states is not the sign of a failed analysis, of a lack of skill on Freud's part, or of mental illness in Ferenczi, but rather a sign of the brilliant success of an analysis to be considered exceptional in many respects.

The constraining conditions in which this analysis had to be conducted made it unprecedented. It was, in fact, for Ferenczi, the equivalent of Freud's self-analysis. Without question, it provided a wealth of learning the two men could not have anticipated at the time. Each of them approached the project with a different attitude: Freud cautiously and even reticently, and Ferenczi with enthusiasm. One placed great faith in the space of reciprocity created by speaking; the other, more cautious, refused to have any certainties. Nevertheless, they both agreed, courageously, to face the trials they would encounter in this demanding analysis. During the *in vivo* experience of this unprecedented analytic adventure, the two men were not aware that the different time segments dividing up the story created a more orderly temporality than might have appeared based solely on the disturbances the experiment provoked.

Even if our reconstruction remains fictional in nature, the perspective we are venturing to bring to Ferenczi's personal analysis by Freud and its consequences for each man's relation to psychoanalysis sheds light on the temporality structuring the transmissibility of the unconscious, and making it possible to become and to stay a psychoanalyst. In our opinion, it is this that constitutes the richness of the unique analytic association between Ferenczi and Freud. Thanks to and despite the stumbling blocks in the analysis of the former by the latter, and thanks to and despite the fact that they disagreed as to whether an analysis could ever be completed, in his collaboration with Freud, in 1928, Ferenczi succeeded in making in-depth personal analysis of the future analyst the second fundamental rule of psychoanalysis. By doing this, he elevated the question of the analyst's training to the appropriate level – that of a debate on doctrine. In the early 1950s, Michael Balint and then Jacques Lacan would remember his teaching.

Note

1 Most of the quotes in this book are taken from *The Correspondence of Sigmund Freud and Sándor Ferenczi: 1908–1933*, Falzeder, E. and Brabant, E. (Eds.), Harvard University Press, 1993–2000.

Chapter I

Before the actual request for analysis (1908–1912)

Teaching, love and trembling (1908–1909)

In 1909, at the end of the summer, Freud and Jung sail for New York; they have been invited by James J. Putnam to lecture at Clark University in Worcester. Freud has asked Ferenczi to join them. Each morning, while the two of them stroll in the countryside, Freud prepares the lecture he will give that afternoon. The two men grow closer. Freud's letter dated October 6, 1909, opens for the first time with "Dear friend," instead of "Dear Doctor" or "Esteemed colleague." Freud did not bestow such marks of friendship easily. On October 22, Freud confides to Ferenczi, for whom clinical work is a veritable passion, that he doesn't feel the same way: "The patients are disgusting and are giving me an opportunity for new studies on technique." On October 30, in response to Freud's request that Ferenczi promote the teaching of psychoanalysis, Ferenczi's letter expresses satisfaction with what has been accomplished over the past 20 months. "Do not be frightened by my talkativeness; I only want to remain true to the tradition of reporting on the progress of my apostolic mission on the basis of fresh impressions." And he reports on his performance: "So, today was the lecture about 'Everyday Life.' I was happy that I could speak before approximately three hundred young and enthusiastic medical students, who listened to my (or, that is to say, your) words with bated breath." The two men have grown so close that when Ferenczi gives lectures on psychoanalysis, it might as well be Freud speaking. Well-versed in self-analysis, Ferenczi adds a few words in parentheses on a matter that he senses may become problematic between them: "(N.B.: I have already determined that it has to do with the infantile wish to be praised by the father.)"

Ferenczi perfectly understands the effect of the transference which develops in a relation of shared work and a common cause, when there is also friendship involved, and even a father/son relation: Freud often places his colleague (17 years his junior) in the generation of his children. He can envisage Ferenczi marrying his daughter, and invites him to hike in the mountains with his sons. In the correspondence, Ferenczi relies increasingly on their transferential relation to discuss his personal life – that of a 37-year-old bachelor. Freud becomes the one from whom he seeks support for, and to whom he addresses, his self-analysis; this analysis becomes part of the content of the letters, along with the exchange of ideas, and information about the progress of the movement. Moreover, as early as the summer of 1908, Freud points out to the man he now regards as a potential successor that he is at a disadvantage for someone who will soon have to bear responsibility for the emerging psychoanalytic movement, because at 37 he is still unmarried and has no children – nor would he have any later – while at the same age Freud was a married man and the father of five children. This was another considerable difference between the psychic structure of the two men. Shortly after their trip to America, as they grew closer, Ferenczi was very willing to discuss this problem. In fact, at first, it was unclear which of the two men considered it more troublesome. Their relationship would soon become more complicated and take another direction which we see as having led to the request for analysis.

Chercher la femme (winter 1910)

On October 26 and 30, 1909, Ferenczi first mentions the existence of a woman with whom he is not yet living (she would become his wife ten years later). On October 16, he first refers to her in a letter, under an eloquent alias:

> My personal well being (psychic) was good right up to the last few day as long as it was possible to keep frequent company with Frau Isolde (I will call her that, which was also her name in one of my dreams).

The drama involved in their love story was, however, more prosaic than the grandiose tragedy of Tristan and Iseult: "The difficult and painful operation of producing complete candor in me and in my relationship with her is proceeding rapidly." In his own past, Freud had to rely on self-analysis at points of crisis in his troubled relations with Fliess, and in his ambivalent relation to his father, Jakob Freud, an old man who had been married three times and was by then on the threshold of death. But Ferenczi was going to request analysis when the unclear aspects of his relationship with women, his sexual relationship with them, brutally intruded into his analytic practice. Now, in the autumn of 1909, he was not yet ready to take this step. Both Ferenczi and his partner looked to psychoanalysis to provide answers that would resolve the predicament of their relationship. Ferenczi thought that Frau Isolde could find there the strength "to allow the [...] resistances to be overcome and the bitterness of the unvarnished truth to be accepted [...]" As for familiarity with, and overindulgence in, self-analysis: "The matter, of course, makes *much* more rapid progress in me; I dream a great deal, analyze my dreams, and find *lots* of infantilisms." He tells Freud that after a recent discussion with Frau Isolde, he was able to identify the tormenting difficulty in their relation:

> I must say that the confession that I made to her, the superiority with which, after some reluctance, she correctly grasped the situation, and the truth which is possible between us makes it seem perhaps less possible for me to tie

myself to another woman *in the long run*, even though I admitted to her and to myself having sexual desires toward other women and even reproached her for her age.

He loves this married woman, Mrs Palos, but desires her daughter. This woman, the mother of two young girls, is seven years older than Ferenczi, making the prospect of parenthood unlikely. This deeply personal difficulty, which apparently had not troubled Ferenczi until then, takes on a new dimension given his entanglement with psychoanalysis and with Freud: "Evidently I have *too much* in her: lover, friend, mother, and, in scientific matters, a pupil, i.e., the child – in addition, an extremely intelligent, enthusiastic pupil, who completely grasps the extent of the new knowledge."

Towards the end of the year, Frau Isolde recovers her own humble identity: her name is Gizella. On December 3, Freud writes that he has sent to Budapest a copy of *Everyday Life*, "for Frau Gizella," as promised. In his letter to Freud dated December 7, there is mention of the fact that "Frau G." sends Freud "the enclosed lines." Soon Freud and Frau G. were to exchange entire, important letters, and Freud learned to appreciate Gizella's qualities. In the letter dated December 7, Ferenczi makes reference to his personal feelings: "What has happened in me and with me otherwise you will find in the enclosed 'diary pages.' I have made an effort to be completely honest despite the fact that I know that you will read it." The editor of the Freud/Ferenczi correspondence observes, in a footnote, that this "enclosed" document was never found. Still, we learn that at the end of 1909 Ferenczi was already keeping a diary. Was he looking for another outlet for his feelings, so as not to overburden Freud in his letters? The latter skilfully and cautiously avoids entering into any further discussion of Ferenczi's complicated love life. Moreover, after the start of 1910 Freud makes no more mention of the confidences Ferenczi made about his tormented personal life, so as to keep him focused on the political circumstances pertaining to psychoanalysis. Ferenczi accepts being the fighting man Freud needs in the social sphere, but does not give up hope for an open and close personal relationship with Freud, in which the most private matters could be discussed.

Trust and combat (1910–1912)

On January 1, 1910, at the end of a letter to Ferenczi, Freud asks for his advice on the institutional processes to be put in place to establish a policy for psychoanalysis: "Incidentally, what do you think of a tighter organization with formal rules and a small fee? Do you consider that advantageous? I also wrote Jung a couple of words about this." The next day, Ferenczi's reply is preceded by the expression to his deep gratitude to Freud. He is emphatic: "[…] you [have] enhanced the lives and occupation of a very large number of people who were previously striving in vain for recognition." Inclined to be very enthusiastic, Ferenczi considers Freud's followers "the predecessors of all humanity, which, for the time being, is still stuck in infantile resistances," and he is convinced that Freud's work "will leave behind strong traces in world history." He insists on making one more thing clear: "I say all of this after appropriate correction, after removing everything that personal adherence, and especially my own father complex, could dictate to me. Without this correction this letter would have come out much more effusive." Ferenczi could not have known then that the passionate tone of his remarks bore a strange resemblance to that of Freud's own letters to his friend Wilhelm Fliess, written 15 years earlier, when he saw Fliess as a genius, "the new Kepler."

After this declaration of love and respect, Ferenczi goes on to answer Freud, speaking as a fighting man: "I find your suggestion (tighter organization) extremely useful. The acceptance of members, however, would be just as strictly managed as it is in the Vienna Society; that would be a way of keeping out undesirable elements." In February 1908 there had already been discussion about reshaping the functioning – admission of new members, external sites, modes of intervention – of the little group constituting the Wednesday Society, whose status was not clearly defined. Admission of new members was decided by a vote, and it was the custom that they give a presentation. The proposition to introduce stricter admission criteria was rejected. But the question of the institutionalisation of psychoanalysis, and of member selection, had been raised. This question was clearly at the forefront of Freud's concerns regarding an international organisation entrusted with ensuring the Freudian orientation of national and local associations bound to be created in the future.

In a long post-scriptum to his letter dated January 2, 1910, Ferenczi points out the extent to which the analytic and political spheres overlap. He specifies that in his own relations with his colleagues, his "tiresome brother complex is still playing tricks on [him]." He never hid his tendency to rivalry and jealousy, surfacing whenever Freud praised one or the other of his followers. Ferenczi adds: "[…] this affect is for me the measure of the work that I still have to do on myself," without specifying if he is referring to continuing his self-analysis, as we suspect, or to another sort of work – personal analysis – an idea taking hold in him more and more firmly. A week later, on January 10, it is Freud's turn to proffer praise: "Analyses and writings, as you now do them, are very significant events for one's own person, and the other – if he comes into it at all – has nothing to do but keep a respectful silence." Freud is impressed: "I can hardly admire perspicacity, for I know that it is made up of honesty and firm decision. Certainly you are right in every instance." We can imagine Ferenczi's emotion when he read these words and the explanations which followed.

Chercher la femme, once again

In this letter, and after having remained silent on the subject for over two months, Freud comes back to the romantic torment Ferenczi disclosed. Freud congratulates him not only for the relevance of the analysis of one of his own dreams – an analysis recently presented to Freud in person (the dream is not included in the correspondence) – but also, and above all, for his attitude: the decision to be completely honest with Gizella. Freud adopts a new standpoint; he no longer draws Ferenczi's attention to a problem that must be solved; instead, he becomes an active participant in the conjugal scenario beginning to unfold. At this point, he has not yet met Gizella, about whom he has an unfavourable opinion, as he would later admit. Thus, Freud approves of Ferenczi's perilous decision not to hide from this woman the doubts he harbours about his love for her: "As to what is real, I have to say that you were by and large undoubtedly correct with your disclosure to the beloved woman." Freud does not yet see a symptom in the fact that Ferenczi is torn between the woman he thinks he loves and all the other women he still desires. On the contrary, Freud seems to find justification for this ambivalence:

> It belongs to the ABC of our word view that the sexual life of a man can be something different from that of a woman, and it is only a sign of respect when one does not conceal this from a woman.

As he would later admit to Gizella herself, when he had come to know her well, he had perhaps believed, secretly, that Ferenczi would make a mistake by becoming tied to a married woman with two daughters, who was, moreover, seven years older than him. Freud then moderates his views: "Whether the requirement of absolute truthfulness does not sin against the postulate of expediency and against the intentions of love I would not like to respond to in the negative without qualification [...]" Having first praised Ferenczi for his honesty, Freud now takes a different course: "Truth is only the absolute goal of science, but love is a goal of life which is totally independent of science, and conflicts between both of these major powers are certainly quite conceivable." But he refuses the tyranny of truth: "I see no necessity for principled and regular subordination of one to the other." Freud knows or suspects that he is speaking to a man who has long been a slave to his belief in truth and in total revelation. Perhaps this is what impels him to remind his colleague of another character trait that makes their relation to psychoanalysis profoundly different, a trait that was to play an important role in the destiny of their collaboration: Freud does not have the therapeutic passion that animates Ferenczi, who never forgets his primary vocation as a doctor.

Far from possessing any *furor sanandi*, Freud finds patients "disgusting," as we have seen. So he confesses to Ferenczi: "This need to help is lacking in me, and I now see why, because I did not lose anyone whom I loved in my early years." Made intentionally or not, does this remark have interpretative value? Freud probably knows by now that, as the eighth child in a family of 12 children, Sándor was three when his little sister Vilma died before she was one. And Ferenczi has told him that he has long been haunted by the love he did not receive from an indifferent mother. But Freud does not have this double experience of trauma.

This first confession leads Freud to make another, more intimate than it appears, and again related to a troublesome need for truth associated with a passion for healing, of which he is wary when he sees it in Ferenczi: "I found this same personal motivation in Fliess. What is both strong and pathological in him comes from this." How might Ferenczi, a sensitive man, have reacted to this comparison between him and Fliess? He must certainly have been intrigued by this reference to Fliess' pathology, and by the fact that Freud was associating him with this man about whom he had talked to Ferenczi the previous summer, while they were in America. What effect did it have on Ferenczi, a doctor, whose father, also a doctor, died when the boy was 15, to hear Freud emphasise the origin of Fliess' medical vocation: "The conviction that his father, who died from erysipelas after many years of nasal suppuration, could have been saved made him into a doctor, indeed, even turned his attention to the nose." Why does Freud insist on drawing Ferenczi's attention to what a theory – potentially delirious in Fliess' case – may owe to some specific wound in someone's personal history? "The sudden death of his only sister two years later, on the second day of a pneumonia, for which he could blame doctors, instilled in him the fatalistic theory of predetermined dates of death – as a consolation." Then, Freud makes a remark that turns out to be more premonitory than he could have imagined: "This piece of analysis, unwanted by him, was the inner cause of our break, which he effected in such a pathological (paranoid) manner." Again, could Ferenczi have remained unaffected by these threatening words, proffered as a delayed response to his recent declaration of love, and to the analysis of a dream sent to Freud? Would he not have been perplexed, or even made anxious, by Freud's reference to a "piece of analysis" which resulted in the senseless ending of a passionate friendship?

Strictest secret!

Who is the Freud who wrote this surprising letter dated January 10, 1910? Is he the father of psychoanalysis, the experienced analyst, or simply a man struggling with his destiny? As an analyst, he guesses that Ferenczi has "a secret reason" for recounting this particular dream to him, a dream which, he says: "must also have a relation to me." He offers an initial interpretation: "It is easy for me to find the motive for equating me with your father." And he does not hesitate to disclose what he sees as a symptom in himself, namely the anticipation of his own death:

> On the trip I behaved like someone who is taking his leave, who wants to set his house in order. In camp [...] I had real appendix pains for the first time, and for at least a day I was quite despondent [...]

In the letter, Freud gives Ferenczi an Oedipal interpretation as massive as it is dismissive: "So, that provides a basis for the identification. Again, as then, the death of the father is the signal for a great inner cleansing for you, and for an effort to bind the mother to you." He even drives the point home by asking whether a certain reference in Ferenczi's letter "is a compliment for the year just past, or whether it is connected with my imminent demise [...]" Half in jest, Freud admits that his symptomatic fantasy is still at work: "Let us nevertheless firmly establish that I myself already decided quite a long time ago not to die until 1916 or 17. Of course, I don't exactly insist upon it." Although all this is asserted in a rather abrupt manner, Freud does not claim to be stating absolute truths, and his postulations remain playful. Still, he speaks with the authority of an analyst addressing a patient, albeit in the absence of any actual context of this kind. Unwittingly, Freud is reinforcing Ferenczi's propensity for a self-analysis whose results are then reported to him. But this ceases to be the case when, after a long preamble, Freud starts to speak like an analyst addressing another analyst, both of them caught up in the work of reflection which unites them when they dare to speak openly, despite their different sensibilities: "As compensation for this unseemly discussion I want to give you a little piece of theory, which came to me while I was reading your analysis."

In this climate of mutual understanding, Freud returns discreetly to the subjective position he blames Ferenczi for having, to his "requirement of absolute truthfulness," be it in their discussions or in Ferenczi's desire to heal and help those who suffer: "It seems to me that in influencing the sexual drives, we can bring about nothing more than exchanges, displacements, never renunciation, giving up, the resolution of a complex. (Strictest secret!)." Freud seems terrified to conclude that an analysis can only bring about rearrangements, and is therefore interminable. He knows that the enemies of psychoanalysis would immediately seize upon such a potentially scandalous admission and use it to their advantage, in view of harming the cause.

But the fact remains that as early as the start of 1910, and in light of his discussions with Ferenczi, Freud had the feeling that psychoanalysis does not resolve conflicts generated by the instinctual disturbances inherent in human life. The end of an analysis cannot be considered a definitive surpassing or overcoming of such disturbances. Some 30 years later, and four years after the death of his interlocutor, in *Analysis Terminable and Interminable*, Freud tried to clear up the "strictest secret" he glimpsed in 1910.

In his January 1910 letter, Freud was not stating a well-thought-out theory; rather, he was setting out a concept whose echoes are to be found in the shared fragments of self-analysis sent back and forth between Budapest and Vienna. This intuition of an impossible end to disturbances in every human being's libidinal life made itself clear not while Freud was reflecting on the case of a particular patient, but in connection with himself and Ferenczi, particularly the latter's fanatical passion for truth and his desire to heal, as well as his own preoccupation with the possibility of imminent death. Freud was haunted by the idea that he could die before he had officially designated a successor able to take forward his new science of psychoanalysis. Worse still, as the founder of this new science, he had to acknowledge the existence of a death wish directed against him by those he considered his most promising disciples: First Jung, his "Crown prince" and heir, and then Sándor Ferenczi. Here, the symptoms encountered are not those of the patient on the couch, but rather those that emerged in the small Freudian community faced with the necessary transmission of psychoanalysis.

Without developing further, for the moment, the richness of this reflection on the separating function of the object the analysand and may leave behind, on the analyst's couch, when the analysis is over, we can assert that here Freud does more than simply refer to the metamorphosis of neurosis into transference neurosis. He is, in fact, formulating this observation for the benefit of a young colleague in whom he already sees a loyal travelling companion. Does this mean that he has a vague feeling that collegiality between analysts necessarily involves a form of transference neurosis? Reference to the shed skin the analysand leaves behind at the end of his analysis enables Freud to provide logical support for his disagreement with Ferenczi's wish for transparency: "[The analysand] has shed his skin and leaves the stripped-off skin for the analyst; God forbid that he is now naked, skinless!"

Who is this cry of distress addressed to if not Ferenczi? Might not the sad fate of a man skinned alive be his own, as he was to admit in the *Clinical Diary*? When Freud speaks this way, is he influenced by the memory of the unfortunate end of his collaboration with Fliess, or does he have, without knowing it, an astute premonition about Ferenczi's future as an analyst?

Is it not the case that, in a manner of speaking, at the end of his journey Ferenczi found himself spent, stripped of his skin, left with no other choice than that between an impossible metamorphosis and death?

In 1910, while thinking about Ferenczi's passionate approach to psychoanalysis, Freud unexpectedly stumbled upon a potential difficulty related to the end of an analysis, a major problem he was to confront again in 1937. But from his earliest discussions with Ferenczi, he was sure of one thing: "Our therapeutic gain is a substitutive gain, similar to the one that Hans in Glück makes. The last piece doesn't fall into the fountain until death." Freud had already admitted that he saw no solution to the inescapable "effect of sexual drives." Now he reaffirms his conclusion by means of the Grimm Brothers fairy tale, and extends its scope: just as Hans in Luck sees the sun melt away the gold ingot, his royal reward for seven years of hard work in the service of his master, the patient who has come to the end of his lengthy efforts on the analyst's couch will not benefit from the treasure he imagined would be his. But Freud emphasises that it is essential for the remaining fragment of the object not to fall. Contrary to Hans who returns to his idle existence, the analysand must now make one last effort in order to transform this final loss of the object into an opportunity to conclude a new pact with life and with the call of the unknown, which he must answer fearlessly. Desire triumphs over hesitation. Clearly, the end of a personal analysis is difficult. But its beginning is not any easier, as Freud and Ferenczi discovered in their shared experience of it.

The nature of the thing

Between 1908 and 1911, Ferenczi acquired this first-hand knowledge he had sought from the start. To achieve this, he multiplied his contacts with Freud and the members of his circle by participating actively in the life of the emerging analytic movement. He wrote numerous articles which earned him respect and, in 1910, he was the one Freud entrusted with writing a proposal for the creation of an International Psychoanalytic Association. Ferenczi's text emphasised the usefulness of this institution for the advancement of the cause, but also drew attention to the pitfalls of group psychology. In the course of this period, Ferenczi perfected his knowledge of Freudian thought, and had the opportunity to discover how the analytic movement responded to the many trials and tribulations it had to face. Among other things, he discovered that the construction and transmission of this knowledge also created friction in the very midst of the community supporting psychoanalysis. Worse still – a bitter experience for Freud – this transmission created friction in the personal relations between Freud and the disciples he considered best suited to lead the movement. Was it not the case that in the early 1910s the man Freud had long considered a son, his "Crown prince," Jung, was distancing himself and embarking on a path of cruel dissidence to which the father of psychoanalysis had willingly remained blind? The deep chasm between the two men's analytic perspectives became undeniable in 1913, and led to a definite break early the following year.

As for Ferenczi, the most loyal of his followers, Freud slowly realised that tensions of a completely different nature were apt to disturb the rich collaboration they both valued. This became painfully obvious in September 1910, in the course of a trip to Sicily. They had both hoped to enjoy the beauty of the places they visited, as well as the pleasure of working together on a project on paranoia. But an incident was to leave deep scars on their future relationship, an incident each of them viewed in his own way. Freud blamed Ferenczi for letting himself be guided like a child, or like a woman, and for not helping to handle the practical aspects of the voyage. He was critical of Ferenczi's boundless admiration, which rendered the latter so dependent and passive, and which Freud did not want, failing to realise that he could not help arousing the admiration of those who came to him in search of knowledge and truth. Ferenczi had his own version of events, insisting on his great disappointment the very first evening, when they started to work together. He was expecting a stimulating dialogue between equals and instead, he was asked to take notes while Freud dictated his thoughts on paranoia. Hurt by this refusal of an exchange of ideas, which he saw as disregard for his own work and a threat of domination, Ferenczi simply refused. Freud put an end to their work session and, to Ferenczi's great disappointment, worked alone from then on. Afterwards, the two men often referred to this unfortunate incident that Ferenczi never forgot.

Thus, in the fall of 1910 Ferenczi had the worst encounter possible: that with a kind of obstacle to transmission. In the collision which, in an instant, shattered his bright hopes for shared analytic work, he had to abandon his ideal of mutuality in analytic research among those who, like Freud and himself, wanted to share in the development and transmission of psychoanalysis. But without the perspective of a harmonious exchange with Freud, Ferenczi found it difficult to formulate and develop the intuitions and hypotheses that presented themselves to him. He never stopped complaining about this growing unease, whose nature was unclear to him. For this reason, he undertook a rigorous self-analysis to explore his own role in the disagreement, but without ceasing to question the part Freud had played in it.

Freud allowed his actions to be questioned, without realising that his initial double reaction to Ferenczi brought him face-to-face with an enigma, unexpected in itself, and much more so because it arose not between himself and a difficult patient, but between himself and a remarkable man he personally valued and whose work delighted him. As a first step to reconciliation, he willingly admitted his own part in creating the Palermo incident:

> Why didn't I scold you and in so doing open the way to an understanding? [...] it was a weakness on my part, I am also not that [psychoanalytic] superman whom we have constructed, and I also haven't overcome the countertransference.

Ferenczi put this admission to good use. In his future work, the analyst's countertransference – or that of colleagues entrusted with transmission – was to become an essential theme leading to some of his most original work. Freud recognised his error, his failure to overcome the "countertransference"; he was left to face his ambiguous relation – a mixture of love and hate – to his own sons. After admitting that there was much more he could say about this, he made it clear that he would say no more:

> I no longer have any need for that full opening of my personality, but you have also understood it and correctly returned to its traumatic cause [...] This need has been extinguished in me since Fliess's case, with the overcoming of which you just saw me occupied.

By saying this, he recognised that Ferenczi demonstrated a certain analytic astuteness when he guessed that Freud had not overcome the trauma of the abrupt ending of his long friendship with Fliess. Moreover, Freud made another remark – on which we did not comment – when he asked Ferenczi: "Why did you thus make a point of it?" – referring to his own lack of need for full disclosure. In response to Ferenczi's insistence, Freud also wants to make a point. He makes it clear that he now understands the traumatic cause of what was tormenting him a short time before. "A piece of homosexual investment has been withdrawn and utilized for the enlargement of my own ego." And then, despite his earlier declaration that he was not a "psychoanalytic superman," he adds the famous phrase: "I have succeeded where the paranoiac fails." Hence his intention not to dwell on this question any longer. But he soon reopens the door he has just slammed shut.

Correctly supposing that Ferenczi would not be content with such a terse explanation, he returns to what he supposes – with reason – to be Ferenczi's wish: "It was plain to see but also easily recognizable as infantile that you presumed great secrets in me and were very curious about them." But Freud does not stop at this reference to Ferenczi's infantile sexual curiosity and his overestimation of Freud as a private person. He gives two reasons for stopping short of total disclosure. The first reason is simple: "Just as I shared with you *all* the scientific matters, I also concealed from you very little of a personal nature […]" Indeed, as his correspondence and his writing clearly show, Freud always shared "all" the knowledge he gained from his clinical practice and the theoretical research associated with it.

His second reason does not concern his legitimate refusal to disclose everything; rather, it has to do with an obstacle he encountered: "My dreams at the time were, as I indicated to you, entirely concerned with the Fliess matter, with which, owing to the nature of the thing, it was difficult to get you to sympathize." By admitting this, he implicitly admits that Ferenczi's need to make a point of it was not due solely to infantile influences; but he does not yet see in this obstacle a major analytic question. That task is left to Ferenczi.

After the 1910 Palermo incident, Ferenczi is faced with an enigma: total honesty, which he sees as the illustration of the expectation of truth inherent to analysis, seems to be impeded not only by a more or less justifiable refusal, but even more fundamentally by an obstacle related to "the nature" of the transferential phenomenon. As a result, Ferenczi undertakes to submit this "full opening of [the] personality" to a veritable analysis. But in these early years of his psychoanalytic trajectory, Ferenczi makes an even more edifying discovery. In 1911, he finds himself in a compromising personal position when he decides to analyse Elma, the daughter of his mistress Gizella. This new undertaking, associated with other events, was what led a distraught Ferenczi, a year later, to request personal analysis.

Elma or the impossible analysis (1911)

On July 14, 1911, Ferenczi informed Freud of his recent undertaking: "I decided to take her [Gizella's] daughter [Elma] into psychoanalytic treatment; the situation, you see, was becoming unbearable. For the moment, the thing is working, and the effect is favorable." He confirmed this on July 24: "Elma's treatment is going along normally for the time being. In the meantime, I will be able to report to you orally on her case." On October 18, Freud, who had so far refrained from commenting on this treatment, was informed of the suicide – distressing for Elma – of a young man in whom she was interested, among others: "The analysis of Frau G's daughter was already making very nice progress […] It is very questionable how the matter will go now." Badly, we would guess, and especially so because this date marks the beginning of what we will call "the Emma Jung affair."

On November 14, the situation has become much more complicated. Ferenczi describes once again the state of disarray in which he finds himself due to his desire for independence both from Freud and from Gizella, Elma's mother, whom Freud has come to hold in high esteem. Ferenczi observes that in this complicated context "an apparent detachment of libido from Frau Gizella was playing itself out in me. An occasion for this was offered by the treatment of her daughter, who is in treatment with me and in the stage of transference." In his own way, he is also in the same stage of transference where the betrayal of love is a threat: "I […] had fantasies about marrying Elma. [Recurrence of a similar condition in the spring.]"

In this transferential imbroglio without any *ad hoc* setting, Ferenczi has more and more trouble conducting Elma's analysis. On December 3 he admits that he has not been able "to maintain the cool detachment of the analyst" and fears that he has lost control of the situation: "Things are proceeding more rapidly than I imagined they would […] and I laid myself bare, which then led to a kind of closeness." Clear-headed, Ferenczi admits his mistake unequivocally, adding that this "closeness" was something "which I can no longer put forth as the benevolence of the physician or of the fatherly friend." Thus, Ferenczi is in the same situation as Jung was in the spring of 1909, with his patient Sabina Spielrein, only contrary to Jung, Ferenczi does not deny it or blame it on the amorous delusion of his patient. Rather, he tries to identify what drove him "inwardly" towards this deadlock involving his patient, as well as Gizella and Freud.

> From an analytic point of view I have to conceive of the matter in such a way as to conclude that Elma became especially dangerous to me at the moment when – after that young man's suicide – she badly needed someone to support her and to *help* her in her need.

Ferenczi admits that despite his efforts he could not restrain himself when he was helping his distressed patient: "I did that only too well, even though I held my tenderness in check with difficulty for the moment." But his attempt to limit the love suddenly awakened in the transference was fruitless: "But the path was cleared – and now, to all appearances, she has won my heart." Torn between his desire for Elma and his love for Gizella, Ferenczi asks Freud to help. The latter's answer, two days later, on December 5, is firm and clear: "First break off the treatment, come to Vienna for a few days […] don't decide anything yet." Ferenczi went to Vienna. Given the transferential events that arose in Ferenczi's practice, Freud finally abandoned his previous attitude of denial meant to reassure by minimising difficulties. He no longer asked Ferenczi to be self-reliant, as he had to be in his self-analysis. In this situation, Freud stopped interpreting and acted.

For the first time, Freud intervened decisively in this analysis Ferenczi was conducting and of which he had been kept informed regularly over the past six months. The situation involving Ferenczi, Elma and Freud became even more complicated when Gizella contacted Freud, who revealed to Ferenczi on December 17 that Frau G., understandably distressed, had asked him for an explanation.

Freud, Gizella, an edifying blunder

On December 17, 1911, Freud responds to the request of this woman he respects, disclosing his view of her companion's situation. After all, he has acquired an intimate psychological understanding of the man who so readily revealed himself to him. In this letter to Frau G., Freud draws a psychological profile of Ferenczi, emphasising the symptomatic nature of his relationships with women. Through this active intervention, he hopes to pacify an explosive situation, to prevent a possible rash decision on Ferenczi's part, and to keep him available as a valuable colleague. Freud also wants to support Gizella.

True to himself, and although not in favour of always revealing everything, Freud wants to be honest: "What I am writing you today will remain completely between us and is totally sincere, without any embellishment, as is commensurate only with my esteem for you." He admits that he has intervened in the situation. "Our friend has hurt me very much and has forced me, myself, to give advice […]" Surprisingly, Freud does not say "my friend" but "our friend," as if he and Gizella were allies. He goes on: "When, years ago, I first learned of the relationship that he had lodged himself in [a relationship with a married woman with two daughters], I made a face […]" At that time, Freud's reaction had been one of disapproval: "I made a face and made it very clear to him that I wished something else for him."

In the name of what ideal of the couple or the family did Freud manifest this attitude? Was he speaking as an experienced father, or as a man who knows the difference between the role of wife and mother, and that of mistress? Once he confided this, Freud reassured Gizella: as soon as he met her, he knew that she was the perfect woman for a man like Ferenczi.

He then advances a first hypothesis as to the pressing desire that was making Ferenczi lose his good sense: "I understand the tragedy of aging; it is, after all, mine as well." He is 65, and Ferenczi 38. And he reveals a peculiar personal belief: "The hard truth is that love is only for youth and [is something] that one must renounce." He then goes on to give this thought a unique turn: "[…] as a woman, one must be prepared to see one's sacrifices repaid with ingratitude […] a natural fate, as in the story of Oedipus."

Freud then advances a second hypothesis, presented in two parts. "In addition [to the tragedy of ageing], it is the case with *him* that his homosexuality imperiously demands a child." What is he suggesting? Is homosexuality what he glimpses behind Ferenczi's infantile or even feminine dependency on him, as he saw it in Palermo? And why would this latent homosexuality demand a child? To hide behind the appearance of paternity? To love in the child to come the child he would have liked to be for his mother? Freud answers these questions indirectly when, in the same sentence, he associates homosexuality with hate of the mother or the maternal: "[…] his homosexuality imperiously demands a child and […] he carries within him revenge against his mother from the strongest impressions of childhood." Clearly, it is because Ferenczi had already revealed to him the wounds inflicted by his early relations with this mother that Freud could speak this way to Gizella. But did he allow himself to speak just as freely to Ferenczi himself?

A little further, Freud presents a third hypothesis which he does not develop, but which seems to us to be the most relevant: "Psychoanalysis may have accelerated this inexorable development still further." We must keep in mind that he is

referring to a hesitant analysis in the process of being constructed by men who –
according to one of our fundamental tenets – have not had the experience of a true
analysis, an analysis that can end. This is particularly true for the prime creator of
analytic theory, Freud. It is much less the case for Ferenczi, who keeps trying to
acquire this experience, without knowing what to expect. But in December 1911,
neither Freud nor Ferenczi have arrived at that point as yet. They are advancing
cautiously through uncharted territory.

In fact, in his letter to Gizella, Freud criticises her hasty consent to the idea that
Ferenczi, whom she loves, might perhaps be happier with her daughter Elma, his
patient at the time. Freud holds Gizella in high esteem, and is not impressed with
the young girl: "You have shown me this daughter. I did not find that she could
place herself alongside her mother."

The tangled web involving Ferenczi, Elma, Gizella and Freud would endure,
sustained by the confusion of intersecting transferences.

Ferenczi, Elma, Freud: a story without end

On December 8, 1911, Ferenczi refers once again to the confusion in which he is
sinking, along with his patient. Although his tone is humorous, he is vague and
speaks of himself to Freud in the third person: "Patient spent yesterday in considerable turmoil […] the awakening of mourning over the loss of Frau G. (that
is to say, over the end of the relationship), clearer insight into his own intentions.
Marriage with Elma seems to be decided." Facing this confusing perspective,
Ferenczi, or rather the lovesick child in him, appeals to the father in Freud: "What
is still missing is the fatherly blessing." Ferenczi is wrong, of course; what is
missing in this situation is the accurate assessment of an analyst, or the vigilance
of a supervising analyst who could point out to his young colleague his ambiguous involvement in a treatment undertaken on shaky ground.

In his answer to Ferenczi, Freud, who knows he went too far by playing the role
of the good father or the older brother in this hopelessly tangled affair, chooses
to step back and say no more: "I have no more to say, perhaps I have said more
than was justified, and I don't want to spoil your future completely." He knows he
committed a serious blunder by writing the long letter to Gizella and, with good
reason, withdraws from the embroglio.

On December 30, Ferenczi still believes in a happy ending; he will marry
Elma, and although he does not have Freud's benediction, he will have Gizella's. On January 1, 1912, the situation has taken a dramatic turn. A comment
made by her father planted doubt in Elma's mind, plunging her into torment.
Ferenczi, already disconcerted by Freud's silence, is further destabilised, before
regains his wits:

> But the scales fell from my eyes, and when, even after this scene, her pres-
> ence did not fail to arouse feelings of tenderness in me, I had to recognize that
> the issue here should be one not of marriage but of the treatment of an illness.

He then proposes that Freud himself continue to treat Elma. The next day, January 2, 1912, Freud answers and accepts the proposition, with some reservations. "Now to the matter of the treatment! If you [...] *demand* of me that I undertake it, then I naturally have to assent." He does so with no illusions, sensing the difficulties of an analysis undertaken, he fears, "with the vague desire for revenge against you, the one who is sending her into this treatment!" And something else is troubling him:

> In addition, if things don't go well, there is the silent ill will between us, or at least between the both of us and the noble woman, the superfluousness of my having to peer so deeply into your very own affairs without having accomplished anything for the effort.

Freud couldn't be clearer: he agrees, through a third party he accepts as a patient, to show concern for his friend and give him the paternal advice he needs, but he firmly refuses to become entangled for good in the private affairs of his valued collaborator. He even admits avoiding this dangerous possibility: "It pains me that I can't be with you now. I was depressed the whole time and anaesthetized myself with writing – writing – writing." It is interesting to note that it never occurred to him that Ferenczi might have been able to talk to someone else about the difficult situation he was in.

As the year went on, this affair slowly resolved itself, leaving Ferenczi both relieved and bitter: in mid-October, he wrote:

> Nevertheless, the case of Elma has been completely settled. I politely but firmly rejected her attempted advances. Even though I long for youth and beauty, I still see very clearly what kinds of dangers I have to look forward to with her.

Was Freud happy to hear that Ferenczi was accepting the Freudian half-hearted solution? "So, the fact remains: intellectual and emotional union with Frau G., on which I can always build."

In the fall of 1912, Ferenczi seems to have come to terms with the reality principle, which Freud certainly recommended, but he remains torn between his cautious distancing from Elma and his tender feelings for Gizella. In this new internal economy, the libido freed from investment in Elma can shift from the sphere of "love" to the sphere of "work." He writes to Freud: "You and science will have to share the libido that is left over." It is an odd formulation, but well-founded. In truth, the body of personal experiences of this first stage of his analytic career was to constitute the central object of the analytic research to which Ferenczi dedicated the next 20 years of his life, until his death. This object concerns the need for the analyst's involvement and, naturally, the unavoidable dangers to which this exposes him. Ferenczi, who was probably aware of Jung's love affair with Sabina Spielrein in early 1909, has now experienced, at his own expense, in the analysis conducted with Elma (his future daughter-in-law), the power of the deep layers of the unconscious which misdirected his own involvement in that analysis.

These difficulties – the Palermo incident, the Elma–Gizella embroglio – bring Ferenczi back to his troubled relations with Freud, to his symptomatic relationships with women and to the limitations of his self-analysis. At the same time, Ferenczi makes another discovery, concerning Freud's involvement in his misadventures. As a result, he questions more or less openly the unconscious role played by Freud's desire on his attitude towards him (Ferenczi) in Palermo, and then on his active intervention in the situation unfolding between him and Gizella and Elma.

It happened that in the fall of 1911, when there was an acute crisis in Elma's analysis, another incident gave Ferenczi an excellent opportunity to attempt, once again, to incite Freud to greater analytic discernment. Now, their roles were reversed: Freud found himself in an awkward position vis-à-vis a woman who questioned him about his desire as none of his disciples dared to do so openly, while Ferenczi was now in the position of witness and third party consulted for advice. The woman in question was Emma, Jung's wife. This brief incident between Emma Jung and Freud – lasting from the end of October to the middle of November 1911 – is worth recalling because it sheds light on the violent confrontation that took place a year later between Freud and Jung, in which Ferenczi was again involved as a witness.

In fact, it was by adopting a contrary attitude to Jung vis-à-vis Freud that Ferenczi was able to lead up to his unprecedented request for personal analysis. He was determined to shed light not only on his own unconscious role in the predicaments in which he found himself, but also on the unconscious role played by the father of psychoanalysis in creating the complications existing in his relations with his two spiritual sons, Jung and himself.

The Emma Jung incident (fall, 1911)

In September 1911, Freud stayed with Emma and Carl Jung in Zurich, on his way to the Congress in Weimar. On October 30, in response to the "voice of [her] unconscious," Jung's wife found the "courage" to address a firm reprimand to Freud: "Since your visit I have been tormented by the idea that your relation with my husband is not altogether as it should be, and [...] it ought not to be like this." She knows that during his stay, surprisingly, Freud said nothing about Carl's recent text *Transformations of Libido*, and did not try to discuss their diverging opinions or, possibly, their complete disagreement. This silence threw Jung into a state of paralysing doubt which worried Emma. She sums up the situation very clearly: "You didn't speak of it at all and yet I think it would do you both so much good if you got down to a thorough discussion of it. Or is it something else? If so, please tell me what, dear Herr Professor [...]" She does not interpret Freud's silence as a deliberate refusal to debate, but rather as a personal reaction closer to resignation. She informs Freud of his "resignation" which seems to indicate that he now considers it fruitless to have an in-depth exchange with Jung, as if the break to come had already taken place in silence. Is it in fact the case that Freud is resigned, or is there something else?

Not content with demanding that Freud give her an answer, thanks to her intuition Emma dares to make a direct and very personal remark concerning his familial relations. She bases her comment on what she has heard him say during his visit to Zurich: "I even believe that your resignation relates not only to your real children (it made a quite special impression on me when you spoke of it) but also to your spiritual sons."

Since we do not have the letter Freud sent Emma in response, its content can only be surmised from the second letter Emma wrote on November 6. She starts by justifying her decision to write him, and persists in her accusations. She insists that she felt she had to step in if only because of her husband's distress and anguish at the prospect of the expected "verdict" of disagreement. She even names the source of her husband's torment: "a residue of the father complex." In her first letter, she had alluded to Freud's filial complex and she now comes back to this. In the second paragraph of the second letter, she provides a different explanation for her actions, returning to the hypothesis that Freud had adopted a resigned attitude towards his own sons, as well as his spiritual sons, whom he sees as disappointing. She confronts him with the exact statement he made in Zurich, in reference to his family life: "You said that your marriage had long been 'amortized,' now there was nothing more to do except die. And the children were growing up and then they become a real worry [...]"

At 29, Emma, was a vibrant woman who did not mince her words:

> This made such an impression on me and seemed to me so significant that I had to think of it again and again, and I fancied it was intended just for me because it was meant symbolically at the same time and referred to my husband.

She even dares to ask Freud if he is resigned concerning the benefits of analysis: "I wanted to ask then if you are sure that your children would not be helped by analysis." And, unaware of the interpretative potential of her remarks, she then makes two superlative observations. The first is a strong defence of sons, be they one's own or spiritual sons: "One certainly cannot be the child of a great man with impunity, considering the trouble one has in getting away from ordinary fathers." Carried along by her own momentum, Emma put forth an interpretation that must have made Freud's ears burn: "And when this distinguished father also has a streak of paternalism in him, as you yourself said!" Fearing that her words could be taken as the insolence of a woman who lacks objectivity, Emma reiterates her reason for speaking out: "Please forgive me this candor, it may strike you as brazen; but it disturbs my image of you because I somehow cannot bring it into harmony with the other side of your nature, and this matters so much to me."

Once she has explained this, Emma extends the scope of her thought, focusing in on her essential concern: Freud's relation to the spiritual son he thought he found in Jung. She writes:

> You may imagine how overjoyed and honoured I am by the confidence you have in Carl, but it almost seems to me as though you were sometimes giving too much – do you not see in him the follower and fulfiller more than you need? Doesn't one often give much because one wants to keep much?

In stronger terms and better than Jung or Ferenczi themselves could have done, Emma brings Freud face-to-face with the dark side of his fierce and symptomatic will, in his role as the sonless father of psychoanalysis, to hasten to find an heir: "Why are you thinking of giving up already instead of enjoying your well-earned fame and success?" Emma did not venerate the heroic image of the inspired guide who, on the threshold of a promised land he will not enter must pass the torch to those who will continue the battle for the cause:

> After all, you are not so old that you could speak now of the 'way of regression,' what with all these splendid and fruitful ideas you have in your head! Besides, the man who has discovered the living fountain of psychoanalysis (or don't you believe it is one?) will not grow old so quickly. No, you should rejoice and drink to the full the happiness of victory after having struggled for so long.

With the superb arrogance of her desire, Emma points out to Freud his ageing complex. Although he accuses Ferenczi of not having to come to terms with his lost youth, according to Emma he himself anticipates death suspiciously early, since he is only 55. And to make sure that she will be heard, she makes her final argument, an admonition followed by advice: "And do not think of Carl with a father's feeling: 'He will grow, but I must dwindle,' but rather as one human being thinks of another, who like you has his own law to fulfill."

There is no better way to formulate this reminder of the symbolic law addressed to the father in Freud, who seems to have forgotten the son he once was.

Ferenczi is well aware of this exchange between the man in Vienna and the woman in Zurich, since he was the one Emma first contacted and it is with him that Freud shares his analysis of the situation involving Jung.

Ferenczi and the Emma incident

Thus, at the end of 1911 Ferenczi is asked by Emma to intervene as a third party, and solicited by Freud for advice. He also becomes more personally involved when the malaise between Jung and Freud resonates with his own. In this troubled context, Ferenczi draws a parallel between what Jung is experiencing in the present situation and what he himself experienced a year earlier, at the end of 1910, in

Palermo. Freud's sharp reaction to this suggestion causes the two men to have a serious confrontation which, in our view, sets the scene for Ferenczi's request for personal analysis at the end of 1912.

In his letter dated October 19, 1911, Ferenczi presented the following hypothesis: "I presume that Jung is now going through a period similar to the one I experienced in Sicily: the dissatisfaction with the *incomplete* intimacy with the teacher (father)." This identification and reference to the Palermo incident provoke a strong reaction on Freud's part, particularly since Ferenczi seems to agree with Emma Jung's frank appraisal of the situation: "Frau Jung [...] could be partly right in her assertions [where she talks about your antipathy toward giving completely of yourself as a friend]."

This is a terrible blow to Freud, who is forced to admit that the Palermo incident left an open wound, and that the troubling question of his relations with his spiritual sons – his heirs – is unresolved. Worse still, Frau Jung seems to be reiterating the same reproach Ferenczi had tried in vain to make a year earlier. But although Ferenczi agrees with her, he does not agree with Jung, who attributes to Freud the desire to "put authority above truth": "It is certainly false that it is your 'authority' that you want to protect." Although he makes his disagreement known, Ferenczi is nonetheless bringing up an innuendo-laden statement.

Indeed, during the trip to America the three men took together in the summer of 1909, when they analysed each other's dreams, an incident took place. While Freud was trying to analyse one of his own dreams, Jung asked him for more details. But apparently Freud "refused to disclose details of his private life," saying: "I could tell you more, but I can't risk my authority." Later, Jung would write: "This phrase remained etched in my memory." Clearly, when Ferenczi and Jung are confronted with the authority Freud assumes as the father of psychoanalysis, each of them has a different reaction. Jung sees it as a potentially persecutory attitude, and an alienating abuse of power. But Ferenczi interprets it as an enigma rather than a threat of which he must be wary; he sees it as a secret tied to the memory of painful and disruptive separations: "More likely the deep aftereffects of the Breuer-Fliess experiences could be responsible for it," he writes in the same letter.

In his answer dated October 21, 1911, Freud adopts a decidedly defensive attitude in response to Ferenczi's strategy: "This is very amusing. I see how you want to triumph, but I will see to it that you will not succeed." Freud justifies his rejection of Ferenczi's analysis of the situation. First, there is no proof that Jung has the feelings Ferenczi attributes to him, or projects onto him. The analogy with his experience in Palermo is only an uncertain hypothesis. Second, "[if] it is merely a product of the little woman, then the similarity dissolves altogether." Still, Freud concedes one point to Ferenczi: "But I do admit the probability that she is being supported by statements from him." Not everything is pure projection on Ferenczi's part, or pure hysterical invention on Emma's part. Freud qualifies his comments. First, he admits that all this affects him: "On the whole, the matter is not very flattering"; second, he refers to his ethics regarding psychoanalysis: "If I were not obliged to psychoanalysis, then I would only smile [...]" Since he can't simply dismiss these impressions of which he is informed, and since he is "obliged to psychoanalysis," Freud makes a real concession to Ferenczi, who proposes that he should show himself open to the questions addressed to him, even if he does it clumsily. So he does not smile at all this: "[...] however, I want to be careful and wait for material to be presented for signs as to whether I can learn something new about myself." Instead of maintaining an arbitrary, authoritarian position, Freud does not stay with his initial closed reaction, and agrees to see what effects all this will produce in him and in retrospect. He trusts the subject of the unconscious. He knows the intimate nature of what is involved and enjoins discretion: "Eternal discretion goes without saying!"

Freud's reference to a wish to triumph on Ferenczi's part leaves the latter disheartened, as he perhaps was a year earlier in Palermo, when Freud responded to his refusal to take notes by saying: "So this is what you are like? You obviously want to do the whole thing yourself." In his letter dated October 23, Ferenczi feels the need to explain himself once again: "I didn't want to triumph over you," and wants to clear himself of blame: "Even if Frau Jung's impressions coincide with those of Jung, the both of us (Jung and I) could certainly be mistaken and consider our infantile needs to be our right." After accomplishing this feat in the art of diplomacy, he rejects the accusation: "If Jung had the same complexes as I, that would still be no reason on my part to triumph over you." This refusal of Freud's interpretation allows Ferenczi to return to what is at stake in all this, and reformulate the question which remains essential to him: "At most it would be an indication of how hard it is for one to renounce the communality of thought with a being akin to a father."

Ferenczi and Freud after the Emma Jung incident

Thus, after the incident that occurred in the fall of 1911, Freud is questioned by Ferenczi precisely on the position he seems to be taking in response to possible transference centred on him: "I noticed that you interpreted my inclination toward you as transference and [...] didn't want to give too much opportunity for this transference." Yet, although Freud does not withhold signs of friendship, particularly from Ferenczi, the implication is that he is careful not to encourage the involution of this friendship between men of combat, and intellectuals who value autonomy, into a relation of transference, such as that of neurotic patients in therapy. Ferenczi, who has already seen Freud take this attitude, recognises it and looks for its motives. He advances a hypothesis: Freud maintains this distance vis-à-vis those of his collaborators who need too much intimacy: "[...] evidently out of educational considerations, perhaps also because in your few free days you were longing for a *free*, not an infantile, person."

Unbelievable but true, Freud's reply on November 17 starts, for the first time, with "Dear son." Freud goes on to say: "I [...] gladly admit that I would rather have an independent friend, but if you make such difficulties, I have to accept you as a son." Divided between the position of potential analyst which Ferenczi assigns to him, and that of leading figure at the head of an expanding school of thought, Freud has trouble avoiding the foreseeable confusion. First he invites his interlocutor not to succumb to hysterical overreaction and not to complicate their relations, which risk becoming neurotic: "Your struggle for liberation doesn't need to take place in such alternation of rebellion and subjugation." And in clear reference to the Emma Jung affair, Freud presents a hypothesis his interlocutor cannot find flattering: "I think you are also suffering a little from the fear of complexes that has attached itself to the Jungian complex mythology." Finally, Freud asks that Ferenczi not be too demanding: "Man should not want to eradicate his complexes but rather live in harmony with them; they are the legitimate directors of his behaviour in the world."

Freud speaks, if not like a mature man to a tormented adolescent, at least like an older man ready to help a younger man see reason. But he does not intervene just then, like a firefighter at the site of a fire who merely advises against playing with matches. A few years later, he would admit that in an analysis of neurosis transference can sometimes create an incendiary situation. In his reassuring letter, his tone changes when he speaks with the authority of the father of psychoanalysis: "By the way, you are scientifically on the right track toward making yourself independent"; and he gives Ferenczi this surprising double advice: "Otherwise, don't be ashamed to be of one mind with me, and don't demand anything more from me personally than I am willing to give." Whether he wants it or not, Freud is faced with an impossible situation in his relations with his closest disciples. On the one hand, he wants to work with intellectually independent men who, like him and with him, can become men of combat, and he is indignant at seeing them tormented in their relations with him as a man. But at the same time he still longs for intellectual exchange unaffected by the confusion of emotions: "One must be happy when a person, for once, comes to terms with himself on his own." This is why he favours self-analysis, the presumed royal road leading to the courage of maturity – when solitude becomes a companion.

At the end of 1911, when Ferenczi is enmeshed in his confusing love life, bogged down in Elma's analysis and involved in the Carl and Emma Jung affair, he finds himself once again in Palermo, like the previous year, facing a frustrating enigma. Why was Freud, who just recently asserted that "the nature of the thing" made it impossible for him to work through his transferential relation to Fliess, now refusing to acknowledge and take seriously the turmoil Ferenczi was attempting to reveal, concerning his relation to Freud – just as transferential? It was a perfect dilemma.

It was perhaps fortunate that at the end of 1912 the tension between Jung and Freud, now extreme, gave Ferenczi the opportunity to find a way out of this dilemma. He conceived of the possibility of a personal analysis which would oblige Freud to listen, once and for all, to his complaints and grievances.

Chapter 2

Freud, the father of psychoanalysis and impossible analyst?

Interestingly, Ferenczi's request for personal analysis with Freud, made on December 26, 1912, was preceded by the request that Freud take Elma into analysis, and by the unexpected suggestion that he take Jung himself into analysis. Ferenczi's request for personal analysis followed immediately upon a pertinent evaluation of Jung's vehement refusal to be analysed by Freud. To put this refusal in perspective, we shall return briefly to the beginning of this year, 1912.

Paternal transference or filial transference?

We don't know whether it is the analyst or the troubled suitor who speaks when, on January 20, Ferenczi describes Elma's paternal transference in these terms:

> It doesn't actually surprise me *now* that Elma is not behaving like a bride. I know, of course, that by far the greatest part of her love for me was father transference, which easily takes another as an object. You will hardly be surprised that under these circumstances I, too, can hardly consider myself a bridegroom any longer.

In the same letter, Ferenczi tries to reassure Freud concerning the infantile curiosity the latter saw in him:

> Strangely, the infantile curiosity to experience fatherly intimacies has subsided noticeably in me lately. The main thing that I was curious about was whether the father loves me. The great and heartfelt sharing that you brought to me in these difficult days seems to have calmed me down with respect to this.

As we shall see, Ferenczi is alluding to his rather clumsy involvement in the recent Emma Jung incident.

The confusion of tongues between the two men has now reached its height. Ferenczi has forgotten that Freud did not reduce his earlier curiosity about the Fliess affair to purely infantile curiosity, or that he did not maintain a position of obstinate refusal when he acknowledged that "the nature of the thing" created an impossibility to say. Ferenczi also refuses the assessment of fraternal rivalry existing between himself and Jung:

> For that reason I can now think and write about Jung entirely without brotherly envy. I suspect that he has – in addition to the money complex, which you emphasized – an unlimited and uncontrolled ambition, which manifests itself in petty hate and envy toward you, who are so superior to him [...] His unsatisfied ambition makes him *dangerous* under certain conditions.

While two months earlier Ferenczi was still thinking that Jung was in a situation, vis-à-vis Freud, similar to what he himself had experienced in Palermo, now he clearly takes a different position and, rightly, condemns Jung's attitude towards Freud: "He is also not very tactful in choosing his methods; the manner in which he responded to you is very significant."

Once he has made this clear, Freud's paladin invites him to take a more open and subtle approach to Jung's lack of tactfulness, to adopt a less militant and more analytic attitude: "Even so, it would be a mistake for you to be too resentful of him on account of this '*gaminerie.*' The best solution would, of course, be a free discussion (with psychoanalytic openness)."

Ferenczi seizes this perfect opportunity to invite Freud to show Jung the "psychoanalytic openness" he himself has been seeking in vain. And he is clearly speaking of his own situation when he takes the liberty of advising Freud: "All in all, I think that some *caution* is indicated with respect to Jung. But in my opinion he doesn't deserve having the Fliessian *mistrust* transferred to him."

Ferenczi may retreat, he may sidestep, but he remains certain that the reality affecting Freud's relations with the most eminent analysts in his circle has to do with the consequences of the traumatic Fliess affair, a wound less well healed than Freud thinks. To surmount this obstacle which now blocks transmission, Ferenczi makes an unexpected suggestion: "[...] it would also certainly be necessary to take Jung into psychoanalytic treatment from now on." This procedure, the analysis of the analyst, applies not only to Jung, but to all of them. Ferenczi goes on, drawing Freud's attention resolutely to a difficulty he seems to want to ignore, despite the many incidents that could have served as a warning in the past. This difficulty, Ferenczi insists, is not caused by the incidental symptom or character trait of one colleague or another, but by an unavoidable fact related to the workings of the unconscious in everyone.

Is Ferenczi trying to change Freud's belief that any responsible adult can become an analyst by following his example? By conducting a self-analysis whose goal does not have to be a complete reshaping of the personality? He reminds Freud of his exceptional status as the discoverer of the laws of the unconscious, and the father of psychoanalysis: "There is no alternative: you have to do everything yourself all your life." He even takes up an argument used earlier by Emma:

> Your successor has not yet arrived; by that I mean that among us analysts there is still not a single one who, having completely mastered his personal weaknesses, particularly his egoism, could work for the cause and also has the necessary talent and endurance to do so.

In other words, Freud must continue to fill his exceptional position. What is urgent is not to designate a successor, but to provide his disciples with psychoanalytic training. And as recent incidents demonstrate, this training must go beyond self-analysis. It must include personal analysis, which only Freud himself can conduct: "This is small consolation for you, but what use is there in denying it!" Of course, Jung did not undertake an analysis – quite the contrary. At the end of this same year, he would violently reject any such idea.

Thanks to this final heated confrontation between Jung and Freud, Ferenczi was able to submit his request for a personal analysis we consider to be the true original analysis.

The confrontation between Jung and Freud (December 1912)

The circumstances of Jung's dissidence, as well as the nature of the theoretical differences between Jung and Freud, are well-documented. We will therefore limit ourselves to quoting a short sequence illustrating the subjective violence of their imminent separation. In a letter sent to Freud in mid-December 1912, Jung made a significant slip of the pen. Wanting to say that even Adler's cronies do not recognise him as "one of theirs," he in fact writes "one of yours." When Freud answers the letter, on December 16, he can't resist pointing out this slip, which betrays Jung's mixed feelings about belonging to the Freudian community. Admittedly, Freud's outlandish interpretation was unpleasant, and the violence of the context caused Jung to react in a symptomatically excessive fashion, which itself raises questions. On December 18, Jung wrote:

> I would, however, point out that your technique of treating your pupils like patients is a blunder, in that way you produce either slavish sons or impudent puppies (Adler-Stekel and the whole insolent gang now throwing their weight about in Vienna).

Jung is not mincing his words.

Thus, in this period when Ferenczi is asking Freud to treat him as an analysand, even as a patient needing his help, Jung, on the contrary, accuses Freud of misusing the analytic authority he personifies. He is vehement, and his attitude is almost persecutory. "I am objective enough to see through your little trick." He sees the abuse inflicted by Freud as consisting of a unilateral art of interpretation Freud deploys outside the analytic setting, generating harmful psychic consequences: "You go around sniffing out all the symptomatic actions in your vicinity, thus reducing everyone to the level of sons and daughters who blushingly admit the existence of their faults." And he gets carried away: "Meanwhile you remain on top as the father, sitting pretty." Despite its symptomatic aspect, this uninvited evaluation contains a grain of truth:

> For sheer obsequiousness nobody dares to pluck the prophet by the beard and inquire for once what you would say to a patient with a tendency to analyse the analyst instead of himself. You would certainly ask him: "Who's got the neurosis?"

Although this metaphor is too confrontational and forced, even interpretative, it nevertheless raises fundamental questions, quite close in nature to those which preoccupy Ferenczi.

Jung's allusion to the submissive and obsequious position of Freud's pupils vis-à-vis the eminent figure of their teacher brings to mind Ferenczi's comments on group pathology, in his text "On the Organisation of the Psychoanalytic Movement." Jung's remark also resembles Ferenczi's subsequent description of the superego of certain analysts, the ones Freud called "Obedient." Indeed, this discussion concerns not only the question of the analysis of the analyst, but also the iconoclastic question of the analysis of the one who embodies analytic authority. Freud is referred back to his own neurosis, left unanalysed. In his impassioned remarks, Jung cannot avoid the dramatic visual metaphor already suggested in the previous allusion to a "technique," the technique of pointing to something that must be elucidated. Carried away, he builds his metaphor to a climax: "You see, my dear Professor, so long as you hand out this stuff I don't give a damn for my symptomatic actions; they shrink to nothing in comparison with the formidable beam in my brother Freud's eye." Far from subtle, these remarks now reach the height of violence in this metaphoric reversal where Freud is the one pointed to, not in his position as the model father, but in his nudity as neurotic brother.

Carried away by his rage, Jung goes so far as to take a peremptory tone, to better express his denial: "I am not in the least neurotic – touch wood!" In support of his declaration of good mental health, Jung presents an irrefutable argument: "I have submitted *lege artis et tout humblement* to analysis and am much better for it." We are not concerned here with the truth of this claim of analysis, or of the reference to respecting the proper rules. What matters is the conclusion of the argument, which sends Freud back to his initial and much earlier self-analysis, which obviously was not a proper analytic process, since such a process was yet to be established. Jung uses this fact as an attempt to embarrass Freud: "You know, of course, how far a patient gets with self-analysis: not out of his neurosis – just like you."

Of course, it is impossible not to hear in these skillfully sardonic arguments the underlying appeal of the author of the letter, and the passion expressed, which reminds us that under the theoretical disagreements other factors are at stake, such as the conscious and unconscious affective currents circulating in the young Freudian community, that we recognise as inevitable.

The effect of this love-hate component of the relation between Freud and his disciples, particularly powerful in Jung's case, is palpable in the next passage of his letter:

> If ever you should rid yourself entirely of your complexes and stop playing the father to your sons and instead of aiming continually at their weak spots took a good look at your own for a change, then I will mend my ways and at one stroke uproot the vice of being in two minds about you.

After his violent protests, Jung's anger subsides and he is able to imagine an analytic step, a "turning around on oneself," on condition that Freud fulfil a prerequisite: that he leave the position – which Jung assigns him – of supreme father of psychoanalysis, and accept the position of analysand.

In the last paragraph of this enlightening letter, Jung, who knows everything is lost and a break is unavoidable, goes ahead and perhaps as a last good-bye, addresses these questions to Freud without, of course, expecting any answer. The first question reads as follows:

"Do you love neurotics enough to be always at one with yourself? But perhaps you hate neurotics." From this, follows a second question: "In that case how can you expect your efforts to treat your patient leniently and lovingly not to be accompanied by somewhat mixed feelings?"

In his answer dated December 22, Freud, probably deeply affected and knowing that it would be no use, avoids engaging with Jung's verbal attacks:

> In regard to your allegation that [...] I misuse psychoanalysis to keep my students in a state of infantile dependency [...] and to the inferences you draw from this contention, I prefer not to judge because it is hard to judge in matters concerning oneself and such judgements convince no one.

He not only forces Jung to revise his own attitude, but he also adds a remark showing that his relations with his pupils are seen differently by others: "In Vienna I have become accustomed to the opposite reproach, to wit, that I concern myself too little with the analysis of my 'students.'"

Poor Freud! In Zurich, Jung reproaches him with using and abusing the analysis of his pupils; in Vienna he is reproached with showing Jung preferential treatment; and in Budapest, where we will return, Ferenczi comes closer and closer to a request for actual analysis on his couch. In fact, on December 23 Freud sent Ferenczi Jung's letter, which had clearly made him angry:

"The embarrassing sensation of the moment is the enclosed letter from Jung, which Rank and Sachs also know about, since I overcame my shame about it. I really must say he is downright impudent." Ready to do battle, Freud intends to counter the strategy of the enemy: "My reaction to this is difficult. He is obviously disposed to provoke me so that the responsibility for the break will fall on me and he can say that I can't tolerate analysis." Clearly, contrary to Ferenczi's advice a year earlier, Freud does not intend to adopt a position of analytic distance: "On the other hand, if I respond calmly and moderately and treat him like one of our patients when he gets into a fit of cursing, he will think I am afraid and will get more audacious." Although the matter affects him, Freud continues the fight and firmly stands his ground. He will not respond to the attack concerning his unanalysed neurosis: "With deference to my neurosis, I hope I will master it alright. But he [Jung] is behaving like a florid fool and the brutal fellow that he is." Surprisingly well-informed, Freud ignores Jung's reference to a personal analysis conducted according to the rules of the art, and he takes a caustic tone: "The master who analysed him could only have been Fräulein Molzer, and he is so foolish as to be proud of this work of a woman with whom he is having an affair."

The next day on December 26, 1912, after reading Jung's letter, Ferenczi answers Freud, proceeding in two stages. First, he comments Jung's murderous letter in detail – a commentary that Freud must have welcomed in those uncomfortable circumstances. Indeed, it would have been difficult for Freud not to ask himself how it was that he only saw in Jung the fighting man and the leader. This, despite the fact that Jung made clear the internal conflict Freud's expectations of him had produced. Ferenczi makes use of this painful situation to remind Freud again of his particular position vis-à-vis his disciples and colleagues. He takes the bull by the horns. He asks the man who was his teacher and became his friend, to become his analyst.

Ferenczi's comments on Jung

Ferenczi's very first words go to the heart of the matter. Rather than drawing Freud's attention to the obvious theoretical disagreements between Jung and the Freudians, he points out Jung's personal relation to psychoanalysis. With formidable astuteness, he chooses not to dwell on the impertinence of Jung's behaviour towards Freud, and to concentrate on his disregard for the defining principle of psychoanalysis:

> Jung's behaviour is uncommonly impudent. He forgets that it was *he* who demanded the 'analytic community' of students and treating students like patients. But as soon as it has to do with him, he doesn't want this rule to be valid anymore.

His criticism is radical: the young President of the IPA would like future students to undergo psychoanalysis with their elders who have not been analysed. Ten years later, Ferenczi was still criticising this aberrant state of affairs where patients in therapeutic analysis are better analysed than their own analysts, since the "didactic analysis" practised in Berlin was, by definition, short and incomplete. Without providing further details about the difference between the "analytic community" of students and the student's experience as patient, Ferenczi starts by pointing out the arbitrary and unclear exceptional position demanded by Jung:

all students must undergo analysis, except him. This explains his recent rebellion when Freud remarked on the slip in his letter.

Then Ferenczi very skillfully employs a logical argument and accomplishes two things at once. He dismantles Jung's arrogant demand and brings Freud face-to-face with the truth of his exceptional position: "Mutual analysis is nonsense, also an impossibility." The mutual analysis he speaks of here is not the analysis with which he was going to experiment just before the 1930s; it is simply the placing in common of the self-analyses of different individuals, as was the case between Freud, Jung and Ferenczi while they were sailing to America. It is the analysis constantly practiced in Freud's letters, especially to Ferenczi. And the latter continues: "Everyone must be able to tolerate an authority over himself from whom he accepts analytical correction. You are probably the only one who can permit himself to do without an analyst." Contrary to Jung, Ferenczi is not reproaching Freud for not having undergone a veritable analysis; rather, he emphasises that reality has shown that Freud is the exception which confirms the rule. Since no other analyst preceded him, the man who discovered psychoanalysis became an analyst without being analysed. He is then the one on whose couch a few other analysts like Ferenczi could be analysed. Unwittingly, and far from suspecting the import of this act, Ferenczi introduces *de facto* a difference between the founding father, the man involved in the imaginary father–son relation, and paternal function, an agency of otherness able to instigate correction of the words and deeds of the other.

Moreover, he is able to discern the most subtle effective tendency underlying Jung's theoretical positions. Theoretical disagreements are secondary to a more secret internal discrepancy. "Jung is the typical instigator and founder of religion. The father plays almost no role in his new work; the Christian community of brothers takes up all the room in it."

Clairvoyant and rigorous, Ferenczi reminds Freud that he is the only one with whom he can consider undergoing the kind of in-depth analysis he seeks. He is suggesting that Freud give up his stubborn illusion that any truth-loving man who has dreams and wants to learn about the unconscious, can embark on the path of self-analysis he himself followed. Ferenczi insists on his conviction – which he would later moderate – that for Freud, who had not benefitted from analysis, self-analysis would have to suffice: "Despite all the deficiencies of self-analysis (which is certainly lengthier and more difficult than being analysed), we have to expect of you the ability to keep your symptoms in check." Implicitly, Ferenczi is differentiating between the art of ordinary self-analysis, in which he has become a master, and the exceptional self-analysis undertaken by Freud in complete solitude earlier. Ferenczi now reminds him of this:

> For better or for worse: in future you also have to content yourself with self-analysis, from which such a rich harvest has grown for the benefit of science [...]. If you have the strength to overcome in yourself, without a leader (for the first time in the history of mankind), the resistances which all humanity

brings to bear on the results of analysis, then we must expect of you the strength to dispense with your lesser symptoms. – The facts speak decidedly in favour of this.

In stark contrast with Jung, who insists on seeing Freud as the all-powerful father wanting to dominate his sons, here Ferenczi portrays Freud as an analyst who must consent to work with his students despite his flaw – in this instance, the lack of personal analysis.

After entrusting Freud with the potential function of analyst which should rightfully be his, Ferenczi speaks of the potential analysand one or the other of the members of his circle might wish to become. This is, notably, his own case. It now seems clear that for a practitioner of analysis a true personal analysis can no longer be limited to the self-analysis recommended at the time, even if it benefits from Freud's benevolent observation:

> But what is valid for you is not valid for the rest of us. [...] The rest of us, however, have to consider ourselves fortunate if you help us to control our affects in the only effective, i.e. analytically legitimate way, and give us hints that call our attention to the weak points of our psychic organization.

Now, Ferenczi has established the minimal preliminary setting required for the possible encounter between an analyst – also the father of psychoanalysis – and an analysand – also a friend and recognised practitioner. The great difference between Jung and Ferenczi has come to light. While the former refuses, with almost deranged vehemence, to be engaged in any form of mutual analysis with Freud, and what is worse, even to entertain the idea of personal analysis, the latter is ready to make an even more important commitment than he thinks. Indeed, Ferenczi will not only undertake personal analysis, but will embark on an original inquiry on what such an analysis could be and should be – an analysis of the personality as a whole which can be brought to an end.

Ferenczi's position is completely opposed to Jung's, although they started out from the same vantage point: a dissatisfaction springing from their relationship with Freud: "I, too, went through a period of rebellion against your 'treatment.'"

Indeed, whether we think of the Palermo episode in 1910, the Emma Jung incident in 1911 or the affair involving Elma in 1911–1912, Freud had not been tender with Ferenczi on those occasions, any more than when he had been quick to interpret his digressions and errors. Still, the difference between Jung and Ferenczi's reactions is startling. Jung experiences as serious abuse the analytic remarks Freud feels free to make, given his work since the origins of analysis; Ferenczi, on the other hand, does not find them arbitrary or harsh, but insufficient, incomplete and too unilateral. Completely convinced of the powers of analysis, Ferenczi was dreaming, but the outrageous violence of Jung's recent retort yanked him out of his reverie. He no longer likened Jung's unease with his own past distress; he had come to a firm conclusion:

> Now I have become insightful and find that you were right in everything, and
> that you could have done me no other service then allowing yourself, in my
> education, to be guided not always by feeling but often by analytic insight.

Thus, thanks to these insights, and quite reasonably following from them, on
December 26, 1912, he finally, and for the first time, asks for in-depth personal
analysis.

The request for analysis (December 26, 1912)

In the second part of the letter dated December 26, 1912, Ferenczi makes his
request in two stages. First, he declares his intention clearly:

> Now on to myself. – I am also a case in need of treatment – but there has been
> an undeniable progress to the extent that I am conscious of that fact. It was
> and is my intention, if you can grant me time (hours), to go into analysis with
> you – perhaps two weeks (maybe three), for now.

The next five pages testify to the firmness of this desire for analysis, as well as the
change regarding the kind of instruction he still expects to receive from Freud. In
1908, he was expecting to learn, from his exchanges with Freud, the art and ability
of transmitting psychoanalytic knowledge.

Four years later, this wish has been fulfilled: Ferenczi has become a master in
analytic transmission. This portion of the letter also provides a glimpse into the
concept of deeper analysis which Ferenczi expects to undergo in his analysis with
Freud, in view of becoming its first emissary. He continues to trust the distinction
he makes between the teaching of a body of knowledge and the transmission of
the truth of a lived experience. Given his experiences over the past two years in
the world of analysis – the Palermo incident, the Emma and Carl Jung affair, the
Emma and Gizella situation – at the end of 1912 Ferenczi knows that he needs
more than this initial training, which nevertheless turned him into a respected
psychoanalytic practitioner. The constant self-analysis of his conflictual relations
with Freud, of his romantic dilemmas and their worrisome intrusion into his analytic practice, confirm his need for in-depth personal analysis. Now, the goal is
no longer the transmission of psychoanalytic knowledge, but the intimate experiencing of its inescapable truth. Ferenczi senses that only a personal analysis can
free him of the bonds of his neurosis, thereby allowing his compelling thirst for
truth to take a new direction. He makes this clear in the second formulation of his
request, at the end of his letter.

Ferenczi is not content with presenting his case; he is not asking for punctual
analytic help; he is not asking for psychotherapy, be it psychoanalytically oriented.
He is asking Freud for in-depth analysis, even if the nature of this deepening cannot be specified. But we can get a glimpse of it in Ferenczi's appeal to Freud:
"Now, I don't know how much of the neurotic symptoms in me is dependent on

the organic substrate, and how much that which is apparently organic is psychogenic. (I would like to be instructed by you about that.)" This question does not relate to the limits of psychoanalysis, but rather, opens a way to extend its usefulness. Thus, the possibility is raised that analytic investigation may shed new light not only on what unfolds at the psychic level, but in the mysterious realm of the body. Not only symptoms inscribed in the body through conversion disorder, but also those associated with various functional disorders. We shall see that, in fact, Ferenczi prefaces his question with a long discussion of a symptom affecting his reproductive tract. If the castration complex controls psychic life, could it be that it also influences the occurrence of physical ailments? Ferenczi is speaking to Freud from the vantage point of his psychic and somatic ills, a suffering which takes on, and to which he confers, the dignity of a new topic of enquiry that could re-energise analytic research.

For Ferenczi, this questioning on the relation between the organic and the psychogenic, between soma and psyche, is not theoretical: it is first and foremost intimately connected to personal experience in his body and soul. In addition, this questioning, rooted in his practice as a physician turned analyst, was to become and to remain the guiding principle of his future work. Thus, Ferenczi's request for analysis is made on the grounds of his own symptoms, as well as in view of exploring the eminently analytic question of the limits of psychoanalytic knowledge. Ferenczi positions himself on this double ground. The Ferenczi who wants to be instructed by Freud in these matters is not passively waiting to receive knowledge; he has already taken possession of the question and is actively searching for an answer.

Between the declaration of his intention to be analysed and the formulation of what he expects to learn in the process, Ferenczi inserts an impressive picture of his symptoms and, being a master of the unconscious, proposes and astute interpretation. He is probably trying to make clear to his future analyst the severity of his personal ills and the relevance of the "Freudian" analysis to which he subjects them, not retreating before the dizzying depths of the analytic questioning he has initiated. Ferenczi, who has based his request for analysis on his multiple physical ailments, and particularly on those affecting his reproductive organs, observes:

> Today (on December 27) I feel significantly better. Hard to say whether my awareness of an improvement in my physical condition or this analysis was of more use.
>
> Please forgive this gratis analysis, which I have gotten from you by sheer obstinacy (if only in writing!)
>
> Yours, recovering, Ferenczi.

He has found the perfect way to say, on the threshold of his analysis, that he is seeking more than merely treatment for his symptoms.

Taking seriously the witty remark about a "gratis analysis," we see this long letter as the "first session" of the personal analysis which would actually begin 20 months later, in September 1914. This analysis obtained "by obstinacy" contrasts with the fragments of self-analysis found throughout the correspondence, and the letter itself marks a milestone, introducing a new phase in the Freud–Ferenczi relation. The analysand who was soon to be Freud's patient is no longer the young man who in 1908 was seduced by Freud's knowledge and his person, nor is he the zealous Freudian follower he became afterwards. The text of this unusual first session gives the reader the rare opportunity of witnessing a session where Freud, the analyst, remains silent. The reader can see this unprecedented request unfold word for word, and has good reason to suppose that Freud never received another with comparable analytic content.

A first session?

Freud is well aware of the complexities of the intricate relations between Ferenczi and Gizella, Elma and certain other women; between Ferenczi and Jung; and, above all, between himself and Ferenczi. But what does he know, and what sense can he make of the multitude of physical ailments associated with them, be they cause or effect? Ferenczi insists on making it clear that his long practice of self-analysis has made him aware of his problems and allowed him to glimpse their origins and meaning, but not to alleviate the serious bodily harm they inflict. He then presents a very detailed picture of the physical suffering he endures:

> The local process (a Cowperitis) is gradually getting better, since I have been regularly sitting on an air pillow and making hot compresses. The swelling is going down in the regional glands, and the pain is lessening (it was, incidentally, never excessive).

Not long ago, Freud consented to making his own dreams public; now, Ferenczi is willing to show Freud his own somatic disorders, like this most recent one, of a very intimate nature.

To this main symptom, Ferenczi adds others: difficulty breathing and low body temperature during the night, "very weak pulse," "belly inflated, meteoristic," and "more or less stuffy nose." He awakens "naturally washed out, depressed and weak." These functional symptoms, not expressed in psychic representations but through bodily sensations and feelings, intrigue Ferenczi, the psychoanalyst who is still a physician at heart. But he can no longer approach medicine as he did before his encounter with analysis: "Now I think I am not justified in judging these symptoms exclusively from the standpoint of an internist. (I did that thoroughly and went through a series of severe illnesses in my mind.)" He realises that taking a strictly medical approach was about to plunge him into a hypochondriac anxiety. But paying attention to other signs of his malaise prevented this: "The psychic secondary manifestations (depression, occasional tearfulness), the rapid change of mood, disturbance of work, etc. speak in favour of the likelihood that these symptoms are in large part neurotic." Where are we to look for a sign, or "the" sign confirming the relevance of this intuition, as yet only a hypothesis? Being an original thinker, Ferenczi expects the sign less from Freud's knowledge or speculations, and more from a manifestation of the unconscious. More Freudian than Freud himself, without yet knowing it or knowing to what degree, he has developed a conviction: the formations of the unconscious and dreams are not only the royal road of the return of repressed desires in figurative form, not only the return of conscious representations later repressed by reason of their pleasure-giving capacity, but also the emergence of the representation of sensations which until then were deeply buried in the body.

To prove it, Ferenczi uses his own case, and proceeds to analyse at length two of his dreams. This is not the first time he describes one of his dreams, but here he presents them in a totally new way, as if he was already on Freud's couch. He has now gone beyond his long-standing habit of showing his skill at using dream interpretation, in the hope that Freud would recognise his merits. Having reminded Freud that he is expected to accept the duties of this position as analyst, if not with Jung, at least with Ferenczi himself, the latter dispenses with linear narrative – a fact which confers a surprising quality to his writing. He is not presenting newfound ideas stemming from previous reflection; rather as he writes, he associates freely, surprised at times by what emerges in this flow of words, where an unexpected inability to find a word is not to be confused with the forgetting of a word, a significant double-meaning unheard before being spelt out deliberately, or with the return of a previous dream fragment, etc. When reading these pages, the reader may have the strange impression of hearing Ferenczi associate out loud, as if unaware of the presence of the man who, as if seated behind him, is listening in silence. We leave the pleasure of this experience to the reader, who can refer directly to the text describing these two dreams which, occurring a few days apart, echo each other so perfectly that Ferenczi treats them as a single dream. Could this dream be for him what the dream of Irma's injection was for Freud: an exemplary dream? Several reasons allow us to think so.

For instance, the dream insists more on the dynamics of pure enjoyment than on the wish-fulfilment function Freud considered to be the very essence of dreams. The narrative testifies to this, the scenes take place in bright light and show the radioscopic contours of an internal landscape Ferenczi dares to claim as his own, without disavowing the secret jouissance now available and avowed. The dream's scenography reveals the unconscious substrate that complicates his love life, the particularities of his sex life, as well as the underpinnings and complications of his relations with Freud. Presented in light of residues of infantile sexuality, Ferenczi's various relationships with his objects are shown to be characterised by a multiplicity of interconnected drives and sexual fantasies. Nothing is missing: "small sadisms," fright at noticing that tormenting a dog was "too much fun for me," and the trepidation at feeling slightly aroused "by the strength of [another dog's] sexual aggressiveness," aggressiveness and hate towards Gizella, "intentions of death (murder)," meteorism (anal explosion), etc. Revealing these feelings in the letter/session brought back memories: sexual games with his sister Gizella, when he was three, threat of castration made by the cook, fellatio imposed by a boy a year older than him, when he was 5, and a memory we consider essential: "colossal rage" against his mother. The letter also gives details about various occurrences connected with his sex life. Of course, Ferenczi presents all this against the backdrop of the Oedipal economy of the child still present in the adult he has become. More fundamentally, this dream acts as a double transferential appeal to Freud: Freud the founder of psychoanalysis with whom he has already shared a portion of his life and established a friendship, and Freud the future analyst whose patient he is asking to become.

Indeed, this dream is a transference dream of a very intimate nature. In fact, in the last scene Freud himself is present. Embarrassed, Ferenczi places this fragment in brackets and underscores its vagueness.

> [(Indistinct) a woman stands on a table and protects herself from the snake by tightly pressing on her dress.] You and your sister-in-law play a role in this dream; (next to it: Italy, a four-poster bed in the following shape [...]

Indeed, two years earlier, in Palermo, a painful scene took place between them, and they still bore its scars. Unable to describe the Italian bed in words, Ferenczi tries to show it in two drawings, which he crosses out at once, scribbling over them, when he realises that its shape resists even graphic reproduction: "[I can't draw it correctly]." What is it about this bed that makes it indescribable? We know what malevolent suspicions arose following Freud's trip to Italy with his unmarried sister-in-law. The nature of the transference is clear. The dream willingly portrays the unconscious vectors of Ferenczi's libidinal life and, with some awkward reticence, Freud's as well.

It is probable that Freud had spoken about his early renouncing of sexual relations, before reaching 40, soon after the birth of his fifth and last child – his darling Anna. But although Freud consented to disclosing his personal life to some extent, modesty or resistance prevented him from revealing everything. While this enraged Jung, who regarded it as abuse, Ferenczi was intrigued and driven to try to solve the mystery. Disguised as a dream, does this curiosity follow upon the more fundamental curiosity he showed in Palermo and afterwards? Not concerning a hypothetical adulterous or incestuous relations Freud might have had, but concerning the earlier relation of friendship and shared work between two men, Freud and Fliess. Why does Freud refer so often to this friendship of such rare and troubling intensity? How did it come to end so badly? Yet it was within the bounds of this relationship that psychoanalysis was born, and that Freud became a great man. Moreover, soon after Palermo, why did Freud refuse to elucidate any further this Fliess affair which tormented him? Ferenczi's curiosity was not rooted merely in infantile sexuality; something else was at stake when Ferenczi quickly guessed that his relation with Freud carried the invisible traces of this initial transferential event. In fact, Freud was the first to recognise the ambiguity of his position, going so far as to admit to Ferenczi, who kept asking, that indeed, in their relationship he has not overcome the countertransference, which bears the scars of the Fliess affair.

Not without reason, Ferenczi is therefore very intrigued by this double tendency of Freud's to accept revealing himself, and at the same time to resolutely hold back, by his ability to maintain a distance in close friendship. What surprises Ferenczi is Freud's openness to dialogue between analysts who are friends, combined with the firm desire to preserve the solitude he needs for reflection. Ferenczi has experienced this firsthand, and painfully, in Palermo; Freud can give everything without making any concessions. The experience was traumatic for Ferenczi. In our view, the presence of this traumatic dimension in the dream we are examining constitutes its third particularity. This is made apparent by a word impossible to say, and only possible to suggest incompletely in writing.

The missing name of the trauma

While narrating and analysing this dream, Ferenczi, like an analysand sometimes, has a very surprising experience: in the middle of the easy flow of words, one word stubbornly escapes him, creating a gap in written account. Under analysis, Ferenczi, astounded, realises that a second unconscious formation has arisen and infiltrated the dream process. To his astonishment, this phenomenon does not indicate the forgetting of a word that could eventually be recalled, but rather a missing word. He would not succeed in finding it. This word gap would quickly be revealed to be tied to what we consider to be two facets of trauma.

Just after describing the peaks of sadism that manifested themselves in the life of the infant and little boy he once was – the pleasure he took in torturing, his tendency to be disdainful, his lack of compassion, his murderous intentions – peaks illustrated in the dream – Ferenczi's associations turn to his mother. This is when a German word escapes him. Although his mother tongue was Hungarian, Ferenczi had completed his medical studies in German in Vienna, and it was in German that he was writing. This is what he says: "As a small boy I had a colossal un………. rage against my mother, who was too strict with me […]" It is precisely at this point that the sought-after word cannot be found; he can't find the words to describe the nature of the rage hidden beneath the various manifestations of sadism. And he continues: "[…] a colossal un………. against my mother, who was too strict with me; the fantasy of murder […] was immediately turned toward my own person." This passage is valuable because in it Ferenczi, without knowing it, draws attention to the possible relation between the missing word and a failure of the fantasy which cannot be formed. The fantasy cannot be constructed when a silent hateful impulse instantly turns into a powerful breaking wave that injures the body, possibly exposing the living organism to the violence of the death drive.

Theoretically, and in the best of cases, the sudden confrontation with a dizzying failing in the essential other – lack of speech or persistent deafness – can cause the unsuspecting subject to be overwhelmed by a primal effect of internal rage that will inevitably turn into externally directed hate. For the subject momentarily in shock, the passage from an inclusive explosive effect to a minimal representation occurs as a reflex action. Through outwardly turned hate, internal rage can take the shape of a fantasy which wards off the collapse or confusion that threaten the subject. But in the case of actual trauma, this beneficial passage from targeted hate to fantasy can remain ineffectual. This is what Ferenczi discovered in this trans-ference dream which initiated his future personal analysis and pointed the way to a discovery yet to be made: the fact that rage and hate can fail to play the role of a protective shield. There is no better way for Ferenczi to show this than by losing the word that would name, not the subject's impotence – momentarily overlooked – but the impotence of rage to turn into a fantasy expressing the desire of a living subject. Ferenczi would say later that in this extreme situation the subject as such is annihilated, is split or fragmented, disarmed and helpless in the face of the other's destructiveness. The aggressive energy that should have been expressed in a murderous fantasy turns inward, against the body and its vital functions. This failure of the fantasy leaves the subject in a state of primal disorganisation, with bodily sensations – more than feelings, in confusion. This confusion of sensations – jouissance, beyond pleasure – will be experienced as hypochondriac suffering, fear of illness, anxiety about organic disorder.

Through this dream and his interpretation of it in transference, Ferenczi stum-bles on a fundamental analytic question, that of primary repression and the sub-ject's initial discovery of alterity.

He glimpses something he would later examine and designate as the "traumato-lytic function" of the dream. Thus, Ferenczi adds to the first function of the dream, that of "wish fulfilment," a second function. The traumatolytic function of the dream, in its aftermath, is not to eliminate secondary repression but, on the con-trary, to repress, through figurative representation, the libidinal energy previously turned inward, when construction of fantasy failed. In this way, some dreams, but not all, and some dream fragments, but not all, can succeed in expelling the bits of jouissance which interfere with a traumatised child in the neurotic adults. Ferenczi needed another 20 years to try, and finally be able, to formulate a theory of the economy of this experience of trauma. But on December 26, 1912, he had not arrived there yet. He was still focused on what he was experiencing at this moment when he was attempting to convey to his future analyst the endless pain he carried in his body.

Could the missing word, the hollowed-out word, be the word of transference, given that our analysand-in-waiting cannot find it precisely in the language of the man by whom he wants to be heard, the man who, in his own way, treated him too harshly? Could it be that rage, as the inability to express the devastat-ing effect of the primordial other's excessive severity – indifference, coldness, deafness, silence – was being repeated in this very session, in the transference already created? Why this stammering? What followed enables us to advance a hypothesis. Ferenczi stammers because he is searching for a word which in itself would account for two totally different dimensions whose clinical manifestations seem to merge. The rage of the speechless infant whose appeal does not encounter a responsible validating witness is not the same as the rage of the little Oedipus humiliated by the distressing discovery that he is not, as he might have imagined, the child-phallus the mother could have seen in him. This child is further humiliated when he realises that his father, endowed with sexual power, seems to have the know-how to satisfy this desire in the mother. His father remains a stranger to him. Occurring late, after a lengthy preparation, this experience of symbolic castration is not to be confused with the unexpected and sudden shock experienced by the child present in every adult, upon his encounter with the real. In the last stages of his research, and with his discovery of the post-traumatic narcissistic split, Ferenczi describes the coexistence of these dimensions in some subjects. At the end of 1912, his relation to the language of his future analysis is still ambiguous:

> The word with the periods after it (an adjective with which I wanted to express my inability, my being bound, my inhibited will) won't come to my mind in German! In Hungarian the word is "*tehetetlen*," which at the same time also means *impotent*. So: "my impotent rage against my mother."

To name the most traumatic aspect of the trauma, not the shock itself but its deep internal resonance, or the consequence of the initial rage, Ferenczi uses, in his mother tongue, the term "impotence." But this substitute word lends itself only too well to the confusion of dimensions Ferenczi is trying so painstakingly to avoid. Yet the impotence of the infant who, in the event of early assault, finds himself in a state of sideration – unable to respond, his ability to act tied up, his flight obstructed – this radical subjective powerlessness, this agonal experience of the abolished subject is not the powerlessness of the child who, at the Oedipal phase, discovers with bitterness and shame that he doesn't have the means to satisfy the woman in the mother; nor is it the anxiety and humiliation of sexual impotence in an adult.

Yet in the second series of substitute words, the traumatic dimension surreptitiously intertwines with the sexual infantile material. The first reference is to traumatic experience: "But the German word still escapes me! Substitute words: without result, gagged, lost labour (?), Loves Labours Lost." Again, the experience of the infant, who feels as if he is gagged, as if his life energy is cut off at the source cannot be compared to the humiliating disappointment of the older child who realises that his mother does not respond to his incestuous advances and does not validate his illusion of being the imaginary child-phallus bringing her fulfilment. But in his second reference, Ferenczi casually shifts from the traumatic to the Oedipal: "A king can be incapable. My father wasn't. He produced thirteen children." A cruel observation for the rebuffed child, wounded in his phallic pride: sexual power is now on the father's side, thanks to his undeniable anatomical advantage. Here, Ferenczi inserts the memory of a playmate one year older than him, on whom he consented to perform fellatio when he was 5, and whose "penis was larger […] was 'nice and brown' and had blue veins." Was this proud penis really that of an older child, or that of an adult, of a father figure? Once again, Ferenczi confuses the traumatic with the Oedipal, so that he observes once more: "But the punctuated word still escapes! Fresh substitute thoughts: raging, Orlando, furioso, *hurler*, *hörögni* [Hungarian = emit death rattles], whore." The verb "*hurler*" is written in French. Thus, he goes blithely from a death rattle, from a scream – like the terrifying scream of the psychotic – from fury to a scream of pleasure. Ferenczi associates these groans with orgasm, and with his own childhood fantasies about intercourse between his parents, as well as his excitement in early adolescence when he overheard his father tell his mother that a certain man had married a whore.

The richness of this associative sequence – which we have reduced to its bare bones – does not deliver Ferenczi from the surprising lack of the German word, despite the number of languages invoked to compensate for the deficiency in German. There is the English *lost labour*, the French *hurler*, the Italian *Orlando furioso* and, of course, the Hungarian. Ferenczi remarks: "My fear of impotence must have been responsible for the strong repression of this word." Thus, he connects back the secondary phenomenon of fear of sexual impotence to the more primary unspeakable inability of rage to turn into hate, the inability to transform pain into suffering (*sub-ferre*), which is subjectivable.

This is what gives rise to Ferenczi's implicit hypothesis: a consequence of symbolic castration anxiety, fear of sexual impotence sometimes acts as an imaginary disguise for an even more radical impotence, specifically the unspeakable fear of being unable to maintain the standing posture of a living, speaking being, for lack of access to the negative dimension, to hate and to the support of fantasy.

Castration anxiety is well-known; Freud has described it in detail. The second fear, that which is felt in the grip of the unspeakable powerlessness of rage, cannot be called anxiety. The cold dread that paralyses the subject is not a reaction, like hot anger. Fundamentally, castration anxiety plays the structuring role of a signal: the child is warned, he knows, even if only unconsciously, what it would cost to disregard the prohibition; just as the neurotic is warned what is at stake if he wants to live or fulfil his fantasies.

The fear provoked by the "immediate turning" of hate inward is not preceded by a signal. The traumatic dimension of the shock cannot be foreseen; it catches the subject off guard and even breaks through the protective shield and attacks the perception-consciousness system.

In 1912, when Ferenczi, in an attempt to justify his request for personal analysis, tries to shed light on his physical symptoms through the analysis of his dreams, he stumbles on a problem of logic and, as a result, strives to clarify the distinction between trauma and fantasy, and to conceptualise the connection between the two spheres. Later, he would introduce his hypothesis of "narcissistic post-traumatic splitting" to solve this problem which by then had become part of his clinical practice and a major theoretical question in his work.

Acting out and questioning

Through this courageous analytic act that becomes the first session dedicated to the dream that introduces his analysis – the dream discussed above – Ferenczi does more than point out the devastating turning back on himself of the rage of the little boy he once was. He also uses an illustration of this destructive mechanism by referring to events in his current life, in which Freud plays an active role, as we have seen. When recounting his dreams, Ferenczi refers to "life's residues," a notion he will later add to the Freudian "day's residues" as a source of dreams. The plot is precise. After describing his unspeakable, crucial rage in childhood and associating it with fear of sexual impotence in adulthood, Ferenczi gives an example based on the memory of his earliest sexual experience: "Before my first coitus: great fear that it wouldn't work; masturbatory stimulation of my member in order to ensure an erection." After confessing this, he goes on to say that he "never had actual impotence (failure)," but adds the recollection of a recent difficulty: "Only about a year ago, when I brought Elma to Vienna for analysis and came back with Frau G., I wanted (without desire, deeply depressed) to make an attempt which failed." In this situation, complying with what he thinks – with reason – to be Freud's wishes, Ferenczi seems to accept giving up Elma – left on Freud's couch – but is unable to reconnect with Gizella. He experiences a momentary loss of desire. To reassure himself, during a stay in Vienna, he has an encounter with a prostitute – an encounter followed by long-lasting anxiety: "With the dangerous coitus in September this year in Vienna (from which I was expecting syphilis) I was – despite unpleasure and anxiety – quite potent." The reference to danger makes it clear: there was unprotected intercourse. Ferenczi does not say how he performed earlier, in the summer, when he had "coitus a few times with *puellis*," in other words, with prostitutes. Ferenczi gives a first interpretation – Freudian – of his actions: the rage he very likely felt when external reality revealed the inanity of his desire to marry the young woman who could give him heirs was instantly transformed into subversive, deadly guilt:

> The mischief that I made when I wanted to marry Elma has to be punished by cutting off my penis; for that reason I am exposing myself to the danger of syphilis (syphilis eats up the penis)." The analysis of his dream also leads him to see his actions as the fulfillment of a forbidden desire: "Or: in intercourse with the person with whom I risked infection I wanted simultaneously to do what is forbidden and get punished for it.

Then, Ferenczi proposes a second interpretation of his acting out in the summer of 1912, which were followed in the fall by a series of physical symptoms whose psychogenic origin had just been revealed by the December dream. Now, his approach is "Ferenczian."

Indeed, he interprets the symptomatic events of the past four months in light of the concurrent ups and downs of his relationship with Freud. The fact is that

Freud had been involved in all the recent events of Ferenczi's personal and ana-lytic life. Not long ago, he had even intervened directly, revealing to Gizella his reservations about Ferenczi's projected marriage to Elma. On January 2, when Ferenczi asked him to take Elma into analysis, had he not exclaimed: "In this humor, a woman can hardly be woo'd!" This open involvement of the father of psychoanalysis in the fluctuating events of his life causes Ferenczi to interpret his dangerous behaviour of the summer as an act of defiance addressed to Freud.

The last scene of the dream provides this opportunity. It presents the great Freud himself in a delicate situation involving the risk of wrongdoing facilitated by a shared room with twin beds while travelling with his sister-in-law: "The last, muddled part of the dream is mysterious. I interpret that as a kind of defiant apology: (father, after all, did something similar with mother)." Ferenczi is per-fectly aware of the transferential aspect of this defiance: "Only you have moved to the position of father, your sister-in-law to that of mother. [Father also said (=acted) 'whore.'" With some embarrassment, he associates this thought with a fact of which he is vaguely aware: "You once took a trip to Italy with your sister-in-law [...]" but hastens to add: "*voyage de lit-à-lit* (naturally, only an infantile thought!)" Although he strives to reduce to infantile speculation his fantasmatic image of Freud as a man whose sexuality is free of conventions, he nevertheless introduces, again in parentheses, a strange comment: "(Similar rumors are cir-culating here about me as about you in Vienna.)" Ferenczi's actions constitute a challenge that could be seen as asking Freud why he should condemn Ferenczi's sexual desire for Elma when he himself takes certain sexual liberties with his beloved wife's sister. In the last lines of Ferenczi's letter, Ferenczi's enacted chal-lenge becomes a spoken accusation.

At the end of this dialogue with the subject of the unconscious whom Ferenczi has allowed to speak freely and whom he trusts, he concludes: "I picture the connection as follows: The game with the danger of syphilis was a vengeance turned against my own person because of the hindrances that made marriage to Elma impossible." And Freud is obviously the greatest hindrance, since what he wants most is to see in Ferenczi a mature man able to love and to work, a man of combat rather than a per-petual adolescent. This is why it is to him that, via the dream, Ferenczi attributes the responsibility for the self-punishment that motivated his actions: "My unconscious placed the responsibility for it in your and Frau G's hands." Although this acting out took the place of what could not be said between Ferenczi and Freud, and although the physical symptoms were silently trying to inscribe something in the organism itself, it is only through the enactment and interpretation of the dream that Ferenczi is able to reveal what is most deeply troubling to him.

Once this truth is finally out in the open, Ferenczi can bring the analysis of his dream to a close – an analysis that has made him aware of the psychic origin of his somatic symptoms, "materialised" in his body and particularly in his repro-ductive system: "When a doctor (in reality) diagnosed syphilis in me (albeit with reservation) – I had to regressively live out the anxiety that I once went through while being threatened with having my penis cut off." We have seen that this targeted threat of emasculation was, in Ferenczi's case, only a secondary manifestation of a more complete threat – irrepresentable this time – of possible subjective destruction (no more speaking subject), of loss of a sphere of desire (no more fantasy) and of a slow death (no more vitality). Ferenczi states this explicitly at the end of his letter: "The local malady (at the base of my penis) was a constant stimulus to maintain this anxiety, which then degenerated at night into unconscious fantasies of bleeding to death and dying [...]"

Ferenczi couldn't be clearer: the castration anxiety by emasculation protects him from what otherwise would become unconscious fantasy, not of local amputation, but of a bleeding away of the complete being of the subject, until death. But despite his eloquence, Ferenczi stammers and comes to see as fantasy certain phenomena which, if not for their ulterior re-consideration in the traumatolytic scenario of the dream, would be left to exert their effect unscripted and silent, in the secret space of the body – becoming physical symptoms: "(deceleration of the pulse, cooling, weakness of the pulse, pauses in breathing, general weakness); during the day I was tormented by hypochondriacal ideas about incurable diseases."

By the end of the unusual first session constituted by this long letter dated December 26, 1912, Ferenczi is able to show "how much that is apparently organic is psychogenic," and explains very well the correlation he sees between the "neurotic symptoms" and the "organic substrate." Still, this does not provide a complete answer to the apparently theoretical question Ferenczi addresses to Freud, and henceforth never ceases to examine in his own work. In both its form and its content, this letter is above all an opportunity for a desperate but experienced analyst to address to Freud the appeal of a man exasperated by his confusing feelings when, for better or worse, his passionate ties with the woman, with Freud and with the theory and practice of analysis intermingle and interfere with each other. This puzzled man, enlightened by five years of persistent self-analysis, knows that clearing up this confusion will require a more radical and in-depth approach. Indeed, he places in parentheses his reference to being instructed by Freud in this regard. He is perhaps unknowingly indicating to Freud, beforehand, the new place he intends him to occupy: no longer that of master revered by his pupil, but that of analyst in relation to his analysand.

In this powerful plea, Ferenczi is in fact asking Freud to consent to take on, besides his role as the father of psychoanalysis generously dispensing his teaching, another task he alone can assume: that of analyst for disciples like Ferenczi, who express the need for analysis. Implicitly and perhaps unwittingly, Freud reminds him of the conditions and responsibilities associated with this new task. Upon reading this letter which solicits him so directly, Freud can't help feeling that he is being asked to reconsider the effects of his active intervention in his friend's personal affairs. His colleague is asking him to "overcome the counter-transference," a precondition which involves another difficulty. Freud must know that in the analysis to come he would receive not only the admiration addressed to the "superior analyst" that Ferenczi sees in him, but also criticism and complaints. From the start, and especially since the Palermo incident, Ferenczi has been searching in vain for the desire underlying Freud's passion for psychoanalysis, or more specifically, for the personal experience that led him to become an analyst, the experience at the source of his own desire for analysis. Thus, the analysis in which Freud and Ferenczi were to engage together was sure to resemble no other: an analysis in which the future analysand has many reasons to invite the future analyst to become an analysand himself.

On the brink of this adventure, Ferenczi's personal analysis on Freud's couch, neither one of them, we believe, is unaware that their enterprise is both necessary and impossible. But they both courageously agree to attempt this impossible task. Freud with some hesitation, and Ferenczi with enthusiasm.

Chapter 3

Laying the groundwork (1912–1913)

Ferenczi ends his long letter dated December 26, 1912, by saying: "[…] please forgive this gratis analysis, which I have gotten from you by sheer obstinacy (if only by writing)!" To this, Freud responds: "Will you believe or be angry about the fact that I have read your auto-analytic letter, but I have not studied it as I should have? […] So, get something from me by sheer obstinacy!" Freud answers his friend's urgent request without haste, but with a certain willingness to go along.

Two years earlier, in 1910, soon after their trip to Sicily at the end of the summer, Freud had indicated in no uncertain terms that he wished to maintain a degree of distance between them, and had reproached him his infantile curiosity:

> I no longer have any need for that full opening of my personality, but you have also understood it and correctly returned to its traumatic cause. Why did you thus make a point of it? This need has been extinguished in me since Fliess's case, with the overcoming of which you just saw me occupied.

But Freud was wrong: Ferenczi did not understand his reserve, especially when he tried to find out more precisely what happened between Freud and Fliess. For the sake of remaining unperturbed, Freud foregoes working with Ferenczi as they had planned. On November 23, 1910, he writes: "As regards paranoia, it would be better for you to make yourself independent of me […] I tell you, it was often nicer when I was alone." In his December 2 answer, Ferenczi objects: "The 'independence' that you have granted me in the question of paranoia evidently doesn't agree with me." The years 1911, 1912 and 1913 involved Freud in a wealth of events of great concern to him, and allowed tenacious Ferenczi to clarify his passionate desire for exchange with him. Defying Freud's reluctance, Ferenczi prepares the ground for his future analysis.

Freud's hesitation

Having put the Palermo incident behind them, Ferenczi and Freud spent two days together in South Tyrolia, in the spring of 1911. A week later, on April 24, Ferenczi expressed his delight:

> [...] the joy of being able to spend two days with you again in intimate con-
> versation, free from the obligations of work, seems to me here in my isolation
> to be so improbable that the impression of the fairy-tale-like quality of our
> splendid excursion is enhanced even more by it.

He went on to analyse what had delighted him so much – the incredible richness
of what he called "intimate conversation" with Freud:

> I never depart from you without benefit. I mean by that not an increase in my
> understanding of mental activity in general but rather a deepening of insight
> specifically into my own mental life, without which there can be no true
> knowledge – but especially no true *faith*. The relationship between *knowl-*
> *edge* and *faith* that has occupied people for so many centuries is only being
> made clear by means of analysis.

This is the first reference to a more in-depth analysis whose value Ferenczi would
henceforth advocate. This "deepening" is neither a new awareness, nor access to
the repressed, or proof of the existence of the unconscious; it represents an experiencing of truth that Ferenczi connects not to the revelation of a certain knowledge,
but to trust. Two years later, he would write an article on the question of belief,
disbelief and conviction. On April 24, 1911, he wrote:

> If one hears something new, then one is really obligated analytically to test
> one's personal relationship to the herald of the new doctrine in the most con-
> scientious manner before one can make a decision as to the real value of that
> statement.

Here, Ferenczi distinguishes the statement from the act of stating, to provide support for his stubborn belief. And what is the new doctrine he has in mind, if not
Freud's own definition of analysis? He obstinately desires to test, not so much
the rigour of Freudian theory, but its solidity, its embodied reality, that he seeks
in the relations of the theory with Freud's psychic life, and even his personal
experiences. This is what impels Ferenczi to force Freud to explain himself and to
become more involved in his private affairs.

The complications of his love life provide the perfect opportunity; he reached
an impasse in Elma's treatment, which he could no longer continue and passed on
to Freud. The latter, in fact, went even further. He wrote Gizella a long letter on
December 17, discussing the Ferenczi "case" with her. But he regretted it at once,
as he confessed to his friend on December 16: "I have no more to say, perhaps I
have said more than was justified, and I don't want to spoil your future completely."
A week later, on January 2, 1912, Freud expressed his misgivings as follows:

> Now to the matter of the treatment! [...] Just imagine under what unfavorable
> auspices I am supposed to begin. After withdrawing the bonus that can spur

her on to recovery, with the knowledge that I was not in sympathy with her intentions, and with the vague desire for revenge against you, the one who is sending her into this treatment! In this humor, a woman can hardly be woo'd!

Freud fears, above all, that his involvement in his friend's personal affairs is likely to complicate their collaboration and shared combat:

In addition, if things don't go well, there is the silent ill will between us, or at least between the both of us and the noble woman, the superfluousness of my having to peer so deeply into your very own affairs without having accomplished anything for the effort.

Ferenczi had also used the opportunity provided by Emma Jung's suggestion to Freud, in the fall of 1911, that he examine his own father complex. Whether innocently or, on the contrary, driven by his faith in analysis, on January 20, 1912, Ferenczi incites Freud to engage in open analytic discussion with Jung, adding: "For this it would also certainly be necessary to take Jung into psychoanalytic treatment from now on." Freud makes no reply, no doubt because the suggestion comes too late and is not to his liking.

Ferenczi considers that the honest discussion he proposes is the least one should expect of analysts who share a belief in the virtues of Freudian methods. He proclaimed this point of view publicly as early as the spring of 1910, in the "Introduction" to the proposal for the establishment of an International Psychoanalytic Association:

Moreover, the older and younger children united in this association would accept being told the truth to their face, however bitter and sobering it might be [...] it can be taken for granted that we should endeavour to tell the truth without causing unnecessary pain [...]

For a community of analysts to avoid the well-known pathology of "organised groups" and to keep personal passions in check – the love/hate relation to the father, attachment and jealousy between brothers – a second condition is required. It concerns the figure of the father:

It [this association] would be a family in which the father enjoyed no dogmatic authority, but only that to which he was entitled by reason of his abilities and labours. His pronouncements would not be followed blindly, as if they were divine revelations, but, like everything else, would be subject to thoroughgoing criticism [...]

The obstacles that arose in the space of two years between the father of psychoanalysis and Jung, his chosen heir, revealed the utopic character of Ferenczi's idealised vision; in fact, Ferenczi himself had since revised his position.

Whereas he initially spoke of "mutual surveillance" between "the psycho-analytically trained" – this training then referring to in-depth self-analysis – he now refers to another training, one acquired through the experience of being analysed on Freud's couch. But Ferenczi's new act of faith, in its turn, met with a reluctance that took tangible form in the organisation of the psychoanalytic movement. In the summer of 1912, Jones and Freud proposed an institutional option instead of the analytic option based on Ferenczi's faith in the unconscious as a tool to define the new relations to be established between analysts. The creation of the Secret Committee sealed the decision against Ferenczi's proposal.

In-depth analysis or Secret Committee

In the second volume of his monumental biography *Life and Work of Sigmund Freud* (1955), Ernest Jones describes the creation of the Secret Committee in the summer of 1912, when Jung's dissidence, added to Freud's conflicts with Stekel and Adler, became a threat to the future of the psychoanalytic movement and of the IPA, presided over by Jung. Ernest Jones writes:

> In July 1912 [...] I was in Vienna and had a talk with Ferenczi about the situation. He remarked, truly enough, that the ideal plan would be for a number of men who had been analyzed by Freud personally to be stationed in different centers or countries.

Early in the 1910s, Ferenczi not only sent Elma, and even wanted to send Jung, to be analysed by Freud; before making the request on his own behalf, he had recommended personal analysis with Freud for all analysts. Anyone wanting to acquire knowledge or solid faith in the power of the unconscious has to go beyond the rigorous self-analysis advocated by Freud; he must, in Ferenczi's opinion, undergo "thorough, in-depth" analysis with "full opening of the personality," on Freud's couch.

   In the summer of 1912, Jones is the first to inform Freud of his conversation with Ferenczi and later with Rank. On July 30, 1912, Jones's description of what took place is ambiguous:

> Ferenczi, Rank and I had a little talk on these general matters in Vienna. They were rather disappointed with the whole Zurich attitude at the moment, and even thought that their faith in the cause was not what it should be. We all agreed on one thing, that salvation could only lie in a restless self-analysis, carried to the farthest possible limit, thus purging personal reactions away so far as can be done.

Based on this account, the notion of a secret committee is still very tentative, since the proposed deepening of analysis refers to self-analysis, not to veritable personal analysis. But in the next sentence Jones conveys accurately the very different proposition made by Ferenczi:

> One of them, I think it was Ferenczi, expressed the wish that a small group of men could be thoroughly analysed by you, so that they could represent the pure theory unadulterated by personal complexes, and thus build an unofficial inner circle in the Verein and serve as centres where others (beginners) could come and learn the work. If that were only possible it would be an ideal solution.

Ferenczi proposes replacing self-analysis practised between well-meaning colleagues well-versed in Freudian doctrine with analysis on Freud's couch. Properly analysed, these analysts would be able to transmit "the pure theory," the very spirit of analysis. Although Ferenczi had not yet attempted to define the basic principles and aims of this analysis, was he going to designate as pure analysis this in-depth analysis he intended to generalise?

Given Jones' ambiguous formulation, in his August 1, 1912, reply Freud was able to ignore the originality and radical nature of Ferenczi's proposal, and orient the discussion in another direction: "What took hold of my imagination immediately is your idea of a secret council [...]" But Jones's letter had, in fact, made no mention of a "secret" council. This term Freud thinks he saw in Jones's letter is one he himself introduces a little father: "First of all: this committee would have to be strictly secret in its existence and actions."

Thus, it was Freud – and Jones – more than Ferenczi, who conceived of this "secret council" against the harm expected from the powerful position held by Jung, now openly a dissident, and President of the IPA. Pursuing his own thought, Freud deepens his misunderstanding of Ferenczi's idea:

> What took hold of my imagination immediately is your idea of a secret council composed of the best and most trustworthy among our men to take care of the future development of psycho-analysis and defend the cause against personalities and accidents when I am no more.

Here, Freud is clearly referring to the recruitment of the best analysts, that is, the small number of members who showed intelligence and creativity in defending the cause. But Ferenczi was proposing another mode of recruitment, different from one based on merit: recruitment based on the personal experience of a demanding personal analysis.

Neither Freud nor Jones took notice of this new ambiguity which led to another misunderstanding:

> You say it was Ferenczi who expressed this idea, but it may be my own, shaped in better times, when I hoped Jung would collect such a circle around himself composed of the official headmen of the local associations. Now I

am sorry to say such a union had to be formed independently of Jung and of the elected presidents.

Clearly, Freud is confusing the idea of a secret committee with the previous proposal of creating an international association. Indeed, he was the one who asked Ferenczi in 1910 to think about the possibility of gathering together into an international association all those who practised psychoanalysis scientifically, and presenting the association at the Nuremberg Congress in March 1910. But in the summer of 1912, Freud is mistaken: Ferenczi is not proposing a new collective body – not even a secret one – but, on the contrary, is introducing the idea of a group of analysts composed of individuals who have engaged in more extensive personal analysis than the others. Their own experience of the unconscious should have freed them from the worship of a father – imaginary – invested with "overwhelming authority" whose "pronouncements would be blindly followed."

This persistent misunderstanding led Freud to adopt Jones's point of view rather than Ferenczi's, which was dismissed out of hand:

> This committee would have to be strictly secret in its existence and actions [...] I had better be left outside of your conditions and pledges; to be sure I will keep the utmost secrecy and be thankful for all you communicate to me. I will not drop any utterance about the matter before you have answered me, not even to Ferenczi.

In a letter Jones sent to Freud on August 7, 1912, the misunderstanding reaches its height. Jones refers to Ferenczi's proposal once again, without noticing the extent to which it is the exact opposite of an inner circle surrounding the father of psychoanalysis:

> In our conversation the only subject discussed, raised I think by Ferenczi, was the possibility of a few men being analysed by you, so that they could serve as representatives in different places to teach other beginners. The idea of a united small body, designed like the Paladins of Charlemagne, to guard the kingdom and policy of their master, was a product of my own romanticism [...]

What secret reservations prompted Jones to compare a small group of analysts charged with transmitting the spirit of psychoanalysis, based on their own experience of personal analysis, with a small battalion of men ready to defend the doctrine of the master – a master Freud, in truth, does not wish to be? He would soon state explicitly that what he wanted was the status of chief of staff of a small battalion, and to enjoy an enlightened authority like that of a professor of medicine in charge of a respected clinic.

Was it in order to dispel these reservations shared by Freud and Jones that Ferenczi seized the opportunity offered by the Jung episode at the end of 1912 to voice his own request for personal analysis? Perhaps. But Freud remained reluctant throughout the next year. Moreover, Ferenczi had to deal with his own unconscious resistance to his desire for analysis. But in the summer of 1913, he found an occasion to reiterate his faith in psychoanalysis and in the profound benefits of personal analysis. Thus, the ground was laid for the first segment of his personal analysis to be conducted a year later.

Conquering reservations

On February 8, 1913, Ferenczi writes Freud: "The contempt for sexuality has evidently also caused as much mischief in biology as it has in psychology." In his own case, he blames his romantic involvements:

> As for myself, I am convinced that my poor health, which has lasted over half a year, was a bodily reaction to the failure of the marriage project. My body has 'played dead' since it saw itself thwarted in its anticipated satisfaction.

Exhausted, he would like to take a vacation with Gizella, and timidly suggest that Freud might join them. Of course, this vacation would put off the start of a possible analysis: "But if I permit my body this recuperation, then I have to postpone the planned analysis. I know, of course, that resistance toward being analyzed is partly to blame for this postponement!" Two days later, in a post-scriptum, Freud encourages Ferenczi's travel plan: "P.S. Stop! I am not thinking about your analysis in such a way that it should disrupt your vacation."

In March, Lou Andreas-Salomé visits Ferenczi in Budapest, probably on Freud's advice, to continue her initiation into psychoanalysis, started the previous autumn in Vienna. On May 4, Freud seems torn between his friend's professional evolution and the persistence of his physical ills:

> I am always glad to hear about how you are, even if you can't report the best. What consoles me is the extraordinary elevation of your intellectuality right at this time. You write better and better and have the nicest ideas.

Then he mentions the prospect of the analysis he reluctantly consented to conduct with Ferenczi:

> If I could be of use to you, then [nothing] else would take precedence over that. But I know that four or six weeks of analysis would be much too insufficient. For that reason something else comes into consideration, namely my dearth of inclination to expose one of my indispensable helpers to the danger of personal estrangement brought about by the analysis. I don't yet know how Jones will bear finding out that his wife, as a consequence of the analysis, no longer wants to remain his wife.

Freud's reluctance is two-fold. The duration of the analysis would be insufficient, and the analysis could be a threat to the future of a couple which has already faced numerous difficulties. The reference to Jones is clear. On May 12, Ferenczi attempts to set Freud's mind at ease:

> I am convinced that my analysis could only improve relations between us. With Jones the matter is different: his wife, not he, was analyzed. I have already gone through this period, in which you analyzed Elma and I subsequently couldn't marry her; I went through it without alienating myself from you or analysis.

On May 13, Freud points out another difference:

> Your case is not quite the same as Jones's. Jones has had his wife for seven years, and she is actually a jewel. It is certainly not my fault that he has lost her, and hardly his own either, by the way. They were no longer together for a long time.

In the same letter, Freud encourages Ferenczi to do battle: "If you can found your local group, then do it right away, and before the Congress, not just because of the votes but also because of the position that it bestows on you."

Keeping in mind Freud's advice to Lou Andreas-Salomé to go to Budapest to perfect her training with Ferenczi, while the latter has been charged with creating a local group as quickly as possible, can we presume that Freud preferred to negotiate with Ferenczi the established analyst, rather than with the future analysand he intended becoming? We might, given that he took a third initiative not likely to simplify these relations where the analytic, the private and the political intermingled. Just before the summer of 1913, Freud, who might have felt ill at ease in his complicated relations with Jones, advised him to go to Budapest to start an analysis with Ferenczi. Both Jones and Ferenczi kept Freud informed, in their letters, of the progress of this analysis. Both are respectful of what is at stake, and avoid case history. We leave the pleasure of discovering this correspondence to the reader; in it, he can glimpse Ferenczi's involvement in the conduct of this analysis which, as we know, precedes his own.

Ferenczi's propensity to transference

On June 8, 1913, Freud reassures Jones, who has started his analysis: "Ferenczi is strong and reliable and you may win him for life." Tactfully, Freud prepares Jones for the unavoidable break with his wife. He also points out that the fact that she was in analysis with him complicated his working relationship and friendship with Jones. In his letter to Freud dated June 17, Jones describes the progress of his analysis:

> I am doing my best in the analysis and think it is going on satisfactorily. Ferenczi discovers in me very strong aggressive tendencies which I have

reacted to by too much suppression and submissiveness, and which revenge themselves in various impulsive tendencies. It is to be hoped that in the future all this will be better balanced.

The conduct of this personal analysis does not prevent the three men from continuing their common combat for the cause. In fact, Ferenczi and his analysand travel to Vienna together to meet with Freud and discuss the unhappy circumstances of the psychoanalytic movement. In Budapest, Ferenczi and Jones's relations are more than therapeutic: "Ferenczi and I have many interesting discussions outside the analysis hours, and are especially occupied just now with the question of symbolism, origin and psychological significance." So far, two weeks after the start of the analysis, Ferenczi has maintained total discretion in his letters. Finally, on June 23, he writes to Freud:

> Jones is my best and dearest patient; he is competent, clever, obedient, and a really dependable friend at the same time; I think we will be able to build on him [...] The brief period of resistance with Jones has been replaced by sound progress.

Freud would soon see for himself.

On June 25, Jones answers Freud, who has asked him for comments on the manuscript of *Totem and Taboo*. Jones ends his letter by saying:

> You will have noticed that in this letter I have ventured for the first time to take it for granted that you are a human being with human reactions, and to write openly and frankly as from one man to another.

Evidently, his analysis with Ferenczi has given him new freedom vis-à-vis Freud, a freedom his analyst does not yet possess. Jones is explicit about the nature of his new-gained freedom: "My analysis is giving me more self-dependence and freedom by diminishing further what was left of my father-complex, and I think you will welcome that as much as I do." Through his experience of the couch, Jones has reached the conviction Ferenczi has maintained for a long time, and expresses it in his own words: "It is better to have a natural and therefore permanent attitude of respect and admiration than a kind of veneration which brings with it the danger of ambivalency." In Budapest, Jones has gained inner freedom in his relations with Freud; Ferenczi would soon try to gain the same freedom on Freud's couch.

On July 8, Jones refers to the progress of his analysis:

> The analysis here still makes progress. Ferenczi is very patient with my eccentricities and changes of mood, and we get ever deeper into things. We also spend much time together in scientific talks, and understand each other very well. He has a beautiful imagination, perhaps not always thoroughly

disciplined, but always suggestive. He has been exceedingly kind to me here, and I shall always remember it. I have nearly a month more here, and hope to get a good deal more done in that time.

It is clear that Ferenczi's aim in analytic work is to "get ever deeper into things."

On July 22, Jones announces the imminent end of his stay in Hungary:

Well, my analysis is drawing towards a close, and I have found it so valuable that I am wondering if I can manage to get in another month next year. It has without doubt been successful in making me face more clearly various character traits and dangerous tendencies, and I trust that it will prove its value also when it comes to be tested in actual life.

We can guess that for Ferenczi deepening the analysis involves analysing personality traits, as if the personality as a whole were a symptom. Jones's letter continues:

I cannot praise Ferenczi too highly for his skill and tact throughout, and he has also succeeded in making it congruous with the analysis to be very kind 'out of school,' so that on the whole I have had a very enjoyable time in Budapest.

What new "out of school" social relation does Jones draw attention to by distinguishing it in these terms from the collegiality between men who share ideas and belong to the same work community?

On August 5, 1913, Ferenczi refers to the end of this analysis in his letter to Freud, confessing: "Jones left me four days ago. I miss him very much. We have become intimate friends; I grew to love and treasure him; it was a pleasure to have such intelligent, fine and respectable pupil." Now that these twice-daily sessions were over, Ferenczi had a strange feeling of emptiness. Was it a state of "unbeing"? As to the benefits of the analysis for his patient, Ferenczi remained cautious: "His convictions were more securely based, his self-reliance increased, and probably also his courage to be somewhat more original." Analysis, Ferenczi is implying, should reinforce the analysand's courage, the arrogant desire necessary to manifest the originality and uniqueness expected of every person. But the success of an analysis is to be assessed as well by the future it makes possible: "Let us hope he will succeed in mastering his neurotic tendencies from now on – but I will not venture to make a definite prognosis on this." This is the vital question of faith Ferenczi is left with at the end of his analysis of Jones. It is not surprising, therefore, that a few weeks later, at the Munich Congress, Ferenczi presents this question as one of the key concepts of analysis. To the firm belief in the existence of the unconscious, evidenced by the symptom, Ferenczi adds "faith" in the unconscious.

Faith, incredulity and trust

In Munich, two years before Freud presented his "Observations on Transference-Love," Ferenczi wrote a pivotal text on what we shall call "transference trust," which he named "capacity for transference." As he continued to prepare the ground for his future analysis, this concept suggested the quality that would give his future work its force and singularity.

On the eve of his second work session with Lou Andreas-Salomé, Ferenczi presented "On the Psychology of Conviction," a lecture later published under the title "Belief, Disbelief and Conviction." In this paper, Ferenczi investigates the conditions needed to arrive at psychological conviction. Without ever invoking the overly psychologising notion of conscientisation, Ferenczi examines how the analyst's interventions are received by the patient, in light of the fact that their analytic effect is entirely dependent on the dynamics of the transference. For instance, how can one judge the reality of the patient's subjective interpretation of events? Would it be enough to trust the emotional nature of his agreement with the analyst's interpretative hypotheses, knowing that this agreement depends on the patient's trust in the image he has of the person conducting the analysis? According to Ferenczi, this is where things become problematic; he points out that this essential trust is never pure, and that when it is secretly absent, it must be regained in the momentum of the analysis.

Is the analysand's agreement with a particular intervention of his analyst the expression of clear and objective reality or of some nebulous subjective reality? What is the difference between transference trust and the excessive enthusiasm and faith often shown by hysterics at the start of an analysis? What must be done to prevent such blind trust from turning into "utmost intellectual resistance," like the resistance of obsessional neurotics suffering from doubting mania? Agreeing with Freud, Ferenczi describes this mania as "characterised by the inhibition of the power of judgement: belief and disbelief come into play here simultaneously, or immediately after each other, with equal intensity [...]" Ferenczi speaks from experience: he recognises that these transference effects in his practice generate intellectual inhibition in him, of a very particular kind, since they affect only his divided relationship with the father of psychoanalysis.

Ferenczi goes on to speak of the difficulty of working with paranoid patients: "The paranoiac [...] does not scrutinize the attempted explanation put before him at all, but sticks to the question, what motive, what interest can the doctor have for making that statement, what purpose is he pursuing thereby [...]" In this state of mind, and given his delusional interpretation, the patient "will not go deeper with the analysis." But even without "delusions of persecution," no analysand can avoid moments of subjective unreason when he is gripped by doubt and distrust as to the secret desire of the one who is listening to him without revealing anything about the motives of his action. Ferenczi is definite in his confirmation of this phenomenon: "Moreover, there is hardly an analysis during the course of which the patient does not temporarily, or for a more prolonged period, identify the doctor who takes the father's place with the devil himself." The patient might ask himself whether there is a hidden intention behind the well-meaning neutrality of the analyst. Just as a disciple, like Jung, might ask.

It is clear that this representation of the analyst/analysand relation resembles the pupil/teacher relation. This is often the case, particularly when the patient "sees in the doctor alternately his helpful, omniscient deity, whom one must blindly believe in all things, and his equally omnipotent but demoniacally malevolent destroyer, whom one may not believe even in apparently obvious matters." Aside from shedding light on Ferenczi's state of mind as his analysis drew near, this short text written in 1913 reveals a particular trait of his analytic research. Given their different temperaments and the different positions they occupy in the history of psychoanalysis, Freud and Ferenczi have divergent views on the clinical manifestations of transference. Oddly enough, this difference is particularly obvious in Ferenczi's 1913 article about belief, disbelief and conviction, just as it is in another article on a related theme, written the same year.

From transference trust to transference love

In his essay "Observations on Transference-Love" (1915), Freud focused on true love present in the transference of adults in analysis. He goes so far as to speak of a woman's "passionate demand for love" in transference, meaning a demand for sexual enjoyment. Freud asserts that transference love, with its erotomaniac potential, is the repetition of an original infantile love characterised by an unconditional demand for love like the incestuous demand of the child Oedipus who wants everything: the disappearance of the father and possession of the maternal object. This is why this transference love can resemble the pathological, even though Freud admits that "these departures from the norm constitute precisely what is essential about being in love." In transference on the analyst, this instinctual demand for jouissance is to be seen as originating in a symptomatic fixation or in regression to a psycho-sexual stage preceding the genital stage. In 1937, Freud would assert that given the biological origins of castration anxiety, neither the man nor the woman can ever reach a genital stage free of the partial instinctual impulses of previous stages. In 1913, two years before Freud, Ferenczi was thinking about the economy of transference and its effects in the course of an analysis, but his approach was very different. Five characteristics distinguish this approach:

1) His focus was not transference love as such, but rather transference trust.
2) Like Freud, he traced back problems of trust to childhood, but not to a particular stage of psycho-sexual development, although according to Freud these stages organise the partial drives "under the primacy of the genitals." He equates "the abnormalities of belief" with "symptoms of regression to or fixation at those infantile stages in the evolution of reality which I have called the magical and projection phases of the sense of reality." Here, Ferenczi refers the reader to another text written in this prolific year 1913, "Stages in the

Development of the Sense of Reality." In this essay, he "attempt[s] to bridge over the gap between the pleasure and the reality stages of mental development" – the stages Freud described in *Formulations on Two Principles of Mental Functioning* (1911).

3) In his second 1913 test, Ferenczi identified the various stages of specific psychic activity which gradually give the infant – before he speaks – access to the field of speech and language, and to conscious thought which this field makes possible. Only then can there be an "adjustment to reality, i.e. by the testing of reality that is based on judgement," which is free from the problems of judgement he is now examining. Thus, he adds to Freud's range of psychosexual development a new level we might call psycho-linguistic, and then strives to connect these two types of developmental stages.

4) By combining his two texts, Ferenczi becomes able to identify as "symptoms of regression to or fixation at […] infantile stages in the evolution of reality" the "abnormalities of belief, extreme ecstasies of belief, doubting mania, as well as disbelief in general and distrust," which can infiltrate transference and disturb the judgement of the analysand about the progress of the treatment and about his analyst. Ferenczi ascribes these transferential disturbances to regression to a specific stage in the development of a sense of reality, the phase he calls "the magical and projective stage of the sense of reality." Clearly, he understands this phase in light of his own interpretation of Freud's discussion of the experience of satisfaction, as described in the *Project*, published in 1897. In that text, Freud emphasised, to begin with, the reorganisation of internal somatic stimuli as a result of the "specific action" bringing the newborn "extraneous help" from his environment; he saw as "a secondary function," albeit "extremely important," the development of "an understanding with other people," originating in this stage. Ferenczi, on the other hand, emphasised the linguistic aspect of this experience of "an understanding with other people," which signals the child's access to alterity. In fact, he seemed to say that an inexpressible wish to encounter or bring back a particular other of the specific action – language action – is present in every request for analysis. Thus, abnormalities of belief originate in this phase where the infant, not yet aware of the mediation provided by an extraneous helper – the other in a relation of care and speech – attributes magical power to his own motor discharges (crying, struggling) which can make the object of his wish materialise. These motor impulses are felt to function like "magic signals, at the dictation of which the satisfaction promptly arrives."

Before awareness of the intercession of an external helper, the infant can believe in the magical omnipotence of what becomes a veritable "gesture-language." Ferenczi compares this subjective impression of the child, in this period of omnipotence, to what a magician might feel when he forgets for an instant that there is a "trick," a technique behind his fascinating and hypnotic gestures.

5) Ferenczi points out that this phase of "omnipotence by the help of magi-
    cal gestures" sheds light on "the curious jump from the world of thought
    into that of bodily processes," which constitutes hysterical conversion. Once
    again, in contrast to Freud, who was more focused on the instinctual econ-
    omy of these processes of reality sense development, Ferenczi emphasises
    their language dimension. They are the means by which a subject emerges
    and the living organism becomes the human body of a speaking and sexual
    being. As we continue our enquiry, we shall see how this orientation takes
    on a radical character with the taking into consideration of what are called
    "hysterical materialisation phenomena" in 1919, and finally in 1929, when
    Ferenczi reproaches Freudian psychoanalysis with remaining too focused on
    ego-psychology, "neglecting the organic-hysterical basis of the analysis." He
    would even speak of the "traumatic-hysterical basis of illness."

This link between "abnormalities of belief" and the phase of magic gestures in
which conversion hysteria originates inspired a delightful passage on the role of
the hand in the repertoire of magic gestures: "In the mental life of the normal the
countless number of superstitious gestures, or such as are in some other way considered efficacious (gestures of cursing, blessing, praying) is a remainder of that
developmental period of the sense of reality [...]" a period, he adds, "in which
one still felt mighty enough to be able to isolate the regular order of the universe."
About this order, Ferenczi remarks in a footnote that this is "of course quite unsuspected," just as, for the newborn, there is an unsuspected external helper who
makes the bottle appear when it is urgently desired.

The persistence of this infantile phase which remains in the adult explains the
fact that: "Fortune-tellers, soothsayers, and the magnetisers continually find belief
in the assertion of such complete power of their gestures [...]" It is easy to understand why, after elaborating these ideas, Ferenczi wanted to examine the nature
of an analysand's agreement with a particular statement of his analyst, or with his
judgement of the benefits or harmful effects of the treatment. The same questioning could be used to assess the views of detractors of psychoanalysis as a new
scientific domain. Are we dealing with hysterical belief, obsessional disbelief or
delusional conviction? How can we distinguish subjective sentimentality from the
objectivity tied to a sense of reality?

Ferenczi raises these questions ahead of Freud, who would turn to them in 1920.

Before the fort-da, there was the gesture

As he continues to reflect on the stages by which a speaking subject gains access
to the sense of reality, Ferenczi tries to understand how the subject leaves behind
the stage of magic, and how the illusion of the omnipotence of the gesture is lost.
Just as Freud would do in 1920 with the game of the bobbin, he invokes a form
of myth to illustrate the initial elusive moment when the prodigious power of
the hand is perceived to have been nothing more than an illusion, a supposition.

Indeed, sooner or later, the trembling hand of the infant propelled by an urgent need is no longer seeking the vitally necessary bottle, but reaches for an unattainable object, asking for the impossible – the moon, we might say. The moon which smiles down on him in the deep darkness of the night. When the toddler stretches his hand in the direction of the moon he desires and wants to seize, "the outstretched hand must often be drawn back empty, the longed-for object does not follow the magic gesture." Similarly, after the moment of jubilation when he recognises himself in the image reflected in the mirror, the baby senses the presence of an illusion and turns away from it to recognise himself in the face of the other, the one who is holding him.

The same thing happens, Ferenczi admits, when the infant or the toddler stretches out his hand to reach the indifferent moon, understands the futility of his gesture and can turn to another who acts as a witness, praises him and formulates the richness of the painful experience of reality testing to which he is being exposed.

These recurrent failed rendezvous with the desired object contribute to bringing about the major evolution that awaits all subjects in the process of becoming: "Till now the 'all-powerful' being has been able to feel himself one with the world that obeyed him and followed his every nod, but gradually there appears a painful discordance in his experience." This discordance introduces the infant to his subjective division, since from now on he is going to be split between his ego and the outside world. Thus, what emerges gradually is not so much a reality principle, but rather the sense of reality. The little human "has to distinguish [...] between the subjective psychical contents (feelings) and the objectified ones (sensations)." Ferenczi's allegory of the hand stretched towards the moon foreshadows the allegory Freud would use seven years later in *Beyond the Pleasure Principle*. Through the bobbin game – the body and an object – and the *fort/da* game – the voice and words – the child takes control of, and symbolises, the mother's absence, avoiding the anxiety related to the radical and deadly disappearance of the other who provides care, and to the terror associated with the imagined permanent nature of this disappearance. This masterful access to the sphere of play absent at the stage of magic can be considered the moment when desire is humanised, and the child gains access to the power of the symbol.

Ferenczi's 1913 essays not only foreshadow Freud's 1920 writings, but they also in fact complete them. Indeed, before the hand reaching for the moon can be replaced by the playful hand, it had to have had time to do the work of laying the foundations of the necessary sphere of illusion. In fact, Ferenczi insists on this point repeatedly: he agrees that the child leaves behind a sphere of illusion, but only after having enjoyed this illusion for a time to his heart's content, under the protection of an attentive environment when the unavoidable and necessary disappointments occur. Both these conditions play a role in whether or not a relation of trust is established with the caregiver. Only after such a pre-traumatic relation is created or recreated can the trial of disillusion be experienced as the promise of a future, rather than a catastrophe inflicting injury on the very construction of the subjective apparatus. Later, Ferenczi was to equate trauma with such a catastrophe. Indeed, this catastrophe is at the origin of abnormalities of belief, of which negative transference is an example. Did Freud, his future analyst, take note of the message Ferenczi was sending him? Would the analysis that lay ahead live up to his expectations? Was it going to contribute to Ferenczi's future, confirming what Lou Andreas-Salomé declared: that "Ferenczi's time must come"?

In September 1913, one year still separates Ferenczi from the actual enactment of the personal analysis he has been anticipating for two years. Now, it is slowly drawing nearer.

At the same time, a woman endowed with great foresight, Lou Andreas-Salomé, feels concerned about the tension she detects in the relations between the two analysts she admires.

Lou Andreas-Salomé

Lou Andreas-Salomé was the first to sense in Ferenczi the intensity of a disturbance not at all due to the imaginary father–son representation, but entirely due to an analytic fact inherent to the act of speech itself in the context of analysis and in exchanges between analysts. As early as 1913, Lou was surprised by the strange inhibition paradoxically experienced by Ferenczi in the midst of the prolific collaboration between the most valued pupil he has become and Freud, the enlightened master. This strange, silent inhibition has the formidable power, on occasion, to leave Ferenczi speechless and unable to think when he is face-to-face with Freud.

Early in the spring of 1913, Lou Andreas-Salomé made a first three-day visit to Budapest, to see Ferenczi and continue her initiation into psychoanalysis, begun the previous autumn in Vienna. She took the initiative of inciting Ferenczi to bring out of oblivion the notes he jots down in a diary and then no longer consults, not bothering to expand on them. Lou is very impressed with the philosophical dimension she discovers in these intuitions Ferenczi is reluctant to put to use. She is particularly struck by his critical reservations about the existence of the "tendency to death" theorised by Freud, since she herself shares these reservations. In her journal, she does not hide her delight: "However fantastic the consequences of some of [his ideas] may yet seem to Ferenczi himself, it would be good if his way of seeing things would influence Freud's philosophical views."

Lou appears to understand Ferenczi's attitude, although he backs away from the paths his thoughts want to explore and clarify: "His ideas worry him […] since they are of a philosophical (synthetic) nature, they don't oppose Freud's, although, precisely for this reason, Freud is not happy with them." More astutely still, she supposes that Ferenczi knows that Freud is too busy and too preoccupied to be able to share his thoughts with him:

> In the conversations with Ferenczi it became very clear to me that all Freud's well-wishers must for the present hope for the most tolerant policy on his part toward the schisms. This policy is best for his own work and peace of mind and hence also indirectly for his cause […]

Indeed, Freud needs to protect himself from the political turmoil agitating the Freudian circle at the time. Lou concludes that the difficulty she senses in the relation between the two men is momentary: "perhaps publication of Ferenczi's ideas is premature with respect to Freud's present and next endeavors, but they really *are* complementary. So Ferenczi's time *must* come."

But fortunately Lou Andreas-Salomé went beyond these reasonable observations. Used to the company of exceptional men like Nietzsche, Rainer Maria Rilke and recently Freud, she perceived with rare finesse another enigmatic characteristic of Ferenczi's relation, not with Freud, but with his own analytic concepts:

> But it is significant that Ferenczi speaks of these, his dearest ideas, those by which he might be said to live in his lonely state (as the manner of his talking about them plainly attests), as "craziness," "pathological curiosity," and his burning "desire for omniscience."

Thus, she reveals that Ferenczi lacks confidence in the ideas formulated in his writings, not recognising them as his own, and apparently experiencing them as emerging from an obscure place with no guarantee, as if produced by someone other than himself. Intrigued by this discovery, Lou proves to be clairvoyant, showing Ferenczi to be trapped in an impossible dilemma, unable either to formulate his thoughts or betray them, without being a coward: "It is interesting how even in the midst of his work he himself tries to run away from [his innermost experiences], although he is passionately determined to pursue them." This fierce determination she senses under Ferenczi's reserve reinforces her conviction: "Ferenczi's time must come." When she makes this prophecy, Lou Andreas-Salomé is both right and wrong.

She is wrong in two ways. The undeniable malaise she detects in the friendship and cooperation between the two analysts she considers the most accomplished does not originate in their philosophical convictions. Moreover, Ferenczi's time would not come as she imagined and hoped.

But now, at the start of 1913, Lou is also right in two ways. She is not mistaken when she detects the fear that grips Ferenczi at the idea of moving away from his position as a loyal Freudian, and letting his own voice and difference finally be heard. To speak "to" Freud, even in self-analysis, to speak of, or based on, his doctrines, is not yet, as Ferenczi knows, to state a viewpoint emerging from a place other than full consciousness.

Lou is also right to suppose that what sometimes stops Ferenczi in his tracks, as if paralysed by the Medusa's gaze, is not connected to fear of the disapproval of the father of psychoanalysis, but to a deeper anxiety. Ferenczi confided to Lou that he was haunted by the ghost of the unwelcome child he had been, the son of a mother with too many children, prematurely widowed: "Ferenczi suffered as a child from insufficient recognition of his accomplishments, and it interfered with his diligence. Now alongside his publications, these works of his that contain his innermost spiritual experiences run a rather secret course because they are unappreciated." With a clairvoyance the two men do not yet possess, Lou differentiates between the works Ferenczi takes credit for, presents before audiences or publishes, and the works in which his dignity as a desiring subject is invested, which he keeps to himself.

But when she made this journal entry about her stay in Budapest, did Lou Andreas-Salomé know that three months earlier Ferenczi had already taken a radical and unprecedented initiative: that of asking Freud for an in-depth analysis? After long years of self-analysis, the time for analysis had now come for Ferenczi.

Chapter 4

The actual analysis (1914–1916)

Little by little

During the latter part of 1913 and the first half of 1914, the exchange of letters allows Ferenczi to refer regularly to his love life. Although, following Freud's implicit advice, he has apparently given up Elma, he has not yet decided to marry Gizella. The correspondence also allows Ferenczi to comment on the political situation at a time when a decisive confrontation is about to take place between Vienna and Zurich. There is complete disagreement about Freud's theory of the libido, and Jung is still President of the IPA and Director of the *Jahrbuch*. On February 11, 1914, Freud informs Ferenczi that in these troubled times he is writing – "very assiduously" – "On the History of the Psycho-Analytic Movement."

In 1912, as the situation involving Jung worsens, the Secret Committee comes into being. Ferenczi feels at ease in this small friendly circle with no institutional power, but endowed with unquestionable analytic authority. He is, however, less comfortable with Freud, who refuses to participate in the analytic reciprocity that Ferenczi seeks. On April 18, he writes to Freud:

> A real circle of friends is gradually coming out of the 'Committee,' in which one feels well and secure. But I had to observe not without pain that my position with respect to you, specifically, is not completely natural, and that your presence arouses inhibitions of various kinds in me that influence, and at times almost paralyze, my actions and even my thinking.

At first, this renewed reference to the paralysing inhibition present in his relationship with Freud seems surprising. Indeed, Ferenczi is clearly not hindered in his contribution to the development and transmission of Freudian theory; after all, in the space of two years (1913–1914), he has written 38 articles of various lengths. What then, is the nature of his inhibition, and what does it have to do with the intuition he had in the spring of 1911 when he engaged in "intimate conversation" with Freud about "mental activity in general" – the only way to gain access to "true knowledge" worthy of faith?

In other words, Ferenczi has doubts and raises questions: is the spirit of psychoanalysis best transmitted by means of classical teaching, or is it better served by another means of transmission? In his letter to Freud dated April 24, 1911, he did not answer this crucial question, merely reminding the latter of his own way of understanding and, above all, of adopting the Freudian doctrine:

> If one hears something new, then one is really obliged analytically to test one's personal relationship to the herald of the new doctrine in the most conscientious manner before one can make a decision as to the real value of that statement.

Does this ambiguous formulation make it possible to sense the nature of the inhibition of which Ferenczi constantly complains? Is the obligation of the one who hears a new theory to examine scrupulously his own personal relationship – transferential – to the one who promotes this theory, or must he also examine in-depth the personal relationship between this herald of the theory and the doctrine he promotes? Is it not this double obligation that causes Ferenczi to stumble on a difficulty inherent to the transmission of psychoanalysis, which could be the source of his stubborn inhibition?

On April 18, 1914, this difficulty is still present and rendered more acute by the fact that Ferenczi constantly questions his relations of dependence and independence to the inventor of psychoanalysis, while Freud is not inclined to dwell on the division Ferenczi introduces between the statement and the stating, or to disclose the personal narrative underlying his writings. But Ferenczi, with his frenzied passion for analysis, always asserted that beyond the Freudian theories he easily assimilated, he wanted to learn about Freud the man and the desire which animated him. This being so, is Ferenczi's inhibition a personal incapacity or the encounter with an impossibility?

And why is this inhibition at once so insistent and volatile? Two months later, on June 4, it seems to have disappeared. Filled with enthusiasm, Ferenczi is effusive in his praise:

> Just read Narcissism with delight. Haven't had such pleasure in reading in a long time. But I also have to admit to you – and you can take this openness as a sign of the uninhibited inner freedom that is beginning to develop in me – that for years I have actually not been able to read anything thoroughly except your writing.

Why does Ferenczi use the verb "admit" rather than "confess," if not because he knows that Freud is reluctant to be confronted with his affective (transferential) reactions?

On July 20, tensions arise once again between Ferenczi and Freud, when the former comments on the latter's firm decision to break off relations with Jung unceremoniously: "Getting rid of Jung has meant for you to return to your original mode of work: to take everything into your own hands and not to rely on 'collaborators.'" Thus, in July 1914 Ferenczi attributes to Freud a need for independence, a desire to go on alone [...] like the desire he expressed in Sicily, by which Ferenczi was hurt, when their planned collaboration on a text on paranoia was cancelled. Now, Ferenczi says that he is ready – reluctantly – to give up the "intimate conversation" whose virtues he values, and to be content with Freud's texts:

> But the main thing remains that we get as much as possible from you in writing, and to this end independence is the most beneficial thing. That also consoles me in the face of the loss that I, too, among your other collaborators, will sustain through this change of course. Petty personal interests must keep silent when it is a matter of such significant values.

Aware of the obvious ambivalence of his statements, Ferenczi goes on to say, dutifully, as if against his will: "As grateful as I am for the personal intercourse with you and for your interest in my advancement, I have been and am most grateful for your words, which have embellished my life and profession." Two days later, appearing irritated, Freud responds with a denial: "[...] you overestimate Jung's significance for my emotional life in much the same way he did. I don't know of any new course with regard to my friends." Freud refuses to be called to account, and in addition to showing his irritation, he firmly sets things straight:

> I have also not sacrificed our usual get-together to comfort but rather to renewed work, for which I can't use comradeship. I also don't work easily together with you in particular. You grasp things differently and for that reason often put a strain on me.

The next day Ferenczi makes amends: "I concede that I may be overestimating Jung's significance for your emotional life, as he himself did, and you can believe me when I say that I am not very [proud about] this symptom of unconscious identification with him."

On July 28, 1914, Austria-Hungary declared war on Serbia. In Vienna, conscription in the Austro-Hungarian Empire was announced on July 31. Freud's sons, as well as Ferenczi, were drafted.

On August 24, 1914, as the start of the planned analysis approaches, Ferenczi tries to reassure Freud, knowing his reservations:

> I promise to muster everything, in order to mitigate the difficulties [...] If things turn out differently to some extent, then that would be material for further analysis, whereby you would have to proceed with all necessary strictness. You know, of course, that I am suffering from the memory of the good father. Perhaps the bad one will loosen my tongue!

Five weeks before the start of his first analytic session, Ferenczi is drawing Freud's attention to the probable presence, underneath the positive transference on the good father, of a negative transference on the bad father. On September 2, he reminds Freud that "I have on no account totally given up the other idea (to be analyzed by *you*)," if he is not called up.

One week later, on September 8, he sends Freud the self-analysis of a recent dream restructured, in view of publication, into a dialogue between an analyst and his analysand: "You will also recognise yourself in it – in the person of the doctor who doesn't want to analyze me." Written three weeks before the start of the adventure on Freud's couch, this dream, called the "occlusive pessary dream," proves to be even more enlightening than the two dreams Ferenczi analysed at length on December 26, 1912, when he made his first request for analysis.

The occlusive pessary dream

Once again, I leave to the reader the pleasure of discovering the daring feat consisting of the self-analysis – Freudian – of this dream in which the dreamer introduces an occlusive pessary into his urethra. Ferenczi presents this dream as a dialogue between an analyst and an analysand, in a session. The analyst questions his patient on the waking material that could have produced the dream just recounted; the analysand answers, embarking on the associative work expected of him. Between them, as one continues to associate and the other to react, the interpretation of the dream reveals a powerful castration complex, feminine identification with the mother as teacher, a feminine position in regard to the father, auto-erotic pleasure and wish fulfilment: by performing this act, the dreamer gives himself the child that the woman does not give him. There is nothing surprising in this classical Freudian interpretation. What we find astonishing about this dream is something else.

The dream sets out, almost word for word, the themes that were to be, and actually were, those of the three segments of the analysis to come: the fear of not being able to have children, the impediment to marriage, and the dissatisfaction of being unable to choose between the older and the younger woman. But this remarkable foreshadowing is not a complete surprise, since these topics were already present, and had been for several years, in the exchanges between Freud and Ferenczi. What is truly startling in Ferenczi's account is the way in which the analyst and the analysand go from analysing the content of the dream to discussing its transferential aspect. This interpretation concerns the very thing that later would, in fact, constitute a stumbling block for the termination of Ferenczi's future analysis. In the fictional context of the pessary dream, Ferenczi shows the analyst going beyond the analysis of the instinctual and sexual content of the dream, and taking the initiative of examining its transferential dimension: "It is an ascertained rule of dream interpretation [...] that mockery and scorn are concealed behind such nonsense dreams."

Thanks to his experience, Ferenczi, the astute analyst senses that behind the rich content of this dream which reinforces his Freudian perspective there is a more cunning intention and more aggressive impulses. Paying attention to negative transference allows the analysand to speak and to expose this negative transference:

> My next ideas concern you, doctor, though I cannot just at once see that connection. I remember that yesterday you suggested to me that presently I should not require your services any longer, and that I could now manage quite alone. This, however, really only caused me regret, as I did not yet feel myself so far recovered as to be able to do without your assistance.

The potential conflict between the two partners involved in the analysis is clear, since one sees the work as nearing completion, while the other thinks that, on the contrary, there is still work to be done. One thinks that the analysand is settling into transference neurosis, while the other thinks his analyst is avoiding having to analyse negative transference. Indeed, this is exactly what happened two years later, in Ferenczi's personal analysis, when Freud put an end to their sessions.

In the fictional context of the occlusive pessary dream, the analyst admits the relevance of his analysand's intuition: "Now I understand. You mock at me by showing by the unskillful introduction of the pessary how wrong it is to leave you alone and to consider you capable from now on of being your own doctor."

In this scenario, Ferenczi presents an analyst eager to separate from his analysand, and to send him back to self-analysis as soon as possible. This is what he tells his patient:

> You may be partly right; on the other hand, the repeatedly confirmed transference to me that makes breaking off the analysis difficult for you shows itself in your dislike of my remarks. This tendency lets you under-estimate your own capabilities and exaggerates my importance and assistance.

Thus, about three weeks before the start of his own personal analysis, Ferenczi dreams of an analyst who could not only refuse to continue the analysis, but would like to avoid being the object of transference. To this end, he adds, to his previous interpretation, an interpretation of the pessary as a child: "The child that you were making for yourself would therefore also be your own self-analysis." Exposed, the analysand responds by pointing out the limits of self-analysis, to justify his desire to continue the analysis on the couch:

> I have repeatedly tried to analyse myself. I sit at my desk, I write what comes to my mind, I fill pages with my associations, without arriving at anything worthwhile. My thoughts flow into the immeasurable, I cannot collect them properly, I find no clue to the tangle. On the contrary I often marvel at the skill with which you can reduce to order what seems so disconnected.

Through the brilliant language of the dream, Ferenczi skillfully reveals the existence, between analyst and analysand, of an accessory misunderstanding not related to the inevitable subjective disparity between their respective positions in the analytic process, but rather to the subjectivity evolving as the analysis unfolds. The analyst, rooted in his Freudian position, rightly considers that the time has come for the analysand to forego the transferential overestimation of the figure of the analyst, and to overcome the powerlessness caused by the underestimation of his own powers. This analyst thinks that it is time for the analysand to emerge from the trance of transference love, to wake up and to enter, at long last, the time of desire of a mortal man.

The analysand, Ferenczian or Lacanian ahead of his time, tries in vain to signify to his analyst that his subjective situation goes beyond the infantile dependence on the paternal figure of the analyst, suggested by the latter. The analysand knows that he is not merely immobilised in the jouissance of a regressive position repeated in the transference. Courageously, he defends his position. In the transference – whose value he recognises – he also needs the echo provided by what we call analytic dialogue, for lack of a better term. This analysand knows that he cannot fully trust the thoughts that fill his mind, he knows that he can only take hold of the sparks of truth in his own discourse through the echo sent back to him by the one who hears them. Without commenting, this "other" answers by letting him hear the words that strove to emerge in his associations on the couch, as he now sought himself in vain in his auto-analytic rantings.

The pessary dream Ferenczi describes is astounding, as we said earlier. A few days before starting his actual analysis, Ferenczi already knows what obstacle will cause the analysis "to end without being terminated," for better or for worse. The analysand in Ferenczi already knows that the analyst in Freud will concentrate on the difficulties in Ferenczi's love life, rather than on the more delicate matter of his transference on his analyst.

The question is, why is it that on the brink of his analysis Ferenczi has this dream and recounts it to Freud or, to be more exact, intends to publish it? And why, in view of publication, does he present it as a discussion on the termination of an analysis? Is it a personal premonition or a preventive warning addressed to Freud? It was in this setting, when the brutality of world history, the upheavals of the analytic movement and the humble personal stories of analysts intersected, that Ferenczi arrived in Vienna on October 1, 1914, to start his analysis.

The first segment of analysis

These three and a half weeks of analysis with two sessions a day are preceded by a parapraxis that Ferenczi announces in an amused tone on September 30, 1914: "[…] missed train [I have] material for two hours that I request tomorrow afternoon." The analysis starts on October 1, 1914, and is interrupted when Ferenczi is drafted as a military physician in the Hungarian Hussards stationed in the town of Pápa, where Freud would later visit him. Of course, we know neither the content nor the dynamics of these approximately 50 sessions – of 55 minutes – and can only surmise something about them by reading what the two men discussed afterwards in their correspondence.

In his letter dated October 27, Ferenczi seems considerably perturbed:

> I will – I believe – have to conduct our correspondence, at least in part, on an analytical basis; the sudden breaking off of our doctor-patient relationship (you see, I am writing as if in free association) would otherwise be all too painful for me. In addition, difficult to carry out.

Under the influence of transference, self-analysis takes another form: "It went smoothly; I imagined I was talking to you" – but it does not replace actual analysis: "I know how much I have lost through the interruption of the analysis." Ferenczi describes his new activities, his moods and his torments, and his "fierce struggle against masturbation." He then tries to pull himself together: "Now, I promise not to burden you so much with my case from now on. The time will, must, come when I can continue and terminate the treatment!"

On October 30, Freud offers support, in the face of Ferenczi's distress: "I take it from your letter how lively your infantile consciousness of guilt still is! The sudden interruption of the treatment at a time when it was most interesting and productive was very stupid. But it couldn't be helped." He encourages Ferenczi to stop tormenting himself: "I will now give you the prognosis that the self-analysis will very soon fail, and that's alright, because self-analysis and that done by another can't complement each other." Ferenczi complies: "Your opinion was, for me – an order!" On November 30, he comments on another regrettable effect of the short segment of analysis conducted:

> The only – and not totally insignificant – disturbance in our relations as a result of the broken-off analysis is manifested in the fact that I have difficulty in finding the tone for our correspondence. I am vacillating between a normal letter and a literary-analytic confession until the resistance which expresses itself in the vacillation prevails and the letter doesn't get written at all

On December 2, 1914, Freud expresses both regret and renewed reluctance:

> Also regret breaking off the promising analysis […] On the other hand, if war hadn't come, you wouldn't have had any reason to spend your vacation in Vienna, and I might have had reservations about taking you on. Still, the situation remains disagreeable.

On December 18, Ferenczi expresses his hope that, if Freud is willing, his analysis might be continued one day: "It is difficult to tell personal things, once one has tasted psychoanalytic completeness […] But why bring up all these problems. Maybe you will take me into treatment again; until then one has to muddle through as best one can." On the last day of the year, Ferenczi seems satisfied: "Looking back [on] the personal events of the year gone by, I must single out the few weeks of analysis with you as the most valuable"; but he regrets the persistence of neurotic traits in himself:

> I – despite my years – have still not reached anything definitive, and am still deeply mired in the juvenile – not to mention the infantile. Perhaps the chronic juvenilism keeps one from aging prematurely; certainly it hinders one from fulfilling one's personal and social task.

The 1915 correspondence between Freud and Ferenczi dwells on concerns related to the war situation, on personal news and on the research work conducted by each of them in this period when the evolution of the analytic movement has been slowed down. Freud expresses his desire to pursue the understanding of narcissistic neuroses, and to explore the question of mourning and melancholia. On April 28, 1915, Ferenczi reveals that he is engaged in a new type of research:

> From purely psychological perspectives, I attempted [...] to approach the problem of coitus more closely. It proved to be unavoidably necessary for me also to seek biological support for my hypotheses; for that reason I had to read embryological, zoological, and comparative physiological material.

This work led, eight years later, to the publication of *Thalassa: A Theory of Genitality*. On December 16, Ferenczi's letter announces his transfer to Budapest, through the intervention of Anton von Freund, the husband of one of Freud's patients – someone who was to play an important role in Freud's life in the near future. In his last letter that year, Ferenczi writes: "I am getting into a section for cases of nervous illness due to war. An opportunity to occupy oneself with Traumatic Neuroses. See you soon, I hope." It is the first time that Ferenczi finally thinks he will be able to see Freud again. The year 1916 was going to be that of the last two segments of analysis.

The second segment of analysis

As soon as he is back in Budapest, Ferenczi is once again faced with indecision in regard to the romantic choice expected of him by Gizella and Elma, as well as by Freud, who is secretly annoyed with his hesitation in personal affairs. On January 17, 1916, Ferenczi complains:

> I was immediately placed into the situation in which I was at the time of the inner division on account of Elma: my libido was withdrawn from Frau G.; after cessation of my sexual overestimation I saw with gruesome clarity the changes brought about by age which were evident in her.

Here, he engages, as he so often has in the past, in a lengthy attempt at self-analysis of his dilemma. The next day, Freud's answer is firm, although it is difficult to say whether he is speaking as Ferenczi's analyst or as the head of a movement which needs men dedicated to the cause: "Your interpretations are certainly correct, but they still leave out […] the most important thing." Freud considers that the time has come for Ferenczi to make a decision, take action, say yes or no to marriage; and that neither analysis nor self-analysis can help him avoid the risk he must take. Hence, Freud's advice is: "So, act now, as swiftly and decisively as possible, and refrain from analysis now, or treat it as an extra enjoyment without real influence." This injunction from Vienna complicates things for Ferenczi, who can't be sure whether he will be acting of his own accord or under Freud's influence. Therefore, he apologises for being drawn once again into a laborious self-analysis of his relation with Freud, who clearly expects something else of him:

> I feel like a wayward son who has only mischief to report. But I am also remiss in complete honesty with respect to you – since this is the first condition for improvement. I remind you of my neurotic behaviour in the Hôtel de France in Palermo. There, too, the fear of succumbing to your suggestion in common scientific work and of not writing my own opinion was to blame for my refusal.

Did Freud perceive Ferenczi's awkward insistence on showing him that under the influence exerted by the symptomatic position of an indecisive and immature man, another symptomatic position was manifest – not that of his romantic relation to the woman, but his transferential position in relation to Freud himself? Still in the grip of tormenting indecision, Ferenczi is unwell and speculates about his physical symptoms. Maintaining his rigorous attitude, on March 12 Freud speaks with the same firmness: "One must be able to decide whether one loves a woman or not even with stuffed-up nostrils. Of course, I know how difficult it is to differentiate between the psychic and the somatic in one's own person." On April 7 Ferenczi refers to his short visit to Vienna, where the two men obviously had a chance to talk: "The stay in Vienna did me much good. As confirmation of the fact that I belong to the 'not-wanting-to-act' type, I can tell you that I already gave up a relationship […] when it was threatening to be realized." Later that month, these rather monotonous exchanges ended when, on April 27, Ferenczi expressed his wish to start a second segment of analysis shortly. Before making his request, he informed Freud that he has just sent a short article on analytic technique to Hanns Sachs. He implied that his scientific work as an analyst was inseparable from the work of the analysand he soon expected to be: "I didn't want to touch on the great and difficult theme of the physician's active intervention in the analysis and confined myself to repeating what I learned from you about the 'Recommendations.'" ["Recommendations to Physicians Practising Psycho-Analysis," 1912]. But Ferenczi is mistaken: he is unable to confine himself to applying – as a good professional should – Freud's technical advice, precisely because as an analysand he is disconcerted by the personal experience of the advice his analyst gives him in a very direct and even intrusive manner.

Ferenczi's short article was published in 1919 under the title "On Influencing of the Patient in Psycho-Analysis." When it was written, in the spring of 1916, Ferenczi knew exactly what he was talking about. He was deliberately diverging from Jones' opinion that "A psycho-analyst should never advise a patient, least of all to sexual intercourse." Ferenczi advances the hypothesis that in certain cases, and at certain moments in the analysis, the analyst can intervene actively without being disloyal to a certain principle of analytic purity. He submits the following argument:

> In many cases of anxiety hysteria and of hysterical impotence, I found that the analysis went smoothly up to a certain point. The patients had full insight but the therapeutic result was always delayed; the ideas even began to repeat themselves with a certain monotony, as though the patient had nothing more to say, as though their unconscious were exhausted.

In the spring of 1916, Ferenczi's interests are starting to focus more and more on analytic technique. Indeed, he is the one who promotes the use of Freud's active technique, which he is experiencing firsthand on Freud's couch.

At this period, when he encounters not only the limits of self-analysis but also those of free association in the analyses he conducts – as is the case in his own atypical personal analysis – Ferenczi finds support in a remark made by Freud earlier, which suggested the possible benefits of an active influence, not to be confused with hypnotic suggestion. His article states:

> In this predicament some verbal advice of Prof. Freud's came to my assistance. He explained to me that after a certain time one must call upon anxiety hysterics to give up their phobically strengthened inhibitions and to attempt to do just what they are most afraid of.

The Hungarian version of the article gave examples: "[…] try, despite painful anxiety, to go out alone, attend social events, go to the theatre, etc." Did Freud consider Ferenczi's fear of marriage an anxiety hysteria? In any case, the influence Freud allowed himself to exert on his analysand had a fortunate collateral effect. It made the latter aware of the importance of technique in the analytic process. But, while Ferenczi, the analyst, takes a step forward, the analysand he is finds himself at a standstill.

On April 27, his desire to continue the analysis is very clear:

> What concerns me otherwise are all the old things: Indecision […] Paralysis naturally extends to all intentions. – Since I am giving up the Berlin trip (I expect nothing from the rhinologist there), I am planning instead of that to spend the whole three weeks that I am aspiring to in analysis. Perhaps the beginning of June. Two hours a day: that makes almost forty hours of analysis.

As he had done just before the start of the first segment of analysis – perhaps as a warning – he points out that the positive or negative effect of advice from the analyst depends on the moment in the analysis when it is given: "Obviously I am not so far [along] that one could successfully 'advise' me. Incidentally, a nice example of how little use in analysis 'suggestions' are, for which one is not yet ripe enough." But this reservation in no way denotes ambivalence on Ferenczi's part; his determination has not weakened: "The relief which this letter also gave me speaks for a real 'hunger for analysis.'"

On May 30, knowing he would be granted three weeks' leave starting on June 15, he lets Freud know: "I would like [...] to spend this time in treatment with you and request that you reserve two hours a day. My long silence is evidently in preparation for much talking in the sessions." On June 7, Ferenczi announces his arrival: "My leave has been granted. I arrive in Vienna on the 13th or the evening of the 14th and will perhaps be able to take the first hours already on the 14th." On June 13, he arrives in Vienna.

Once he is back in Budapest, on July 10, he writes a letter to Freud describing the immediate effects of his recent experience on the couch: "Above all, I think I can establish that these three weeks were the decisive ones in my life and for my life." He enumerates the changes he sees in himself. He has revealed the most important one to his companion:

> Today I told Gisella that I have become another person, one who is less interesting but more normal. I also admitted to her that something in me pities [the loss of] the old, somewhat unsettled man, who was nonetheless capable of such great enthusiasm (and certainly often needlessly depressed).

Undeceived, he knows that his dreams and his discomfort are telling him that he is not completely cured of his cruel indecision vis-à-vis Gizella, nor of his ambivalence towards Freud. Not fully convinced, he says he counts on the correspondence as a way to continue the analysis: "Probably an indication that I still have work to do on myself. If you permit, instead of simple autoanalysis I want to attempt to analyze the particular occurrences in my letters to you; the transference will certainly 'fecundate' me." As he did two years earlier, Ferenczi suffers from the sudden breaking off of this segment of analysis: "The feeling of gratitude that I owe you for your kind assistance will – I hope – permeate me more and more. For the moment the break in our doctor-patient relations was too sudden not to have caused a certain shock effect."

What he has just experienced and discovered on the couch leads him to draw a conclusion he sees as a theoretical advance:

> Theoretically, it is very interesting to learn why the analyzed patient cannot be grateful to his doctor. The doctor has certainly made him 'healthy,' i.e., taught him to comply with the real demands of life. But he took away the pleasure which in the unconscious accompanied all his [no matter how] uncomfortable, indeed, perhaps lethal, symptoms.

Here, Ferenczi is making a double discovery, which he is going to keep in mind. To psychoanalysis seen as the deciphering of unconscious formations, he adds psychoanalysis seen as an intervention in instinctual economy, and particularly in the economy of jouissance, which Freud would soon show to aim at something beyond the pleasure principle. Moreover, Ferenczi implies that this unavoidable loss of pleasure brought about in the treatment must affect the transference, inevitably calling attention to its negative aspect sooner or later.

The rest of the letter makes clear that once again Freud has taken an active role in the treatment of his analysand, who, in his work as an analyst, draws useful conclusions from this. "Analysis suddenly makes out of a man who has remained childish, therefore basically carefree, another who really becomes conscious of all responsibilities." But the letter dated July 28 reveals that Freud's probable injunctions to Ferenczi have not been altogether successful:

> [...] of my earlier symptoms, two important ones still persist: the inability to make a decision in the question of marriage – and my inability to work. – The parallelism of both symptoms is too striking to have escaped me. But the deeper connection is still missing.

As a result, he decides to do what is needed: follow up the previous segment of analysis: "I have the right to claim an additional two weeks' leave in the course of this year. I want to take it at the end of September [or beginning of October] and dedicate it to terminating or completing the treatment."

Ferenczi does not forget to mention what he has learned from his own experience of analysis, as if to point out the deepening of his understanding of what had previously been a theoretical concept: "I am incredibly much indebted to the last analysis for my analytic technique. It occurs to me that I have only now grasped the significance of repetition in the treatment in all its depth." This remark on repetition is significant, since it indicates the point of origin of a major clinical interest that Ferenczi would soon place at the centre of the revision of analytic practices he undertook in 1922.

On July 31 Freud answers a letter from Gizella in which she asked whether he considers it fair that she wait for her daughter Elma's return before making her own decision regarding the desire for marriage she senses Ferenczi would soon express. Freud resolutely avoids giving her answer, and urges her to be clear about what she herself wants. Then he makes a confession which sheds light on his countertransference in Ferenczi's analysis:

> After containing myself for years with regard to our friend, I have finally come forward with advice, because I believed in the meantime to have arrived at the conviction that there is no other possibility, and because I am in general disposed to believe in the imminent end of all things – youth among them.

Thus, Freud has advised his analysand directly to marry the mother rather than the daughter, to help him leave behind his illusions of youthfulness. But, wanting to be frank, Freud also tells her how frightening this is to him as an analyst:

> Now I am becoming frightened and would [...] not like to have advised any-thing. Not out of cowardice about taking responsibility, but because I feel uncertain and am naturally much too engaged to be able to judge without error what is best.

Thus, Freud, after exerting, in all probability, an active and unambiguous influ-ence on his analysand, reveals to his future wife that he is not free of doubt and indecision. The image of the analyst asserting the inevitable renunciation of a fantasy of youth unaffected by castration and by the arrival of the time of desire is covered over for an instant by the man who doubts and expresses indecision. On August 2, 1916, Freud consents to Ferenczi's request: "Your intention to dedicate two more weeks of leave to the analysis has my full approval. The when and where then depends on the extremely [uncertain] cir-cumstances of this summer." On August 14, Ferenczi confirms the new direc-tion his analytic research is taking – in our opinion – as a result of his personal experience in analysis: "My interest in the subtleties of technique has taken the place of my earlier bio-psychological interests." *Thalassa* has become a secondary interest.

Thus, in the summer of 1916 Ferenczi starts to use, in his own analytic prac-tice in Budapest, the active technique he experienced in Vienna as an analysand. Although the two men don't know it yet, this is the beginning of a change in Ferenczi's perspective, which would continue to deepen until it created a gap between them that ultimately broke the magical thread of their dialogue. Freud always considered *Thalassa*, in which Ferenczi expounds his genitality theory, his colleague's most accomplished work, and always associated him with this contri-bution, despite Ferenczi's vehement protests. Much later, on September 21, 1930, he made his objection very clear: "The 'theory of genitality' was the product of pure speculation at a time when, far removed from my practice, I totally gave way to contemplation (military service)."

But in the summer of 1916, Ferenczi didn't know yet that Freud would never adopt this new perspective which now leads him to focus all his interest as an ana-lyst on the treatment, the technique and the analyst's training. We can assert with confidence that this new orientation is the result of his experience in the personal analysis he is determined to continue. On September 15, Ferenczi makes his great desire for analysis known: "For certain practical reasons I am postponing my trip until the 25th of the month – but I ask you to reserve three hours per day [...] for me. I don't dare ask for four." He finally arrives in Vienna on September 29, and returns to Budapest on October 13.

The third segment of analysis

This third segment of analysis – about 40 sessions – turned out to be the last. The state of upheaval in which Ferenczi is left testifies to the violence of the internal work that had to be accomplished and which, when left in suspense once again, leaves him divided between exaltation and his disillusion, between the certainty of progress and the awareness of persistent attachments to the past. This is made clear in the letter started on October 17, 1916, a breathless seven-page letter written over a period of six days, in which Ferenczi specifies the place and time of each entry: "October 17, 1916, 11:15 P.M.," "October 18, Wednesday evening 11:30," "Evening of the 19th, 12 o'clock/ before bedtime," "October 20, afternoon. Between two [sessions] (a late patient)," "October 21. Morning [at] the hospital," "Sunday. October 22. Night." The formulation of the letter gives a glimpse of his internal turmoil. He senses that he is no longer exactly the same man, in his relations to Gizella, to his patients, to psychoanalysis, to himself and, of course, to Freud. Not wanting to "give […] a false picture of the situation which has occurred," Ferenczi allows himself some time before reporting on the internal changes that leave him temporarily destabilised.

As for his love life, although there is progress, nothing has really been resolved. In a moment of exaltation, he has asked Gizella to marry him, but she chose to postpone her decision because Elma is going through a difficult period. Although he seems to have finally made a commitment, Ferenczi is still attached to his fantasies of erotic adventure: "[…] the familiar motif of infidelity returned." But, at the same time, being aware of the transferential nature of the declaration of love made by a woman patient, his "clear insight" "cooled [him] off" and prevented any inappropriate action. His disappointment in the face of his lover's cool response to his marriage proposal leads him to reflect on the maternal nature of her relationship with him. He even supposes that his own inhibition could stem from the fact that for a long time he wanted to believe that she should make the decision; as a maternal figure holding the key to his future, she was the one who had to decide. This is another thing he learned from his analysis: "Only I am still hindered in deciding to want […]" Thus, he has discovered, at the heart of his neurosis, the fear of his own desire and his tendency to hide it behind his concern with what he supposes the other to be asking.

Ferenczi does not hesitate to describe with precision the quality of his sexual relations with Gizella, pointing out that he is now less perturbed by the visible signs of ageing he sees in her. It even seems that he has an unprecedented experience on the occasion of a "quite normal" coitus:

> A significant difference from before is that forepleasure – which was almost absent before, especially the satisfaction in pressing my face against her – was very pronounced. So much so that, despite [complete] preparedness, I decided only reluctantly to go through with the intercourse. The satisfaction was complete. Immediately afterward still great feeling of tenderness (as before coitus).

Ferenczi becomes aware of the possibility of overcoming the split he has created in himself between the tender and the sensual currents of sexual relations. But this awareness does not prevent him from observing that the problem is not yet solved: "The second coitus was a conscious attempt, which, however failed; it came to an action that wouldn't quit, which twice gave her satisfaction, but me not a single time." But he remains optimistic about his progress in the analysis: "I have already attained so much that – I think – I am less dominated by unconscious forces and decidedly more capable of love than before." He intends to put to good use this opportunity created by the strengthening of his capacity to love:

> I am also determined not to let the present situation last long. Either we suc-
> ceed in bringing our wishes into accord or it will have to come to a complete
> break in our relations. The capability for the latter has – strangely – also
> increased with the increase in the capability for love.

An imagined separation weakens the threat of fatal hold, love ceases to be an absolute which can swallow one up, and the fear of uniting dissipates.

The other internal change Ferenczi observes in himself is that in Gizella's company he recovers the passion for psychoanalysis which he now sometimes finds lacking: "My interest is not totally there. But where is it then? The solution came to me through [this] realization: after the sessions I met Gizella, and – all of a sudden I was in a good mood." He attributes this effect to his analysis:

> Ergo: my libido has become partly [available] through the analysis in Vienna. –
> The attempts to choose a new object floundered (as up to now, always). Only
> in Gizella's company am I in a better mood and at the same time feel an inter-
> est in science.

To what extent is this recovery of Ferenczi's capacity for love, which used to fail him as a result of an internal split, due to the waning of transference love? How closely is it tied to entering a time when Freud's thinking is no longer the only means of access to his own inspiration? But is this new desire not opposed to Freud's principles, given that Ferenczi rationalises the need for marriage as follows: "Consequently, she is the one whom I must finally secure for myself. My capacity to be able to work seems to depend on marriage to G. Tomorrow I intend finally to get serious with this thing." With this relative progress in his relation to love and desire, to tenderness and the sexual, which Ferenczi welcomes, comes a change in his manner of practising analysis.

Ferenczi reports that the desire he invests in his activity, in his way of relating to patients in his daily practice, has changed:

> In the analytic hours I notice that I judge the case of the patients much – much
> more soberly. In the process, to be sure, my earlier, almost passionate interest
> in analytic work is partly lost. At least, that is what I have noticed up to now.

To what extent is this new sobriety in relation to his patients the outcome of a less constraining transferential link to Freud, due to the latter's firmness as Ferenczi's analyst? Ferenczi tries to uncover what has changed in the quality of the desire which underlies his work with patients, by shedding light on its nature: "That is certainly the consequence of the cooling off of the narcissistic relationship to everything that I accomplished myself." This narcissistic devaluation concerns specifically his ideali-sation of the image of himself as a man animated by a desire to treat and to heal. He questions the effect of this passion – that of the physician – on his analytic practice:

> It would be a pity (a great pity!) if it turned out that I can't objectively bring up enough interest in scientific work and am actually one of those in whom the higher interests are pathologically determined and whose cure brings along with it the renunciation of certain accomplishments.

Later, Ferenczi would come to consider this passion for healing a consequence of post-traumatic maturation. A child traumatised by being unwanted, or by bad treatment involving abuse and its denial in the first years of life becomes – through a splitting mechanism – a wise child who will have to take care of his inadequate family environment, as well as of the crushed child he carries in himself. This des-perate healing vocation is that of a child who had no childhood; even if it can lead to sublimatory successes, it remains the vocation of a wounded child. Ferenczi wants to believe that desire for analysis is a means to work through this childhood and overcome it. This attempt to define the distinction between a medical voca-tion and desire for analysis leads him to certain discoveries and to the acquisition of knowledge he attributes to the recent analytic work accomplished in Vienna.

For instance, he reports on a first scientific discovery made as a consequence of his psychoanalysis. When the treatment is at a standstill, when the patient takes advantage of free association to talk endlessly about any subject – no matter how elegant his discourse – Ferenczi notices that insistent covert masturbation is going on, achieving a degraded form of substitute sexual satisfaction.

> A small scientific discovery seems to be the idea of onania perpetua (incom-pleta), which I – as a supposition – believe I have found in my own case (as you perhaps still recall). My 'rape patient' seems to be such a person – masturbating literally day and night, however.

Speaking to complain endlessly, to contain the unknown or to make oneself dizzy could also be a substitute pleasure, loyal companion of secret imaginings or of unconscious fantasy. This allows Ferenczi to expand the application of the active technique initiated by Freud. Speaking of his patient, he describes the effective-ness of this new technique:

> The treatment has been stalled for some time. – She spoke for hours only about the highest artistic and human accomplishments that she has attained

or wants to attain. – I noticed that she lies for the whole hour with her legs crossed, and I instructed her to stop it.

Trusting his intuition that the unconscious expresses itself through representations constituting unconscious formations, but also through bodily events – sensations, gestures – Ferenczi interprets this position on the couch as a masturbatory activity, which he forbids. Once this pleasure revealed, the effect is evident at once:

> An uproar ensued, an attempt at disobedience, etc. Finally, she relented, and in a single stroke the picture of the analysis changed: she remembered new details about the story of her 'rape,' especially those which made her complicity clear. Early erotic screen memories also came.

Ferenczi remained loyal to this hypothesis, which he developed further: the unconscious speaks not only through interpretable unconscious formations, but is also expressed in the life of the body, in that which is repeated through the traces and scars whose memory it bears. As early as the fall of 1916, Ferenczi had the intuition that analysis can unearth material buried in the farthest depths of the unconscious, a fact he attributed to the insistence of certain wounds (rape as the primary figure of trauma) which resonate with early childhood experiences.

As far as he himself is concerned, Ferenczi has just made another discovery, thanks to a slip that brings him face-to-face with a false fantasy. Returning home after a rendezvous with Gizella, he finds hidden in his wallet the key of a cupboard, that he was sure he had lost. He interprets this slip in light of his previous reflections. For a long time, he had wanted to believe that the key to his destiny was held by the other (Gizella) in the love relation; now, he discovers that he holds the key to his own future. In the transference, he understood that he had only "simulated" its loss, adding "for my father's sake." He submits this strategy to an Oedipal interpretation. In order to escape the father's scrutiny, he presents himself as the one who has lost the key – the key giving access to the mother – even though this is a lie. Of course, it is clever to present oneself as a man inhibited in his thinking and circumspect in his words, as someone seeking ultimate knowledge which resides with the other (Freud), because this preserves a secret onanistic pleasure; but Ferenczi discovers that this is also dangerous: "With time I succeeded in leading other people but also myself astray (through my 'disinterest' in believing in the mother)." Thus, the tables have turned. "Out of conscious deception arose unconscious deception (i.e., also self-deception)." Ferenczi is aware of the importance of discovering this lie in the fantasy, which associated pleasure with the unpleasure of the symptom. He had learned long ago the classic art of interpreting such an unconscious formulation, as the psychopathology of everyday life teaches it, but now he was able to distinguish between his previous theoretical knowledge and this other knowledge that informs him now that his experience on the couch places the parapraxis in a sharper light. Thus, this ordinary slip is transformed into a fundamental fantasy which, as Ferenczi suddenly discovers, has long been orchestrating all his neurotic life experience, his relations with the opposite sex, his relationship with Gizella and, what is more, even his relationship with Freud: "Everything that I wrote earlier about the supposed mistake was misplaced, even if something in it can be true. – This is my first scientific accomplishment since Vienna." This new relation to knowledge, not Freud's or his own, but the knowledge emerging from the experience of the analysis, renews his desire to work. He therefore includes this post-scriptum in his letter: "I wanted to have the notes in this letter sent back, in order to revise them partially into essays."

In this long letter dated October 17, 1916, in which he describes the effects of his recent segment of analysis, Ferenczi discusses one subject at length – the one that matters most: his relationship with Freud, as the analyst analysed by his master, colleague and friend. He realises the very complex nature of this plural relationship. He speaks at once of the unease he feels now that he is writing to Freud about their recent speaking-and-listening work together: "I notice that for the moment I haven't found the tone with respect to you. Evidently the transition from penitential child to amicable letter writer has been too rapid." He now has trouble free-associating in writing, as he felt himself able to do before the analysis, and he asks himself: "Do I want to conceal something? – I am supposed to be finished with my analysis already! So say you, at least. I, too, notice the progress, but perhaps I am still not quite capable of action." But although he now has trouble associating, he does not hesitate to speak of the disagreement that has come up between the analysand and the analyst. We can guess that Freud considers his patient, if not cured, at least able to act on his own and to decide, and that in his opinion the analysis is finished.

When Ferenczi expresses satisfaction at having overcome the split that denied him access to tenderness in his sex life, he attributes to Freud some of the reasons for the meandering that delayed the resolution of this problem.

> In the process the following thought came to my mind: I have been occupied for more than 1 ½ years with the problem of coitus, which I wanted to explain from the perspective of biology (– with the use of psychoanalytic experience, to be sure). I recently told you that that was perhaps the reaction to your statement that you can't explain pleasure (i.e., I wanted to know more than you).

This lengthy labour accomplished dispassionately was completed in 1924, when *Thalassa* was published. It had been not so much freely chosen research as an investigation motivated by Ferenczi's transference to Freud.

Finished but not terminated?

On October 24, Freud answers Ferenczi's letter without delay. He is brief: "When I said the treatment was at an end, I did not mean it was terminated." The treatment ended when Ferenczi's leave was over and he had to return to his duties as military physician. Freud does not foresee continuing the analysis, and he justifies his decision in no uncertain terms: "[…] it is at an end because it cannot be continued for at least six months and would thus place itself in the service of avoiding the neurotic intention." Ferenczi understands quickly that there is not going to be a fourth segment of analysis. He has no choice. He must decide on his own about marriage. Freud also reminds him that his bank has not yet received the payment for the analysis (1245 crowns). Rigorously, Freud is careful not to engage in more free association that would lead to endless speculation. But by placing his focus on Ferenczi's neurotic relation to women, isn't he ignoring the transferential complaint that concerns him?

Ferenczi's ambivalence is clear on October 30, when he describes his growing discomfort, while defending the position he has taken:

> The affects unleashed by the treatment have been undulating up and down in me. Whether I want to or not, I must admit you are right about the interpretation. – Gizella's refusal promptly rekindled all symptoms – but [the prospect of] more pleasant hours was able to banish them and make me happy with life and more or less capable of work.

On November 13, Ferenczi's state has worsened:

> To tell you the most onerous things right away – [I am going] through tormenting times. Initially only psychically – but for some time the effects have again found their way to corporeality. (Accentuation of the Basedow symptoms. Breathing disturbances one or two times).

These are the same symptoms he described at the end of 1912, in his letter requesting analysis. He tries to explain his harshness with Gizella: "I recognize in [my angry outbreaks] (at the time suppressed) outbreaks of rage against my mother, whom I loved in vain." And he adds, somewhat ironically: "Frau G.'s refusal is thus at least good to the extent that my analysis can be deepened by it." In addition, the "incapacity for work" is complete, "except for the analysis in practice, in which I can demonstrate the most beautiful successes." While commenting on a dream, Ferenczi insists: "Frau G. is now repeating the bad treatment I received from Mother. At the time I said to myself, proudly – and defiantly: 'It doesn't hurt […]' when my mother hit me." When Freud plays the role of the father, does he guess that in the transference he is also, in part, this violent mother?

Speaking as Ferenczi's analyst and faithful friend, Freud sends an answer on November 16. He confirms his position:

> You know that I consider your attempt at analysis finished – finished, not terminated, but rather broken off because of unfavourable circumstances. If you were still able to make your decision dependent on the continuation of the analysis, then you would have forced it into the service of delay, which shouldn't be.

And Freud ventures to confess: "With that I think I have regained my freedom to tell you what you would have been able to hear earlier if you had not come into analysis, namely, that I have no [good] opinion of the whole matter [...]" A feeling he had before the analysis is now confirmed. He goes on to speak of the somatisation: "Now, since you react to Frau G.'s refusal with a renewal of your being sick, I am all the more sure that the matter has long since been exhausted and cannot be redressed." Finally, Freud feels he must specify that he never intervened in reality: "Naturally, I have never done the slightest thing to influence her, I have only foreseen that she would act that way." Did Freud know that after being badly treated for so long Gizella would refuse the marriage proposal, just as Ferenczi knew from the start that Freud did not want to be his analyst? We can imagine how shocked he is by this new position taken by Freud, who after encouraging him for so long to marry Gizella, suddenly announces that the prospect is definitely lost. Two days later, Ferenczi sends a breathless six-page letter taken up five times in four days.

A second letter written in the après-coup of analysis

In this letter written at 6 AM on November 18, 1916, Ferenczi discusses at random his complicated relation with Gizella, his moods and state of health and, of course, the dynamics of transference in this period when it is not clear to him whether the analytic sessions with Freud are definitely over or simply suspended.

His relation to women remains confused. For instance, he allows himself an episode of mutual sexual caresses with Saroltà, Gizella's sister, and tells Freud that he once had intercourse with her, just after being with a prostitute. As punishment for this – he says – he was afflicted with a great fear of syphilis. He tries to analyse the episode that just took place:

> My relationship with my mother has worsened significantly in the last few years. I think there is a causal connection here to my relationship with Gizella. I am taking out on my mother what I am sparing Gizella and am thereby returning to the original source of my hatred of women.

Despite the clarity of this insight, he plans to show Gizella Freud's last letter: "I will show your letter to Gizella. (At the same time I am sorry that Gizella, who reveres you so, also has to be injured from your part.)" The prospect of a separation allows Ferenczi to realise all that this woman he has known since 1900 has meant to him: "Only now do I see how I experienced my whole life, the smallest triviality, 'sub specie Gizellae.' Twenty times I caught myself with the idea, 'I will tell her that when she comes in the evening.'" Then he points out how greatly this emotional dependence weighs on him. "It now appears to me very plausible that, now freed from the compulsion to love her, my relationship with Gizella will become more normal."

These continuous and tormenting psychic contortions affect him body and soul: "In the morning very sad, hour-long funeral-march melody in my head. Tears [...] But [this separation] seems more and more impossible to me." His despondency is severe: "[...] deepest states of depression with uncontrollable inclination to cry (tears flowed inexorably). I must interpret this symptom, which can almost be called hysterical, as a sign of mourning; they were expressions of feeling caused by Gizella's departure." Devastated, Ferenczi seems ready to accept Freud's last assessment claiming that the situation is without reprieve. At the same time, he still ventures to imagine other possibilities: "Afternoon, analyses. A free hour; restlessness. Nasal breathing very disturbed, tachycardia (continuously 120 beats per minute)." Ferenczi relates his physical symptoms to his romantic situation: "I make plans to mediate, e.g.: 'I am only lacking the legality of the relationship. That's why I was healthy until G. made her refusal known.'"

Informed of Ferenczi's somatisations and involved as his analyst and as a third party in reality, did Freud have any other option than to acknowledge that in these circumstances the analysis could in no way be continued? Ferenczi records the aggravation of his state:

> I notice how greatly my mood, which was so passionate yesterday, has been alleviated since the talk with Gizella. Had dinner with her last evening. During the meal very strong palpitations; I hardly had the strength to give your letter to Frau G. to read. I made ten false starts before I did it. It was as though I were handing the death sentence over to her.

Fortunately, this deathly terror does not last; Ferenczi explains how he manages to put an end to it: "As long as I saw expressions of pain in her, I was almost cold. Only when she regained her kindness and became forbearing with me and spoke tenderly again – albeit wistfully – with me did I thaw out again." Now he finds himself in a paradoxical position. While Freud, making firm use of the active technique, treats him harshly and rebuffs him, he discovers that Gizella offers another kind of listening and consolation.

In the immediate aftermath of this third segment of analysis, Ferenczi the analysand is still in the furnace of transference – and Freud the analyst is caught up in his madness. The letter started on November 18 is ample proof:

> I know that I no longer have the right to speak to you as if to my physician, that I must not speak freely and out of context but rather measure my words against reality. But I can't refrain from taking an hour one last time (is it really the last time?) [...] I have been suffering [...] increasingly since Gizella's refusal.

Ferenczi is in the grip of an unthinkable double mourning, as if he had to give up his love relationship with Gizella, and at the same time his still passionate transferential relationship with Freud. And yet, he is suspicious of his own pain:

"I notice something forced, unreal-dramatic in my manner of writing. Does all my sadness conceal my joy about [...] becoming free?" Similarly, he asks himself if the breaking off of the analysis, which he so greatly regrets, might not be something fortunate: "Perhaps analytic monologue will bring me inner peace." He also wants to know Freud's position. Does he really intend never granting him another segment of analysis? He even wonders if Freud really thinks that his situation with Gizella is hopeless:

> Naturally I thought (with the malicious distrust of all analysands) that it was a trick on your part when you gave your definitive view of my relationship with Gizella. You wanted to free me from the suggestive influence of your earlier view (to marry G.) so that I can decide freely.

Strangely, in this moment of defiance, Ferenczi borrows a word once employed by Jung: he believes Freud capable of using a trick.

The next day, in a calmer state of mind, and without doing it deliberately or even knowingly, he reminds Freud of something the latter had taught him: that through and beyond the person of the analyst, the transference is addressed to a specific psychic agency. And he adds that he can't imagine doing without the mediation of this agency, clearly indispensable to his psychic life: "I still don't want to refrain from noting the internal and external process further. The psychic contents (at least in me) only become completely conscious through communication to a third person." Here, Ferenczi adds a valuable dimension to "third person" as the term is used in the context of the joke. The one who lends his voice to the words that come to him cannot grasp the cleverness of the quip falling from his lips until his interlocutor returns them to him. As a third person, in the silence conducive to the effects of resonance, he can become the receiver of the message that he originally emitted. In the aftermath of analysis, Ferenczi tells Freud once again what he has been repeating since their first meetings before the analysis. Ferenczi maintains that this applies to analytic treatment as much as it does to working relations between analysts engaged in a common combat for the development and transmission of psychoanalysis. He asserts that a psychoanalyst is created in this analytic mode not reducible to any particular teaching.

> Even in scientific things I have my best thoughts while I am communicating. This must have a connection with the fact, ascertained by you, that with me the scientific interests have not been entirely sublimated but are still closely bound to the love object.

We can glimpse the divergence existing between what Freud and Ferenczi consider the nature of transference. Freud thinks, with good reason, that transference love, nourished by the idealisation of the knowledge supposedly held by the "other" as a paternal figure, is alienating and creates dependence. But this transference love is not at all faith in the unconscious knowledge that can emerge in the space of discussion between truth-loving men. Ferenczi, who holds dear this faith in the unconscious, does not see it as sterile alienation, but rather the guarantee of a space of freedom in which thought can flourish. The fact that the two men are unaware of this divergence leads to a misunderstanding in the transference.

Misunderstanding in the transference

In his answer written on November 26, Freud remains deaf to Ferenczi's appeal, and maintains his position: the analysis on the couch was interrupted, the time for analysis is past. To insist, in thought or in writing, is abusive. Freud's condemnation is definitive: "Dear friend, I don't want to leave your letter for long without a reply. It seems to me that you are now using your analysis as a means of confusing your affairs, as you earlier used it to delay." Still true to his active technique, he bolsters his analysand and prompts him to take up the reins of his life: "It remains your task to regain health and ability to achieve, since there is little to be attained in the way of happiness in love under these circumstances." He brutally rejects Ferenczi's hypothesis regarding the "compulsion to love" that weighed on him, and points, on the contrary, to his desire for enjoyment: "Perhaps you meant the compulsion to coital intercourse." Freud is forbidding his patient to escape into analytic repetition and to use illness as a shield. Indeed, he casts doubt on the physical problem Ferenczi describes: "You seem to be making much too much out of your Basedow."

On November 27, Ferenczi describes his depressive state following the four-week separation from Gizella:

> After [...] there came very sad hours [...] Deeply sad music was constantly going around in me [...] I had to force myself to talk [...] It will require an effort to restore a part of my relations to the remainder of humanity.

His suffering takes hold of his body: "Today, changeable mood. I made an attempt to displace the neurosis onto the somatic sphere (hypochondria), but I caught myself with this intention. I have, to be sure, constant palpitations." He even advances the hypothesis that this somatisation has a transferential component: "The physical illness ought to force me to put myself into [your] care [...] again." This, by way of justification of a fourth segment of analysis. He then speaks of his exclusive attachment to Gizella, and for the first time disagrees with Freud's opinion about their relationship: "In the end, of course, your – essentially correct, to be sure – opinion about our relationship – could be exaggerated." One or two days later, after receiving Freud's letter, Ferenczi responds by writing two long paragraphs on the transferential dilemma in which he finds himself: "The immediate reaction to your categorical assertions was a worsening of my condition. The hypochondriacal ideas strengthened to the point of anxiety (now Basedow already means carcinoma thyreoïdeae)." Ferenczi senses that there is "a defiant rebellion" in the "sensual longing for Gizella" he now feels, a rebellion directed towards Freud, who went so far as to advise his friend to give up the idea of this improbable marriage.

Ferenczi refers once again to the transferential dimension of his chaotic situation: "I must also concede that I haven't achieved anything with the self-analysis. Possibly I really confused the situation. So, I will give it up." Not without some trepidation, he even considers breaking off all contact with Freud for a time:

> At the same time I also want thereby to free myself from your influence on my decisions – in the way that I made myself independent of Gizella through the separation. So, in these weeks I will write little – at least about my condition – to you, even though I don't know how I will bear this release of all libidinal cathexes.

But he questions his own motives: "Perhaps I only want to punish myself [...] but – that would already be analysis, so I will conclude my letter." Still, carried away by his transferential torment, he can't help adding a post-scriptum, to point out what the present situation owes to what happened between them at the end of the summer in 1910:

> P.S. I know only too well that it is in here a matter of the repetition of the defiant rebellion in Palermo – I already knew this while I was writing the letter – but I didn't want to withhold these characteristic associations from you.

But just as he had once taken offence when Freud asked him to take notes while he dictated, he now rebels and dares to correct Freud. When the latter insists that Ferenczi uses his desire for analysis to escape his responsibilities and duties, which would be to stay healthy, to work and to love, is he not ignoring the other aspect of his psychic economy: not what is at stake in the love affair with Gizella, but what is at stake in the transferential relation with Freud himself? With great lucidity, Ferenczi points out to Freud the negative aspect of his transference on him:

> But even after mature consideration I am of the opinion that, even if I yield to the presumed, indeed, certainly present tendencies of my unconscious toward flight (separation from G.), I must also allow the tendencies of the unconscious which are hostile to the father and also present in me to operate undisturbed.

Therefore, Ferenczi opts for a period of separation between them:

> So I am – as I said – fully conscious of the transferential character of my reaction to your letter, and consciously I am even grateful to you. And still, I believe that I must remain as uninfluenced as possible in these weeks.

Ferenczi included a note dated December 9 explaining that he had put off sending the letter, since he had "noticed very well the neurotic defiance in the concluding sentences." As a result, Freud had had no news from his distressed analysand for two weeks. In the note, Ferenczi confirms that he has stopped seeing Gizella, although this makes him suffer: "[…] my sadness about it has abated but only made room for a general apathy, and […] the physical symptoms and the inability to accomplish anything persist." He adds: "I rationalized the cessation of our correspondence by the assertion that I must now decide about the future without being influenced from any quarter (neither by the moral obligation toward G. nor by your advice)."

> Freud lets two weeks pass before reacting to his analysand's list of complaints. He places himself in a different role and uses a different tone; tireless in the pursuit of his intellectual work, he invites his analyst colleague to resume the development of ideas – in other words, his work of reflection – which personal analysis should not cause him to forget.

The "pleasure animal" returns to work

On December 22 Freud makes no mention of the two letters he received. He does not consent to continuing the analysis by correspondence, as Ferenczi is ready to do; instead, loyal to the active technique, he invites him to collaborate in a common project: "Today I was in the university library to order the Lamarck for myself. I cannot stay completely idle, and our project, 'Lamarck and Psychoanalysis,' suddenly came to mind as hopeful and rich in content." By refusing to interpret and continue the last segment of analysis in writing, and inviting Ferenczi to take up his work again, is Freud acting as an experienced analyst, or is he looking for a way out of inextricable transferential entanglements? Perhaps, as we suppose, both motives are at work. The request is formulated in unambiguous terms: "I would only like to have the assurance from you that you will maintain your collaboration and do something serious in the near future, even though you don't have as much free time as I." Freud is also speaking as a friend worried about this immersion in the murky waters of tormented subjectivity, to which Ferenczi seems ready to dedicate all his energy. He warns him against this and advises some respite: "For that reason you seem to me to be just as urgently in need of a diversion."

In his letter dated December 28, Ferenczi also uses a different tone. He has "attained a certain degree of normality," and is capable of "putting thoughts on paper" once again: "I will gradually put forth proofs – possibly in connection with our joint plan of work." And he says that he "still figure[s] on the possibility of […] marriage" to Gizella. He describes his very busy working days: "I don't know whether I (the pleasure animal) will be able to stand this life-style." Without going into great detail as he did before, he makes an observation:

> A basic symptom of my illness (indeed, of my character) is an exaggerated quest for pleasure (as you know, a reaction to deprivations of childhood). I

was never able to bear suspense; loneliness was identical to boredom to me. –
I was probably always waiting for some miracle or other, which would bring
me happiness and ecstasy.

It is with this in mind that Ferenczi interprets the two symptoms that impelled
him to request analysis: reluctance to settle down to intellectual work, and his
complicated love life.

> Working was always laborious for me (for that reason I first became a phi-
> losopher). Later, as well, I wanted to solve problems more speculatively, but I
> didn't want to 'espouse' my ideas. As happiness in love I must have expected
> something that was not yet there. I wasn't able to bear the difficulties that the
> relationship with G. brought along with it.

The year 1916, in which two arduous segments of analysis were conducted, seems
to end with a promising renewal of friendship and collaboration between Freud
and Ferenczi, who, nevertheless, remains cautious:

> I hope that I will be satisfied with less than before, educate myself (old chap)
> some more, and give up the [previous] nonsensical melancholia (to which I
> still tend). But I don't want to promise too much – I also know that it won't
> [be] without relapses.

During this trying war period and after the three segments of analysis in 1914 and
1916, the year 1917 would usher in a six-month period of convalescence, before
Ferenczi's triumphant return to the forefront of the analytic scene in 1918.

Post-analytic convalescence?
(January–May 1917)

The year 1917 started under the best auspices; peace became possible to imagine,
and after the turmoil of the analysis, the working relations between Ferenczi and
Freud seemed promising.
　On January 1, Freud was very hopeful:

> I am pleased to see that you are coming back to yourself from your depths.
> The first dove that you sent out was very pretty. Today I am enclosing a
> sketch of the Lamarck work, since I gather from your letter that you are keep-
> ing to the intention that you expressed back then.

Freud is referring to a common work project he had proposed to Ferenczi at the
start of the previous year, while he was in a rather sombre period. Indeed, on January 6, 1916, Freud ventured into a sphere of research which was to hold an important place in Ferenczi's future work: "Don't we already […] know two conditions

for artistic endowment? First, the wealth of phylogenetically transferred material, as with the neurotic; second, a good remnant of the old technique of modifying oneself instead of the outside world. (See Lamarck, etc.)" It was in January 1916, before the two segments of analysis, that the "Lamarck project" was conceived; and it is this project that Freud proposes to Ferenczi at the end of the year as a diversion, and as a means of distracting him from his exhausting preoccupation with the personal analysis. Very quickly, Ferenczi accepts these "auto-plastic" and "allo-plastic" functions. Many years later, he was going to develop the hypothesis Freud put forth at that time:

> This ability, applied to certain unconscious activities, would result in the peculiar mimicry of the artist in being able to make his ideas about things similar to them and then being able to re-create these ideas – back to the outside world – anew, in the form of words, materials, colors [...] In the final analysis, the same roundabout way that is characteristic for the wish fulfill-ment of the artist in general.

Illustrating the richness of their dialogue, at the end of his letter dated January 17, 1916, Ferenczi presents an idea that emerged as a response to Freud's proposition:

> something that came to my mind [...] You say that the preconscious psychic cathexis is essentially word cathexis of thing presentations. But observation of the deaf and dumb shows that one can also perform preconscious psychic func-tions without word symbols. (I am thinking of [untrained] deaf and dumb people.)

Stimulated by the work of reflection in which Freud invites him to participate, Ferenczi puts forth a hypothesis advanced earlier: "It is also conceivable that [...] the preconscious can perhaps also form out of things other than word symbols (in the deaf and dumb perhaps out of the traces of sensations of imitative body innervation)." This valuable living dialogue with Freud allows Ferenczi to voice his difference and his singularity: "I have not yet completely understood your idea of artistic creation, but I feel that the solution is to be found in this direction."

A year later, in January 1917, Freud counts on the fact that Ferenczi can cer-tainly be persuaded to succumb once again to the charm and the benefits of this exclusive intellectual relationship, which is much less exhausting for him than the analytic relation in which his analysand would like him to remain. The events that followed seemed to prove him right. On January 2, Ferenczi replied: "So I am making a solemn decision to collaborate on that nice plan (Lamarckism). I will consider your notes as a basis for the work." It seems that Ferenczi believes once again that collaboration with Freud on common projects is possible, despite his painful experience in Palermo in 1910, when this type of collaboration had seemed impossible. Now, he is enthusiastic: "First I want to copy and send in the notes that I made on this theme. Then I will ask you to designate what is useful in them and to propose specifics about the division of labor." Freud replies on

January 4: "I conceive of the work on Lamarckism in such a way that each of us reads, if possible, everything that is noteworthy, until more specialized areas can be separated out [...]" Could it be that both men have finally emerged from the furnace of transference? Was Freud, the analyst, right to demand that his analysand decide about his love life and return to work?

On January 9, Ferenczi confirms his commitment to their common project: "I am sending you enclosed, with the request that you return it, the copy of the aphorisms, which perhaps justify my collaboration on the work on Lamarck." His consent is somewhat cautious: "In principle, I agree with the manner in which you conceive of our working together. But how it will be in practice very much depends on the condition of my health." Indeed, aside from the memory of what happened in Palermo, there is the reality of Ferenczi's poor health. Despite the fact that he seems cured of his neurotic symptoms, he is plagued by physical symptoms:

> The psychic upswing that I last informed you about was immediately wrested down by influenza. I felt physically very weak, even after the cessation of fever, and Dr. Levy ascertained an increase in the Basedow symptoms, as well as a renewed flare-up of the nephrosis. Naturally I immediately used this situation for a psychic depression [...]

The situation is alarming enough for the doctor to prescribe "[...] eight weeks' leave [...] of which, according to his way of thinking, I would have to spend at least four weeks in the mountains." Ferenczi finds this state of ill health perplexing. For the first time since the end of the third segment of analysis, he asks himself if it might not be useful to have a fourth: "The leave (which, in Dr. Levy's view, can still be extended) would allow me to collaborate properly on the Lamarck work. – Or should I also pick up the thread of the analysis again? I await your advice." In fact, Ferenczi spent three months in a Semmering clinic in the Tatra Mountains. During this period of convalescence (after the analytic procedure?), far from Gizella and from Freud, he took the time to clarify the elements in his body and soul that the analysis had stirred up.

On January 12, less adamant than usual, Freud sends a carefully worded answer: "I am sorry to hear that your health has again been shaken. I also don't know how to advise you about anything expedient from here [...] We don't want to consider resuming the analysis." In the same letter, he informs Ferenczi of the progress of the Lamarck work. He also proposes a slight change in the manner of their collaboration: "I think each of us should complete the thing as though we were alone, and then we should get together." Freud feels helpless, both as Ferenczi's analyst and as his friend.

Freud in distress

On January 23, 1917, Freud humbly confides to Gizella, with whom he identifies, that he is disconcerted: "I now receive little news from our friend. I, too, expect good things from his stay in the Tetra [Mountains]. I, too, have endured much with him." He reveals his true feelings: "Since I know you and know about your relations, it was an [ardent] wish on my part to see you united. He is not a person who can live and work without intimate belonging to another, and where would he find anyone more excellent than you?" More unexpectedly still, Freud goes so far as to enumerate, for Gizella, the different positions he adopted in an attempt to help Ferenczi, whose dismay irritates him as much as it distresses him: "Although I, too, had the impression that the best time has been missed, I have worked on the realization of this wish with the most varied means, directly and indirectly, in friendly intercourse and through analysis, carefully, so that my preambles would not produce recalcitrance in him, and with blunt demands, in order to bring my influence to bear." Freud admits that, faced with Ferenczi's indecision and, later, with Gizella's hesitation, he adopted a different attitude: "I have urged him to make himself free of you, as a test of whether he is capable of doing something else for himself, and then I referred him to you, after it became evident that he is incapable of doing without you and replacing you. I have really left nothing untried and have met with no success." He explains that his inability to change the situation drove him to his last intervention: "Finally, I had to come out and tell him [straight out] that he doesn't want to do anything decisive and that he is even misusing the analysis in order to conceal his [refusal]." Freud admits how dismayed he is by his friend's (and analysand's) inability to decide: "It is not even a no; he just doesn't want to change anything, do anything [but] wait passively to see if something comes to his aid." While until then Freud thought that Ferenczi was exaggerating the seriousness of his ill health, he now has to accept reality: "Then this stupid, trifling, but nevertheless undeniable organic affliction, morbus Basedowi, came and [...] permitted him to free himself from the snare in which I was hoping to catch him." Freud is distressed by his obvious helplessness: "It troubles me deeply that he should have no more of you and of life as before. But I can do nothing." In his discomfiture, Freud turns to Gizella for help: "In these dismal times I accept your [generous] assurance that you will not turn away from me, with heartfelt gratitude and respectful affection."

On January 25 Ferenczi has nothing reassuring to say; a chest X-ray has revealed a possible problem. He doesn't trust his doctor, who denies "the tubercular nature of the illness". Just as Freud has been known to do, Ferenczi imagines the worst: "[...] my first idea after discovering the organic illness was the following: First organize all notes so that they can at least be published posthumously." But he also knows "very well (in the unconscious) that it could be a matter of a mild case". On January 28, not intending to take up Ferenczi's analysis, Freud suggests to him that "it would be very nice if [he] came to Vienna for a day" before leaving for a treatment centre.

On February 8, Ferenczi writes from Semmering. He reports that he has seen Dr Kraus, who gave him "dietary prescriptions" and recommended that he lie out in the open before and after meals. This doctor, the house physician of the cure house where Ferenczi was to stay for two weeks, "reassured [him] about the prognosis" from the start. Ferenczi thanks Freud for the friendly invitation:

> I am, to be sure, already accustomed to and spoiled by being warmly and kindly received by you, but this time it has especially touched me, perhaps because, in my consciousness of being ill, I was more in need of tenderness.

Soon, Ferenczi would make this tenderness component a part of the active technique.

On February 11, Freud informs Gizella of his relief upon receiving confirmation that Sándor's disorders are benign. He wants to stress that this illness, curable in a few weeks, has no subjective significance, so that Ferenczi "doesn't need to assign any particular role to the illness in the economy of his life." There was no attempt to relate Ferenczi's physical collapse to his romantic torments or the subjective effects of the latest discoveries made in his personal analysis. Freud thinks the causes are elsewhere: "Work as intensive as it has been lately in Budapest is, of course, not suitable for him, nor is constant excitement. I.e., there should be peace, once and for all!" Freud asks Gizella to be discrete: "My last letter to you was meant for you only; it was too straightforward for him. He has also not said anything to me about having read it."

On February 16, Freud writes Ferenczi a letter full of dismal news of life in Vienna. He encourages the latter to draw the fullest benefit from the care he is receiving in the mountains.

> So imbibe the comfort from your situation that is contained therein. The flight into illness is this time very much justified as flight from a miserable reality. Recover so soundly that with war's end you will be able to come forth as a worker at full strength.

Recovery and good resolutions

On February 21, Ferenczi writes that his physician is not persuaded by his hypochondria, and not overly worried about his minor functional complaints. He advises "some X-ray treatment of [the] thyroid [...] in Vienna by one of the best [radiologists]." The patient reads a great deal, and has begun writing an article on "The Amphimixis of Partial Instincts in Genitality", which would later be included in *Thalassa*.

On February 27, he reports that there is "a noticeable improvement in [his] condition: gain in energy and body weight, lowering of pulse rate. Satisfied with this success", he includes a small work with his letter. On March 2 Freud reassures him: "[...] you need not worry about neglecting our work on Lamarck. I have not progressed either [...] My motives for work have been partly extinguished, partly forced back, at present. The suspense over what is about to happen in the world is too great. I am warming up to the idea of taking up the work in the summer [...]"

After three weeks of silence, Ferenczi announces that his health has improved: "I didn't want to write before I was in a position to report significant improvement. I must confess that a kind of being ashamed of being ill has contributed to that." But he is not yet cured, and still hopes that Freud will visit him in Semmering. Without going into details, he mentions that his "abstinence and the sexual fantasies aroused by it have cost me two nights." Then, Ferenczi finally makes the announcement Freud has long been waiting for: "The statement in your Theory of the Neuroses: rather go under in battle than make a foul compromise with neurosis, has finally made an impression on me. I am determined to legitimize the relationship with Frau G." He speaks of having matured in this period of reclusion away from both Gizella and Freud, and makes an unusual request of the latter: "I must beseech you (the only authority in this matter) to explain to her, if only briefly, the unconscious motives for taking such a position [...]" Freud replies promptly: "Your will be done. I will write to Frau G. [...]". But although he is glad to know that Ferenczi is recovering, he remains cautious: "I think that you need an extension of your stay and your leave."

The same day, Freud fills his "mission of trust" and writes to Gizella without hesitation: "What makes my task easier is the assurance that you are just as certain of the honesty and interest from my side as I am of yours." He goes straight to the point: "Our friend writes to me that his previous neurotic uncertainty is at an end, feels the unambiguous need to put a constant being together in place of your hitherto impeded and unsatisfactory relations, and is asking you through me to give your consent [...] Postponement has already spoiled more than can be remedied." Freud explains the nature of the neurotic indecision present in the personality of the man so passionately and sincerely dedicated to psychoanalysis: "It has probably never looked any different in him than is now evident. But as long as he felt young and healthy, he continued the game with his fantasies of not wanting to give up any possibility for pleasure and enjoying all fluctuations." Now, Ferenczi is the first to admit this. To explain what provoked and reinforced Ferenczi's decision, Freud refers to the recent illness, an organic symptom that he refuses to relate to the upheavals generated by the last segment of analysis and its immediate *après-coup*: "But now this condition, which does bring along with it a certain need for fostering and care, may have told him that it is time to do the only serious thing to set matters straight." In the weeks that followed, Gizella was still hesitant and asked Ferenczi to grant her some time. Also hoping for a clarification of the political situation, so that an amicable divorce might be negotiated with Geza Palos, from whom she has been separated for years, but not officially divorced. In the letter he writes to Ferenczi on April 30, 1917, Freud does not refer to his friend's marital situation.

Like in the happier period before the personal analysis, he speaks only about things relevant to their common combat aimed at gaining recognition for psychoanalysis. For instance, now that intellectual projects with Ferenczi are ongoing once again, Freud requests that he revise the critique of "a genuine German piece of ineptitude and worth all the rudeness you can muster." After the psychoanalysis which actively prompted him to have the courage to decide – to make a commitment to a woman – now it is the leader of the psychoanalytic movement who addresses the fighter in him: "In brief, you are not superior, and, for that reason, not contemptuous enough."

The letter Ferenczi wrote on April 30 is dedicated to the death of his friend Miksa Schächter: "After my natural father, he was actually the one whom I loved and revered as a model. He was an Old Testament character, also a fighter by nature, very conservative and religious." Ferenczi is surprised by his own strong emotions: "I must have transferred much of my love for my father onto him back then; I surprised myself with the strength of my reaction to his death." On May 4, he informs Freud that he has rewritten the critique: "Forgive me if this time I became somewhat rude in my critique. But the fellow doesn't deserve any better, believe me." He specifies that he will leave Semmering on May 7 or 8, and hopes to be in Vienna, for two or three days, on the afternoon of May 9. He thinks he will go to Budapest on May 10.

Battle orders and transference disorder (May–December 1917)

On May 13, Ferenczi sets the tone: "Immediately after my arrival I plunged into work and am bearing it well for the time being." He also mentions, in passing, that the reunion with Gizella went as he had hoped. The next day, Freud expresses his delight: "I count your news that you have reported back [...] so fresh in all your relations among the most hopeful." Freud would like to believe that the difficult five-year period when their relationship was marked by turmoil while being punctuated by segments of Ferenczi's analysis is now behind them: "That makes the impression of a final settlement." In his reply, written the same day, Ferenczi is reporting on his search for a place where Freud can spend his summer holidays. He is also happy to announce the publication of "the first psychoanalytic work by an ethnologist of the first [order]", his patient Dr G Róheim.

On May 27, Ferenczi reports that he has had a telephone conversation with Dr Freund about Freud's stay in Hungary over the summer. In 1915, Freud had Rozsi, Anton von Freund's second wife, as a patient in analysis. There is another piece of good news: "A young pupil of mine (therefore indirectly of yours) is about to write a book about children's games in psychoanalytical [terms]." On May 29, Freud thanks Ferenczi: "So, your extensive energetic care seems to have bestowed an ideal summer place upon us." But, given his "medical connection" to Freund's wife, Freud hesitates to accept the latter's hospitality. And now, after having awakened Ferenczi's interest in the Lamarck project, Freud takes a step backwards: "I am not at all disposed to doing the work on Lamarck in the summer and would prefer to relinquish the whole thing to you. I also can't take along so many books." Strangely, on June 3, just when he is starting to back out of the common project, Freud informs Ferenczi about a new and promising contact with a newcomer. He intimates that Georg Groddeck could be Ferenczi's interlocutor in the Lamarck project, since he himself intends to withdraw from it: "Next time I will send you the most interesting letter from a German physician that I have ever received, the contents of which impinge lavishly on your pathoneuroses and the Lamarck idea. I have still to reply to him." In fact, Groddeck was to play an even greater role in Ferenczi's life than Freud would have wished. Soon, it was to this man, who became his friend and physician, that Ferenczi would be able to speak of his analysis in a very different way than he spoke of it with Freud.

Ferenczi is as pleased as Freud that they have rebuilt their friendship and work relations at this time when the psychoanalytic movement seems to gain momentum. He is also pleased – just as Freud is – that his relationship with Gizella is now untroubled. On August 18, he thanks his analyst for having weathered the transference: "[…] there became apparent in me the breakthrough of hitherto well-repressed feelings, which convinced me that your view that I have always been fixated on Frau G. […] is justified." He is emphatic: "I thank you for having, in disregard for all my, in part, well-constructed objections to it, insisted on settling the matter in this way." On August 20, Freud applauds his friend's decision: "That is good news! You imagined it to be much more difficult. Now, no more hesitation; speed things up as soon as it goes. I have no doubt that you will bless the decision. But you won't understand then why you made it so late." The same day, Freud tells Frau G. how happy he is: "Hearty congratulations! Now you can cast aside all regrets that are left to you as remnants of a bad time and get serious, finally making a beautiful life for yourself and for him. I am enormously happy about the easy outcome."

Ever since the announcement of Groddeck's letter on June 3, Freud and Ferenczi never stopped discussing him. Freud disagrees with Ferenczi's initial reservations about the newcomer. He reiterates this on October 9: "I know and share your objections, but the heart of the matter coincides with your pathoneuroses and our Lamarck idea, and is certainly noteworthy." At the same time, Freud sends him a little article by Groddeck, asking him to write a "detailed, benevolent review" of it. Freud's insistence that Ferenczi return to work soon bears fruit. On October 10, Ferenczi notes that his physical health and state of mind have returned to "normal": "It appears to me as though I made the right decision about marriage after all; I see that from the consolidation of my physical health as well as the condition of my mind, which [could] be called normal." He knows that this is due in great part to his analysis and to the psychic and physical turmoil that followed, the onslaught of affects and the worsening of his state of health: "Sometimes I feel as if I could observe with a kind of inner perception the displacements that are taking place with my libido." He also knows that his present feelings towards Gizella are related to elements in his relationship with Freud which were revealed and transformed: "I get, for example, moods of tenderness and feelings of friendship with respect to you, as if I had previously been hindered in that by [certain] inhibitions." These internal shifts are promising for the future: "I hope confidently that – when I can finally carry on a normal family life – I will also be capable of work. I think I will then get serious with the work on Lamarck."

On October 14 he writes that he appreciated Groddeck's work, and that he has written the requested review. In addition, he is pursuing an endeavour that goes counter to the thrust of his two segments of analysis in 1916: "Now I will continue my history of illness (cure)." The perspective he has gained assured him of his progress: "As a sure sign of [the] fact that we have taken the right path, I can report an increase in potency; in relation to this I have become quite youthful, or more correctly: it turned out that I was only neurotically aged." This recovery, both physical and psychic, releases and energises the work of reflection now transferred into the sphere of work created between Freud and Ferenczi, instead of remaining captive in the transference onto Freud.

Now, becoming more detached from his analysis by undertaking its account in writing, Ferenczi is able to seize and soon truly make his own an idea casually proposed by Freud two years earlier. So that, on October 14, 1917, Ferenczi feels free to announce to Freud that he has had a new idea:

> Something also occurred to me about the Lamarck idea. Man has almost completely renounced autoplasticity and is adapting heteroplastically. But he is enabled to do this only with the aid of a remnant of the old plasticity which has been preserved. I am thinking of the plasticity of striated musculature, which, under the influence of the will, immediately assumes precisely the form and consistency required. It is this alteration of self which ultimately makes possible the alteration of the outside world.

Through the effect of transference in collaborative work, a casual observation of Freud's became, for Ferenczi, an idea he would develop at length, and make into one of the pillars of his future research on the practice of analysis.

On November 3, Ferenczi reports that he is very busy in his practice. He has an abundance of patients: "I could easily have two or three times as many patients as I can accept. But I don't seem to like to separate from old patients – most have been with me for over a year! There is some error in this!" True to his inclination to provide in-depth treatment, Ferenczi is the first analyst to conduct long-term analysis. On February 6, Freud grows impatient, seeing that Ferenczi's matrimonial arrangements "are going […] too slowly for me."

In his reply, in a long letter dated November 18, Ferenczi speaks as Freud's analysand: "After all, you are not only my friend, whom I have to spare my 'transformations of libido,' but also the physician to whom I owe a report about – the last, I hope – phase of my neurosis." He has trouble putting into words not the self-analysis he is forced to carry out, but the slow working through – work of the unconscious – that unfolded in him. Indeed, how can he speak of something that took place unbeknownst to him?

> Now, how should I tell it to you? And how did this come over me? I certainly can't call it "illumination," since it was [only] able to penetrate with such difficulty – mostly only as a small glimmer, which was soon extinguished, in order to make room for darkness again. But I don't want to get poetic. Let's rather remain precise.

He then explains that since the summer, when they met, he went through "a peculiar time" he finds it hard to describe. This strange experience showed him that the obvious improvement in his physical state doesn't guarantee that the same is true of his psychic state: "But I was not completely satisfied with myself, mentally." He discovers that he has been lying to himself, that he has been playing his role as Frau G.'s future husband "[as] if mechanically, dutifully [...]" The "duty-like character of the execution of this love" forces him to admit that this is not "true love". But he has made progress, because he kept all this to himself instead of cruelly confessing it to Gizella. He knows that it is he himself who has to understand these things and work through them. He now acknowledges that his analyst was right a year earlier, when he insisted forcefully that his patient make a clear decision. "You were right again. It was difficult for me to get anything analytically; I had to be really obligated, as I am now, in order to bring about significant psychic progress." After analysing one of his own dreams, Ferenczi again thanks his analyst: "I have decided to thank you for the tenacity with which you have held to your original view and not let yourself be scared off from the necessity of marriage by my pessimism." Now that he can be attentive to the subject of the unconscious in himself, Ferenczi can finally take it into account and adopt a new position in regard to his symptoms: "I won't let myself be made a fool of by these hypochondrias anymore." At last, he accepts the obvious:

> I finally think that I believe that I have summoned both Gizella's outward appearance as well as childlessness, the psychic and somatic illness, as bogeys against marriage to Gizella, with whom I have obviously been in love, irretrievably and for a very, very long time.

This is what became very clear to Ferenczi, the obvious that was so difficult to describe because it was not an awareness gained after lengthy reflection. But another event was even more revealing.

This awareness, gained in a flash of lucidity, regarding his conflicting love interests and his relation to Freud brought with it an unexpected theoretical discovery, at a time when his "otherwise very rich scientific fantasy even dried up for a while." "In this dull tension [...] the solution first [emerged] a few days ago from a scientific quarter." This fertile moment in his intellectual work came about before the clarification of his romantic feelings, which the dream revealed to him. Learning from the in-depth work with his patients, Ferenczi takes a crucial step in determining the orientation of his analytic research: "From the analysis of a [female] patient which is meeting with complete success, and from similar earlier and present observations, there arose a plan for a work on 'hysterical materialization phenomena.'" But for now, he is content with pointing out the possibilities of the new research field he intends to open: "I don't want to speak now of the interesting connections of this theme with the theme of Lamarckism [...] about the roots of genitality [...] That should really be written down some time." The article on this theme would be written in 1919. In addition to the reference to Lamarck, a few paragraphs further Ferenczi makes a playful reference to the man in Baden-Baden: "Aha! Dr. Groddeck!"

Transference disorder

In his letter of November 20, and perhaps in view of "significant psychic progress", Freud asserts:

> Your letter has strengthened all my convictions, both with respect to the fact
> that there is no other way out for you but to marry Frau G., and that you will
> not cease with the production of "avoidances" until you are confronted with a
> *fait accompli.* If only the miserable six months were already over!

He sheds light on the perspective that guided him during Ferenczi's analysis: "You emphasize that the signs of age in Frau G. have scared you away. There are undeniable, but are seen by you from a false perspective." It seems to us that Freud provides further clarification because he supposes that Ferenczi might be asking himself what role countertransference plays in Freud's convictions: "Perhaps you think, since I myself have grown old and have no access to youth, that I am also wishing an old woman on you. No, I wouldn't have asked that of you [...]" Is Freud taking a defensive attitude on account of his involvement in the delicate private affairs of his friend, or even to account for a part of his countertransference? Is there another factor at play – perhaps to do with both men's fantasies regarding temporality and age – a recurrent theme in their correspondence? At 44, Ferenczi seems to be in the grip of a longing for youth and a search for youthfulness. Freud, who is 61, has long been living with the certainty of his approaching death, and its corollary: the urgent quest for an heir to succeed him.

This is Freud's state of mind when he responds by referring to his own tiredness to the feeling of renewal Ferenczi is enjoying: "The times also demand achievement from each of us; they will become hard. I alone perhaps have a right to flirt with peace and quiet. I have worked hard, am worn out, and am beginning to find the world repulsively disgusting." Moreover, as he once did with Jung, Freud suggests to Ferenczi that he could soon be the heir he needs: "The superstition that has limited my life to around February 1918 seems downright friendly to me. Sometimes I have to struggle for a long time until I regain my superiority." Ferenczi refuses to be drawn in; on December 13 he writes:

> I have already participated in a few such 'leave-taking moods' with you.
> They were always followed by a rejuvenation and something [good] for us,
> your pupils. So pardon me if [...] I don't take this mood of yours in all too
> tragic a light and hold fast to my optimism.

An active professional life, along with his acceptance of marital life, seems to have brought Ferenczi relative serenity: "My life-style is gradually being organized in a bourgeois fashion," like that of "every proper husband." On December 16, Freud declares himself pleased: "I gather with satisfaction that you are leading an idyllically peaceful life as an introduction to one still more comfortable and richer in content."

A few days later, Ferenczi's missive must have been a letdown. The fact that he now lives a stable life with Gizella does not mean that he is through with the pangs of desire, nor with his analysis: "Unfortunately, I must again – *in absentia* – take an hour from – or with – you, since a sad occurrence of the day does not let me sleep, despite sleeping pills. Perhaps this peculiar technique of self-analysis – by letter (i.e., in the constant presence of an imaginary analyst) – is not altogether unsuitable for terminating a treatment." Indeed, Ferenczi has just received tragic news which concern precisely the seriousness of matters of temporality in the treatment, and of the crucial character of the beginning and the ending of analysis.

A criminal refusal?

Ferenczi has just learned that a former patient has shot herself. But analytic honesty forces him to be more precise: "It is actually not a case of a 'former' patient but rather of one who had 'begun' – and was then dismissed." He saw the young girl, was moved by her distress, and since he could not take her into analysis right away, he advised her to write a journal and record in it her childhood history – that of an unwanted child, who was now haunted by thoughts of suicide. Thus, the treatment began and was quickly interrupted and put off indefinitely. The description of the patient as "one who had 'begun' – and was then dismissed" cannot fail to awaken an echo. Indeed, this experience of Ferenczi's as an analyst occurred at a very significant moment: "She came to me – a very poor, very beautiful, very intelligent, affectionate girl – a year ago, before my therapeutic trip to the Semmering." The young working girl was cruelly subjected to the experience of an analysis that started and was quickly interrupted by her future analyst, around Christmas 1916 or the start of 1917, when Ferenczi, the analysand, was still suffering the traumatic effects of the sudden and definitive ending of his own analysis with Freud. Dismissed just before the promise of analysis made to her was to be kept, the young girl killed herself. Was Ferenczi's letter trying to tell Freud that playing with transference has serious consequences?

Indeed, Ferenczi uses this tragic event to allow himself to benefit from another analytic session in writing. He does not conceal his troubling involvement in the young girl's tragedy. "But I happened to be in a period of vacillation with respect to Frau G. – her youth and charm enchanted me. – I gave way to a kiss. [The repetition of the case of Elma.]" It was in this transferential context, confused and difficult, that the beginning and the end of the working girl's treatment were negotiated:

> She wouldn't allow herself to be dismissed in this manner and vehemently demanded analysis. I […] gave her two hours a week – on principle charged three crowns an hour – she yielded something but seemed to want to stay longer in the transference (which is no wonder, in view of the above).

The analysis proved to be difficult: "The analysis flattened out more and more; after the interruption in consequence of my illness she returned – for a short time – but soon asked for a new hiatus, which I granted her. I didn't see her for a long time." Thus, the analysis, which could have been resumed in May 1917, soon stopped. Ferenczi advised the young woman to put her story in writing.

Ferenczi did not see her again until the beginning of December, shortly after the suicide of a brother-in-law who desired her: "She came about two weeks ago – quite resigned with respect to the brother-in-law, but with the plan to continue the analysis. I avoided her – citing military agendas, etc., and consoled her with a later time." But five days before Ferenczi wrote this letter to Freud, "[last] Friday she came for the last time. She inquired about the analysis again, told me she wanted to shoot herself, already brought and old revolver, etc." Just as Freud had done with him, Ferenczi remained firm in his decision: "I beseeched her to wait for treatment." The girl's sister, who had come to inform him of the suicide, suspected that Ferenczi had wrongly suggested to the young girl that she was in love with her brother-in-law, to better cover up the fact that

> her sister had died only because she had been in love with me, and, in fact, she had wanted to love the man and not only the doctor in me; since I didn't love her, she went to her death. She bases this surmise on obscure statements of her sister's.

Ferenczi is deeply affected: "The case depresses me extraordinarily; but I maintained my composure [before] the bearer of bad tidings (Which I interpret as a sign of [my] health). Nonetheless, my sleeplessness shows me that I unconsciously want to guilty of this death." Ferenczi is unable to lie to himself: "The truth of the matter is also that my conflictual attitude ([towards the end]), perhaps, the fanatical refusal) […] did not favorably influence the case – which was certainly [doomed in any case]." This is the sad analytic tale which prompted Ferenczi to extort another session *in absentia* from Freud.

But we could easily imagine that such a letter, once written, has already filled its allo- and self-analytic function. Why, then, does Ferenczi send it to Vienna? What unconscious transferential impulse prompts him to do so? He asks himself this question: "To this extent the matter is clear to me. I probably wouldn't have needed to send the letter off at all. But it would be nonsense to withhold from you just this chapter." Why should Freud not be deprived of precisely this chapter, if not because it has close relevance for him, given that it is an account illustrating the dangers of an analysis that begins and is left in suspense, not terminated, like Ferenczi's analysis with Freud? A few weeks after the end of his analysis, when he was still obsessed with dreams of triumphant youth, which Freud expected him to give up, Ferenczi, perhaps as a gesture of defiance, Ferenczi gave free rein to his demons with this touching young girl. But the careless solicitude he showed in the face of her distress, overlooking the furnace of transference – which he himself lit – left the young girl more alone than ever with her painful experience of life. Whether intentionally or not, the interruption of the treatment promised and expected proved deadly. Contrary to Freud, who didn't give this case particular attention, we venture to say that Ferenczi never forgot this dreadful experience.

In fact, in 1929 he had the story of the young girl published – this young girl whom he had advised to write while waiting for analysis. His account was entitled "From the Childhood of a Young Proletarian Girl". In his foreword to this publication, Ferenczi makes no mention of the intersecting transferential elements between himself and the young patient, and between him and Freud. But the fact that this text was published the same year as "The Unwelcome Child and His Death-Instinct" allows us to suppose that its subtitle could have been: "The Unwanted Analysand and His Death-Instinct".

At the end of December 1917, Freud is not moved by these tragic events, and draws no conclusion from them. He does not intervene now, as he did so promptly six years earlier, when Ferenczi found himself in an awkward situation in Elma's analysis. On December 25, 1917, Ferenczi's letter makes it clear that he has noticed Freud's reserve, when he speaks of putting the incident behind him: "I don't want to leave you [...] in the belief that the gruesome story about my patient that I told you has had a lasting influence on me." But he goes on to say that someone else provided the possibility for dialogue he probably would have liked to have with Freud: "But the correct estimation of the case did not come in a logical way, but rather according to – and in consequence of – a talk with Frau G." Strangely, and despite evidence to the contrary, Ferenczi wants Freud to see him as being free of any neurotic guilt about this affair:

It corresponds completely to your views on the feeling of guilt – as far as I know them – that, since this moment, I don't feel the slightest trace of guilt over the case that I reported, even though I am still genuinely sorry about the girl.

He presents himself as a man fitting what he supposes to be Freud's ideal: "You see – I am beginning to live the life of a normal husband, with the obligatory fantasies of infidelity and reconciliations." On December 27, Freud is laconic and justifies his silence: "You will probably have understood why I haven't answered your next-to-last letter. I saw that you are filling up the waiting time with a repetition of the same trick – now, to be sure, already diminished, and not without good support from external events – and I consoled myself with the conviction that you won't do it anymore when the provisional [period is past]." Freud is counting on his conviction that marriage will put an end to Ferenczi's habitual subterfuges. His letter makes no mention of the young woman.

In this last letter of the year, Freud announces the bad news that their common project on Lamarck will very likely not be completed.

Indeed, at the end of 1917 Freud relegates Ferenczi to the solitude of his own responsibility for his marital affairs, and to the freedom of choosing the direction of his thinking, now that the personal analysis of the past two years has made him the analyst he is. The analytic adventure on Freud's couch had been preparing in the wings since the two men first met in 1908, even though the request for analysis was only made at the end of 1912. The actual analysis that took place in three segments conducted in 1914 and 1916 was followed by immediate aftermath effects throughout 1917. We think we are justified in equating the year 1917 with a five-year subjective period extending between 1912 and 1917.

We might even say five years or more, since it was not until 1918 that Ferenczi took the leading role he deserved in the movement, and not until 1919 that he carried out Freud's wish by marrying Gizella.

Despite this clear progress he and Freud were both happy to acknowledge, Ferenczi had to wait until the end of 1921 to form a more nuanced judgement on his treatment, with its benefits as well as its serious failings or impasses. And it was not until 1922 that he attained independence of thought. From then on, he was able to cope with what had not been worked out in his analysis. Better still, what he failed to find in his personal analysis served as the basis of the analytic path he never ceased to define and explore, and which would be uniquely his. After the analysis, and thanks to its enlightening and its shadowy aspects, Ferenczi resolutely enters the time of desire. More determined than ever, he advances on the analytic scene. In September 1918, the fifth International Psychoanalytic Congress was a true consecration for Ferenczi.

Chapter 5

Budapest: Great expectations (1918–1919)

Hard at work

In 1918, the year the war ended, the letters Freud and Ferenczi exchanged concerned primarily their analytic work. Having left behind, to a great extent, the torments of recent years, and free of the need to show himself to be a zealous Freudian, Ferenczi could now dedicate all his energy to psychoanalytic research that gradually acquired a new and more original character. In fact, he undertook to make a critical revision of analytic practices. He used the term "revision" in early February, in a letter to Freud: "Having returned after an uneventful trip, I am up to my neck in work. The time constraints caused me to undertake with a few patients, instead of a strict psychoanalysis, at least a cursory psychoanalytic revision [...]"

Caught up in his characteristic enthusiasm, he was unwittingly venturing into a sensitive sphere by attempting to find an alternative to classical analysis, which he had just experienced. His transferential grievances were replaced by technical experimentation. Later, he would write "The Elasticity of Psycho-Analytic Technique" (1928), to counter the lack of flexibility in rigidly structured classical analysis.

In the above-mentioned letter, dated February 5 and 9, Ferenczi specified that he was rewriting his paper on hysterical stigmata, that he was still working on the Hungarian translation of *The Interpretation of Dreams*, and that he hoped to "attack biology" shortly. On February 15 he confirmed the power of transference between work associates:

> Your two essays [Metapsychology of Dream Processes, Mourning and Melancholia] are occupying me constantly. Only now does one comprehend the structure of the psychic apparatus. But I fear you are correct in your assumption that at most one [or] two people will grasp the extent of what is being revealed. It will become necessary to revise the *concept of introjections* on the basis of the new findings. I will reflect on this.

He then announces the planned publication of four of his articles in German, in a special volume, explaining that in Hungary this is likely to earn him "scientific significance." On May 4 he sent Freud three short articles, and on May 18 he seemed almost ecstatic when he described his newest practice, that of long-term analysis, a treatment he considered closest to the Freudian model: "I haven't been working lately, except for my hours [...] In the next few weeks I am hoping to terminate a three-year treatment victoriously after hard final struggles. It will be a triumph for psychoanalysis." His obvious confidence could be a due to several factors. The end of his own analysis has left him slightly euphoric; in addition, two men have entered the scene, and can serve as go-betweens between him and Freud: Georg Groddeck and Anton von Freund.

Over the past year, he has gradually gotten to know Groddeck's ideas. The latter's unusual therapeutic practices interest him, and allow him to legitimate and enrich his thinking about his own practices. On June 14, he revealed to Freud a discovery which, unbeknownst to him, was going to offer strong support to his critical re-evaluation of the practices of so-called classical Freudian analysis:

> It strikes me altogether as much more probable that Groddeck is not curing at all *with analysis*, but rather that with the aid of transference he puts the plastic power of hysteria into the service of the organic tendency to heal. Precisely because he doesn't analyze but rather displaces the tendencies as a block, he is able to perform such feats.

This faith in an innate tendency to heal stops him from fully agreeing with the Freudian hypothesis of a death instinct. In addition, Ferenczi has the support of Freund, whom he met in 1915, and who takes a very active part in the activities of the local group of Hungarian analysts. In fact, he would play an important role in the major analytic event of the year, an International Psychoanalytic Congress, which was originally to be held in Germany.

On June 26, Ferenczi is looking forward to Freud's planned visit to Budapest, before going to the Breslau conference in Germany: "We will only forge plans for your program on the spot. Nice walks in the surroundings of Budapest should play a considerable role in that, a good restaurant should always serve as a goal for an outing." Very happy with this prospect, Ferenczi is looking back at the evolution of their friendship, its setbacks and its renewal:

> I often think now about the 'honeymoon' of our acquaintance in Berchtesgaden just ten years ago. In the meantime, some changes have taken place in me – the newest one may give me the inner freedom that still eluded me in Palermo.

On June 29 Freud confirms that he will be staying at Freund's house in July. Freund had been in analysis with him after Freud had treated his second wife. Speaking of this analysis, Freud made a remark Ferenczi must have appreciated: "The analysis with our host was very interesting. Since it has as its aim the remaking of a person, I am permitted to continue it beyond the disappearance of symptoms." This comment must have bolstered Ferenczi's opinion that an analysis must be deepened, and cannot limit itself to eliminating symptoms. Freud's letter also contains this bit of information about Freund: "He himself will develop for you his intentions of helping out psychoanalysis." This is another reason for Ferenczi to feel hopeful: Freund had told Freud of his intention to make a substantial financial donation in support of the Freudian project. This donation would make it possible to plan the setting up of a psychoanalytic outpatient clinic in Budapest, with an affiliated training institute for future psychoanalysts, whose analytic activities would be headed by Ferenczi.

In these favourable circumstances, the International Psychoanalytic Congress provided Ferenczi with an opportunity for double recognition: political and analytic. On his own initiative, and without consulting Freud, he took charge of organising the Congress. During the proceedings, Freud made a momentous declaration, saying that the therapeutic way forward was "first and foremost" connected to activity on the part of the analyst, as advocated by Ferenczi – this master of psychoanalysis who, thanks to his personal analysis, had become acquainted with the good and bad consequences of the analyst's close involvement in his practice.

The success of the 1918 Congress

In principle, organising an international congress is the responsibility of the President of the IPA, in this case, Berlin analyst Karl Abraham. In a letter dated August 27, Freud wrote Abraham: "I am […] quite specially looking forward to our meeting at the Congress in Breslau," planned for September. He seems to be in high spirits, and says: "I can venture to join [in the dance] again," explaining: "I ascribe a good share of my better spirits to the prospects that have opened up in Budapest for the development of our cause." He is full of praise for Freund, "the sort of person whom one would have to invent if he did not already exist." Freud ends his letter with a prophecy: "Budapest is well on its way to becoming the center of our movement." But it was still uncertain whether the Congress could be held in Germany; Abraham was still waiting for authorisation from the German War Ministry. On September 2, Abraham still thought that everything was set for the arrival of the participants on September 21 and 22.

What he didn't know was that Ferenczi, with support from Rank and Freund, was about to make an important decision, of which he only informed Freud afterwards. The three friends proposed that the Congress be moved from Breslau to Budapest. On September 10, Ferenczi explains what led him to take this independent action:

> When I made the suggestion of holding it in Budapest, it turned out that I [had] only put into words the secret wish of Rank and Dr. Freund. "En petit comité," we thereupon decided to proceed on our own recognizance; we sent telegrams "to all" concerned and began preparations for the "Psychoanalytic Congress in Budapest."

Perhaps Ferenczi thought that his former analyst would be impressed with his decision-making capacity. "It would have cost us much time to seek out your opinion; we also knew that [faced with] such questions you like to reply: 'I am [staying out of it!]'." On September 13, not knowing that Freud had written him the same day, Ferenczi worried: "I, Dr. Rank, and Dr. Freund all feel a strong uneasiness, since your concurring reply to our – to be sure, energetic – action still hasn't arrived." In his answer of September 17, Freud expresses only one reservation: "The hints that you want to develop the Congress in a ceremonial – official direction have less of my sympathy."

Thus, the Congress was held in Budapest on September 28 and 29. It was a resounding success. Ferenczi was elected President of the IPA, and Freund its Secretary. Thanks to the anticipated donation, a new German-language international journal was created (*Verlag*), and the idea of awarding a prize for exceptional psychoanalytic work was considered. Back in Vienna, on September 30 Freud expressed his warmest thanks to Ferenczi:

> On the day of our return, at the threshold of the new work year, I can't refrain from thanking you for all the evidence of your warm friendship these last few days, and [congratulating] you for the beautiful success of the Congress as well as for your elevation [in rank].

And he adds: "Remember the prophetic words [...] I told you before the first Congress in Salzburg, that we had great things in store for you." It is becoming clear that Ferenczi holds a privileged place among Freud's potential heirs: "I am swimming in satisfaction, I am lighthearted, knowing that my problem child, my life's work, is protected and preserved for the future by your participation and that of others." On October 4, Ferenczi also confirms that the Congress was a success: "We seem to have greatly impressed the Budapest physicians. I am being congratulated from all sides. I must admit, however, that this elevation hasn't made me any prouder; it has only increased my sense of duty."

Aside from the political success which granted Ferenczi a central place in the activities of the psychoanalytic movement – which was regaining vigour as the terrible war was about to end – the Congress also proclaimed the new analytic direction to be pursued. In the paper he presented at the Congress, "Lines of Advance in Psycho-Analytic Therapy," Freud declared:

> Developments in our therapy, therefore, will no doubt proceed along other lines; first and foremost, along the one which Ferenczi, in his paper. "Technical Difficulties in an Analysis of Hysteria" (1919), has lately termed "activity" on the part of the analyst.

A mitigated achievement

Delighted with this recent success and with their future perspectives, neither man is surprised to have gone, in one year, from the torments caused by the scalding consequences of transference, to an unexpected upturn in their fortunes. We can legitimately ask ourselves whether Freud saw the transferential aspect of the Ferenczi article he cited. Was he aware that when Ferenczi describes the technical innovation he dares to make – tracking down the jouissance of his hysterical patient – he is also pointing out what was missing in the technique Freud employed when analysing him?

In this article, Ferenczi discusses a technical question: that of the limitations of an analysis that simply follows the rule of free association – on the part of the patient, and free-floating attention – on the part of the analyst. He describes a patient who

> was endeavouring with great intelligence and much zeal to carry out the directions for psychoanalytic treatment, and who left nothing to be desired in the way of theoretical insight, [but who] nevertheless, after a certain degree of improvement, probably due to the first transference, made no progress for a long time.

Faced with her excessive free association and with transference love resistant to analytic elucidation, Ferenczi "decided on extreme measures" and set a date up to which he would continue her treatment. In his own way, Freud had done the same thing with him in October 1916. But, Ferenczi notes, the effects of these measures were short-lived: "she soon relapsed into her former inactivity, which she concealed behind her transference love. The hours went by in passionate declarations of love." When interpretations remained fruitless, the analyst took concrete action: "On the completion of the period set I discharged her uncured. She herself was quite content with her improvement."

A few months later, the patient came back to resume analysis, when her old troubles resurfaced. But after some improvement, Ferenczi notes that: "she began the old game again." This time, the analysis was interrupted by extraneous circumstances, and the treatment "again remained incomplete."

The renewed exacerbation of her symptoms brought her back for the third time. But the patient remained fixated on her fantasmatic love for the analyst. It was while she spoke of these fantasies that Ferenczi observed her more closely; he noticed that while describing erotic genital sensations, she always kept her legs crossed. He then brought up the subject of onanism, but the patient vehemently denied engaging in this discreet form of masturbation. After a time, says Ferenczi: "an incipient new point of view erupts into [my] consciousness." Just as he had forbidden inexhaustible free association by ending the analysis, Ferenczi now forbade her to adopt this position on the couch, which, he explained, allowed her to carry out a "larval form of onanism," that discreetly discharged unconscious impulses, distorting the associative material by reducing it to the love fantasies focused on him.

The effect of this active measure was "staggering." As a result of this prohibition, the patient "was tormented during the interview by an almost insupportable bodily and psychic restlessness; she could no longer lie at peace, but had to constantly change position." The energy bound up with unsatisfied impulses was transformed into bodily experience, producing a change in the patient's discourse. As a result of this opening of the unconscious, speech revealed the fantasmatic context of unconscious erotic pleasure, and the associative process, moving to a different level, finally allowed the emergence of fragments that were of use to the analyst: "Her fantasies resembled the deliria of fever, in which there cropped up long forgotten memory fragments that gradually grouped themselves around certain events in her childhood and permitted the discovery of most important traumatic causes for her illness." Under the words of transference love, there is the patient's fantasy and secret jouissance, and under these, the childhood traumas from which they spring: this is Ferenczi's first discovery. But he makes a second discovery: "although she conscientiously carried out the above rule," the patient reconciled herself to this abstinence and again ceased to exert herself, taking refuge, once more in the "sanctuary of the transference love."

The tricks of the unconscious led Ferenczi – who was very determined – to escalate the measures aimed at reinforcing the patient's psychic work in the session. He set out to track down her secret auto-erotic activity: "Having had my wits sharpened by these previous experiences, however, I could now rout out the hiding-places in which she concealed her auto-erotic satisfaction." Consequently, he extended the restraint applying to the sessions, to the whole day. Because this also resulted in only temporary improvement, Ferenczi finally forbade all "larval onanism," including symptomatic acts that were its equivalents (such as muscle tremors, certain tics, hands in the pockets, needlework). Cut off from investment in "parts of the body that are not by nature prominent erotogenic zones," but are only substitutes for "genital erogenicity," her sexual pleasure found its way back to its normally indicated genital zone.

As Ferenczi shows by describing the case of his hysterical patient, this returning home of masturbatory erotic pleasure takes time and requires explicit prohibitions to be made by the analyst, who is invited to leave his position of well-meaning listener. In the case Ferenczi describes, he was forced to take a fifth measure during the sessions, when faced with the patient's "need to urinate at unreasonable times; the gratification of this was equally interdicted." At the end of this hard-fought analytic battle, the analyst had reason to be satisfied with the results: "Parallel with the reconstruction of her infantile defence reaction, she achieved, after all these worries, the capacity of obtaining satisfaction in normal sexual intercourse, which – although her husband was unusually potent [...] – had hitherto been denied her."

The novelty introduced in the classic analytic technique is clear. A new task is added to the activities expected of the analyst – providing the setting, interpreting the productions of the unconscious, and handling the transference. He must also resolutely put an end to the secret erotic satisfaction of the patient. Ferenczi points out that the hysteric suffers, as we know, from reminiscences that need to be remembered, worked through and freed from repression, but that she also suffers from autoeroticism she endures like a sleepwalker. The most striking aspect of his discovery is the intuition that the necessary frustration of the demand for love inherent in the dynamics of transference contributes to reactivating in the sessions masked auto-erotic pleasure which makes itself visible through repetition. Ferenczi stresses that making active use of this diminished form of pleasure in the analysis gives access to the most deeply hidden elements of fantasy life and of the traumas that have created them. A cure is thus brought about, with the ability to experience pleasure acquired through a slow bodily acceptance of castration.

At the Budapest Congress, Freud was praising not only Ferenczi himself, but most of all this technical innovation he attributed to him. However, certain details in "Technical Difficulties in an Analysis of Hysteria" deserve closer attention.

In this article, Ferenczi, not without reason, did not take the position of promoter of a subversive new technique, but rather that of an enthusiastic disciple: "We owe the prototype of this 'active technique' to Freud himself," he wrote. He then described the stratagem Freud sometimes employed when he encountered stagnation in the analysis of cases of anxiety hysteria, when he enjoined the patient to face, in reality, the anxiety-provoking situations from which their phobias protected them. The desired goal was to "free the wrongly anchored affects from their connections." Freud was the first to use the most spectacular, but also the most questionable of these stratagems: setting a date for the end of the treatment, as he did with the Wolfman.

When Ferenczi praised Freud's active technique, and then rendered it even more radical, and when Freud gave official approval to Ferenczi's – Freudian – approach, what shared amnesia prevented them from noticing that these matters of setting a date for the end of an analysis were related to transferential residues overlooked by both of them when Ferenczi was on the couch? How was it that Ferenczi did not remember that, as was the case for his patient, his treatment was interrupted by external circumstances at one point, and declared "finished but not terminated" afterwards? Could Ferenczi have forgotten that taking active measures – deferring the analysis and asking the patient to write – had had disastrous results in the case of the "Young Suicide"? Were both Freud and Ferenczi using the success of the Congress, and the promising prospects it opened in Budapest, as a substitute "happy ending" for the past analysis? How could they both tacitly agree to leave its persistent transferential residues in suspense? Indeed, is the article "Technical Difficulties in an Analysis of Hysteria" not an outcome of these residues? Could it be that Ferenczi felt such a great need to justify and make a model of Freud's active technique because unbeknownst to him he was already uncertain of its merits? And why did this former military doctor familiar with the traumatic neuroses of war limit himself in his article to discussing only morbidity rooted in fantasy, although he relates the morbid state to traumas masked by fantasy?

Wind in the sails

On October 4, 1918, Ferenczi answered Freud's letter of thanks sent after the Congress: "I, too, can report only pleasant things to you about my affects in these last days." And he adds, on an unexpected note: "The ground on which we will certainly always find ourselves, is, of course, science. All fog dissipates in its

light, and in that way also the ridiculous little irritations of the summer months."
But the next sentence shows Ferenczi's joy to be somewhat tempered: "In the
summer I was probably only disappointed that the planned collaborative work
was left undone." The Lamarck project they planned together would not be carried out.

On October 8, Ferenczi informed Freud of a promising project:

> The day before yesterday I was called on the telephone by the chief medical
> officer of the Budapest Military Command, the general staff physician, who
> attended the Congress. He informed me that he is finished with his report to
> the War Ministry, in which he recommends instituting a *psychoanalytic ward*
> in Budapest. He asked me for suggestions about this plan.

Ferenczi accepted the planned project immediately: "I said: first we should have a
smaller experimental ward for about thirty patients. At his request I then assumed
its direction in principle, but I immediately remarked that I definitely needed an
assistant who knows the field." Ferenczi added that he was ready to fight for the
nomination of Max Eitington and Istvan Hollos as assistants. Clearly, Ferenczi
foresaw that this project could lead to the creation of a polyclinic destined to
become an invaluable institution for the training of analysts. On October 11, Freud
wrote that he approved of Ferenczi's tenacity in obtaining his chosen assistants
for the "psychoanalytic ward." On October 25, Ferenczi had more good news for
Freud and for psychoanalysis:

> A number of medical students have asked me to give lectures about psycho-
> analysis. I assented, provided they have an appropriate place. In a flash, a
> movement had started! 180 signatures are being directed to the rector of the
> university with the request that I be given an opportunity to teach!

On October 27, Freud saw it fit to temper Ferenczi's enthusiasm, reminding him
of the uncertainties of the political situation: "Withdraw your libido from your
fatherland in a timely fashion and shelter it in psychoanalysis." On November 7,
Ferenczi acknowledged the worsening of the political situation in Hungary, and
feared that his country would be dismembered, and that with the social upheaval
to be expected would come a return of antisemitism. But he still hoped to be able
to teach psychoanalysis at the university:

> The two hundred students who want to learn psychoanalysis from me seem to
> have included this plan in a larger movement that involves university studies
> in general. If this government stays, I hope to get to a lecture hall one way
> or another.

On November 11 the Armistice was signed; the war was over. After the defeat, the
dismemberment of the Austro-Hungarian Empire led to the creation of new states.

On November 17, 1918, Ferenczi sent the members of the Secret Committee a circular letter. He reiterated his intention of using the interest from the foundation (Freund's donation) for the creation of two annual prizes for works of exceptional quality. On November 24, he was sounding hopeful after the return to power of progressive Social Democrats. Setting caution aside, he joined the newly formed Social Democratic Physicians' Union, and participated in the Association of Creative Artists and Scientific Researchers, where he intended to give a lecture on "the central significance of psychoanalysis in the humanities." His letter went on to say: "At the same time, some psychoanalysis disciples at the university have gathered signatures for a petition (up to now already about 1,000); they are demanding to be given an opportunity to study psychoanalysis." Ferenczi ended his letter with a reference to the conference he was about to have with Freund about the distribution of the main endowment. The small committee entrusted with administering the funds would receive the support of a political figure: "Minister Garami has accepted membership on the board of trustees." Ferenczi the activist takes on a leading role in the fight for the undisputed recognition of psychoanalysis. He remains euphoric: "The home of psychoanalysis is indeed Budapest and not Vienna; you should move here!" On November 27, Freud reminded Ferenczi to keep his focus on psychoanalysis: "Your suggestions for awarding the prizes don't quite square with my intentions. I don't want to distinguish authors but rather works." He is more cool-headed than Ferenczi: "Budapest is decidedly more favorable for psychoanalysis, not that I am thinking of moving on account of that." On December 3, Freud's questions about the political situation reveal his concern: "How do things look with you under foreign domination? Do you really have censorship of the mails?" And of course, he asks about the upcoming marriage. On December 6, still busy with a number of projects, Ferenczi sounded confident: "The chances for the 'academic psychoanalysis' are changing a great deal; the last reports don't sound unfavorable." He also reassures Freud that Gizella will soon be officially divorced, and that their long-awaited marriage can then take place immediately.

On December 26, in the aftermath of his analysis, and taking into account the political situation in Hungary and the success of the recent Congress, Ferenczi makes a mixed reassessment of the year which is ending: "Another year gone by – and what a year! I think we still actually have no idea of the emotional effect that the upheaval of the last twelve months will have on us all." He knows that there is no guarantee that the new government will keep its current promises: "No lesser, however, is the test of strength that we will be subjected to in the near future […] Truly, no shining prospect." In these times of uncertainty, Ferenczi holds on to his faith in psychoanalysis:

> The only thing that kept me going in these days and still keeps me going is the optimism that I owe to the circumstances that, as a collaborator in psychoanalysis, I feel I belong to an intellectual movement which is without a doubt a part of the future.

He is committed, and does not hide his hope that psychoanalysis could exert a favourable influence on "a still very primitive social organisation contributing thereby to the progress of humanity." Still hopeful, he tells Freud: "I won't abandon the idea that you may yet move to Budapest." But he is lucid and foresees the possibility that "a clerical-reactionary tide will come and also harm the young Hungarian psychoanalysis." Still, he believes he can count "on a certain sense for freedom of thought, even among our opponents, so that we can still maintain our problem child in this country for the future."

Boldly forward, analysts! (early months of 1919)

On January 1, 1919, Freud confesses that Ferenczi's last letter was "doubly welcome." "I know you to be in smooth sailing, in a commanding position, surrounded by students and adherents, soon, very soon, let us hope, in possession of your own warm house and a woman unsurpassed in many important respects." At last, what the father of psychoanalysis had always wished for his young colleague, even before acting as his analyst, was coming true. Now, Ferenczi could work and love in peace, and become the most accomplished and trustworthy analyst in Freud's circle, and in fact the one who could ensure the transmission of psychoanalysis and the training of analysts. Freud wrote reassuringly: "I know that much work and great inner torment will confront you, but one shouldn't wish it otherwise." This clairvoyance incites Ferenczi to consent to his share of torment, and to convert to work energy the residue which resisted analysis. Freud the thinker knows that an analyst must – like any man – accept the part played by destiny, by the inevitable [Ananké]: "Success will then be the way it indeed can be under all the interplay of external forces and inner powers. In any case, very honorable and, let us hope, also happy." In the next paragraph, Freud revealed his worries about Freund, his analysand who had become the protector of psychoanalysis. Seeing his "strange behavior of being a candidate for death in the morning and healthy in the afternoon," Freud hesitated between attributing this to neurosis or some organic cause. On January 6 he sent news of Freund, and also asked Ferenczi to be resolute in his role as leader of the new journal *Zeitschrift*: "But I would still like you to keep your role as a leader secure and to express it by taking a critical position with regard to really significant publications in literature." The same day, Ferenczi informed Freud about rapid changes in the political situation, which was becoming less favourable to psychoanalysis: "Everything is pressing toward a showdown between the extreme parties: the Communists on the one hand, the reactionaries on the other." In this turbulent context, psychoanalysis no longer had true allies. But despite this, a letter from Budapest dated January 19, 1919, testifies to intense analytic activity among members of the local group: "The Budapest Society is functioning well, beyond expectations." Yet Ferenczi's mood fluctuates:

> I actually couldn't say much about the depression which you notice in my letters. I am fully capable of work, and I don't allow myself to be influenced

much by the moderate physical and sleep disturbances. To be sure, I can't report about any particularly boundless feeling of happiness, either.

On January 24, Freud expressed his concern about Freund's analysis again: "Toni is naturally much better than at home, but in [a state of] neurotic defiance because I don't want to accept any more gifts from him. In some areas his primitive savagery has not yet been dismantled." On February 9, Ferenczi also spoke of Freund, after seeing him: "I found Toni churned up. I have the impression that resistance is giving rise to the deeper, rougher layers of his personality. Perhaps that means recovery for him, but he is useless to us – at least for the time being." But Ferenczi goes on to say that despite this, his chances of teaching are not altogether lost: "The matter now stands in a not entirely unfavourable light; the new Minister of Education is amicably disposed to the thing, and so is the newly appointed government commissar of the university." On February 13, Freud reminds him to remain cautious:

> As to the chance at the university, it certainly should be considered that all your patrons won't remain in office long enough for a decision to take place. Marriage and living quarters are certainly more assured, but I would very much wish for you to get the teaching position [title of Professor].

Freud, who doubts that any recognition will come from the political sphere, brings Ferenczi back to more solid ground – that of the analytic research in which they are passionately engaged: "Your paper on technique is pure analytic gold, and can only be completely appreciated by the worker. In a few places I would have felt like adding a continuing or concluding statement." The compliment probably provoked a certain wariness on Ferenczi's part. Was Freud telling him that he found this remarkable article – loyal to Freudian concepts, as we said earlier – somehow lacking, needing further development and a conclusion?

Freud was still worried about Anton von Freund: "Toni is, as you yourself have found, wild and in an uproar, subjectively very well, objectively in resistance." But Freud remained hopeful: "I expect with certainty that the sublimation which has now been removed will be restored on a more secure basis after the treatment." But, wisely, he could foresee another possibility: "Provided that the real conditions [...] don't [...] bring about a new illusory cure!"

By counting on self-analytical work to take place for Freund after his analysis, Freud was staying loyal to the conviction that caused him to put a definitive end to Ferenczi's hopes of pursuing his analysis beyond the third segment.

Mission accomplished – game over?

On March 1, 1919, Ferenczi was finally able to give Freud the news he had long been hoping for: "Our first greeting goes to you, whom we would so very much like to have chosen as a witness to our marriage." In his letter of March 4, Freud does not hide his joy, which could be said to be triple, since it is at once that of the man, the analyst and the father of psychoanalysis:

> Finally I receive from you the so-long-awaited news that you have both carried through your union and have let a marriage lasting half a lifetime, which has proved to be indissoluble through all the pushes and pulls, be crowned by a civil ceremony!

Ferenczi's analyst knows all about the internal struggle his analysand went through to finally consent to marry, and about the active techniques he himself had to use in the treatment. Freud, the man, is also happy to see his valuable and difficult colleague finally adopt the conjugal model he, Freud, considers ideal – that of self-realisation in the couple:

> I know how much each of you has gone through in the process and how much [each] has finally renounced, but I remain firm in my conviction, which has grown in the course of a decade, that all happiness that awaits you both could only have been assured in this way, and that, despite your having left such a long time unused, it will turn out to be something irreplaceably beautiful after all.

Very early, long before analysing him, Freud drew Ferenczi's attention to a sad reality that made them different: at the age Ferenczi was when he met Freud, the latter benefitted from a major advantage: the presence of a loyal wife, the mother of their many children. During the summer of 1908, when they shared their first vacation, Freud suggested that Ferenczi pay attention to his love life. Ferenczi later remembered what Freud told him then, obviously moved to speak by a secret suffering he perceived. In 1910, in a letter dated April 5, Ferenczi had confessed to Freud how much and how absolutely he needed the latter's presence, needed to hear how his thinking about the work developed, and needed the reassurance of his friendship:

> Your letters always gave me extraordinary satisfaction in my intellectual and emotional isolation. This time your letter had this effect to an increased degree; being together for days with people of like mind spoiled me – and this evening I caught myself singing a Hungarian song with the following text: "On the great ball of earth no one so orphaned as I."

Ferenczi remembered what Freud had told him in the summer of 1908: "You told me once in Berchtesgaden: 'Man *must* love something.' That could also be craft and science. But obviously not exclusively. One must also love *people* if one wants to be happy." It's clear that Freud was already thinking that a woman was missing in the life of this pupil, whose remarkable intelligence and passionate investment in psychoanalysis were obvious. Was Freud speaking as a family man reminding the younger man of the benefits of married life, or was he speaking as a potential analyst frightened by the ambiguous request for love and recognition addressed to him? This question needed an answer again in the spring of 1919.

When, during Ferenczi's analysis, Freud demanded that his analysand make up his mind to marry, even to a woman who could no longer have children, was he using the active technique or was he also promoting the ideals that conformed to his desires – desires never examined on an analyst's couch?

In the letter dated March 4, 1919, the joy and relief expressed are also those of the father of psychoanalysis who is burdened with the symptom and fantasy Emma Jung had identified and denounced some years earlier. Here again, Freud is speaking from the imaginary position of a family man who feels death approaching and needs to ensure the secure position of the son who will succeed him and to whom he entrusts his heritage:

> And since you have given me the honor of wishing me to be a witness to your union, I may speak personally and admit that often, when I had to think about putting things in order and saying good-bye, I was troubled by a concern about you both, as to how you, who have become so dear to me, would get on – a concern which has now been allayed.

When Freud "speaks personally" and "admits" his very personal "concern" of recent years, who exactly is speaking? Is it the analyst who ended the analytic exchange, or the father of psychoanalysis who feels he has accomplished his mission?

A few decades later, Jacques Lacan did not hesitate to do what Ferenczi had done: question Freud's desire. In 1955, in his seminar, Lacan pointed out the important role held in Freud's oeuvre by the latter's relation to a woman:

> We know the immense importance of the role which his wife played in Freud's life. He had not only a familial attachment to her, but also a conjugal, highly idealised one. It does seem, nonetheless, given certain nuances, that on certain levels, she brought him a certain disappointment.

The allusion is clear: Freud apparently gave up conjugal relations after Anna's birth, when he was nearly 40, precisely the age when Ferenczi was going through a mid-life crisis. Could this disparity have contributed to the complexity of their transferential relations? In 1964, in his seminar on fundamental concepts, Lacan developed his earlier intuition and connected the question of Freud's relation to women and to "his" woman with the question of the father and his function:

> As far as Freud and his relation to the father are concerned, let us not forget that despite all his efforts to understand, he was forced to admit, to a woman of his acquaintance, that, for him, the question – *What does a woman want?* – remained unanswered. He never resolved this question, as we can see from

what was in fact his relations with women, his uxorious character, as Jones rather delicately puts it.

Jones goes so far as to say that Freud might have wandered off in totally unfounded directions had he not listened to women intent on achieving fulfilment as women more than as wives or mothers. Lacan adds: "I would say that Freud would certainly have made a perfect impassioned idealist had he not devoted himself to the other, in the form of the hysteric."

On March 18, 1919, Ferenczi confirms that he is happy with his new status, and thanks Freud for his support:

> I find myself in the acclimatization stage of marriage. Aside from small vacillations, which pass quickly, everything seems to be getting on the right track. The future may prove you right, you who did not allow yourself to be diverted from this solution, despite my often very dramatic displays of resistance.

Clearly, Ferenczi was eager to believe that the neurotic symptoms which drove him to ask for an analysis had now been vanquished: "I have the feeling that the final settlement of my personal matter will significantly increase my capacity for work. In any event, new work plans are always emerging, e.g., that of the final realization of the paleobiological speculation." This "speculation" was to be *Thalassa*. Although, Freud attempted to situate his analysand's ill-being in his relation with Gizella and to women in general, Ferenczi had not forgotten the other source of his distress, his relation with Freud himself. But he wanted to believe that this too was in the past:

> Your dear letter gave us much joy. We both hope that our friendship will always remain undisturbed. I think that henceforth I will sooner be permitted also to show you all the gratitude that I always felt toward you. Neurotic inhibitions, which from time to time prevented me from doing that, may finally have been banished from the world.

At last! Ferenczi can now enjoy the stability of his own home, which his analyst deems essential for the full flowering of the man of science. Now, Freud can hope that Ferenczi, free of his neurotic preoccupations, will once again be his ally in defending their common cause. Their intellectual collaboration can be taken up again, and will be particularly welcome because Freud is about to make fundamental changes to his theoretical edifice. He is writing a new essay: "I am still heavily booked up, but at the same time I am writing the essay 'Beyond the Pleasure Principle' and, as in all instances, I am hoping for your understanding, which has not yet abandoned me in any situation." But in addition to the unstable political situation in Hungary, Freund's uncertain state of health casts a shadow on the otherwise bright prospects that have opened up with the newfound vitality of the analytic movement, and the new promising perspectives in Vienna.

Light and shadow

The political situation in Hungary is unstable, but the promises of official recognition for psychoanalysis seem to be coming true. They brighten the spring, but, at the same time, there is concern about the physical and psychic health of Anton Freund, the generous donator who has become Ferenczi's most valuable ally in the enterprise that was to make Budapest, as Freud said, the "center" of the analytic movement which was now enjoying a revival with the return of peace.

On April 1, Freud informed Ferenczi that Freund was returning to Budapest after a stay in Vienna dedicated to his analysis: "In a few weeks a member of your Society will be cured of his excursion into psychosis and will return to you as a halfway analysed neurotic, Anton Freund. Let us hope he is also well in other respects."

On April 4, Ferenczi cautiously enumerates a series of accomplishments:

> The chances for psychoanalysis "fluctuant necmergentur." Today I was visited by 1) a delegation of students who want to found a psychoanalytic society of medical students. I intend to encourage them. 2) The chief physician of the Workers' Health Service, who wants to set up an outpatient department, that is to say, put it at the disposal of the university [...] 4) In the name of someone empowered by the people I was invited to claim a requisitioned private sanatorium for the psychoanalytic institute.

But along with these promising but not absolutely certain prospects, there was less fortunate development listed by Ferenczi: the rumour of the nomination of two enemies of psychoanalysis, entrusted with reorganising the teaching of neurology. Nevertheless, these tenuous promises were enough to hope that favourable conditions would allow the creation, in Budapest, of an Institute of Psychoanalysis – the first – with Ferenczi as its Director, responsible for its analytic orientation. It was with this Hungarian context in mind that Freud wrote the article "Should Psychoanalysis Be Taught at Universities?" On April 5, Ferenczi admits in the post-scriptum of his letter that he has taken a considerable liberty: "I permitted myself (for tactical reasons), to interpose a little sentence into your little essay on psychoanalytic training. Something like: 'A psychiatric section would be used for psychoanalytic investigation on the psychoses.'" Thus, Ferenczi felt free, once his analysis was over, and thanks to the success of the Budapest Congress, to take a position that would have major consequences for psychoanalysis. Ferenczi, like Lacan would later, thought it possible to apply analytic therapy to the psychoses, as he himself had already done; but Freud did not agree. On April 13, Ferenczi wrote that he continued to receive promising propositions:

> Psychoanalysis is being courted on all sides; it is costing an effort to defend myself against the solicitations. But yesterday I was unable to avoid a direct invitation to take over a section of a state hospital. In the new era they want

to *communize all medical practice: private practice will cease completely.* Psychoanalysis will have to devote itself to hospital material.

But Freund's state of health throws a shadow on these happy prospects: "Toni is quite hypochondriacal again. He has strong pains, which are localized in the back and the liver area, he turns more and more to being sick."

Ferenczi's letter dated April 15 opens with news about Freud's analysand:

First, something about Toni's case: Since the moment at which the possibility of your coming here emerged, I stopped conducting thoroughgoing analytic negotiations with him – he is also *completely* primed for your coming. If you are impeded, then I can still jump in. Incidentally, we haven't yet actually gotten into the proper analytic mood at all.

Ferenczi is reminding Freud of Anton's very strong transferential dependence.

Very busy with the political context to be established for psychoanalysis, and very concerned about the analytic treatment of their friend, Ferenczi had not seen Freud since the Budapest Congress six months earlier. He is very frank about the painful weight of this isolation which now goes hand in hand with his independence:

It has been a frightfully long time since we talked to each other – and now, of all times, when every day is an eternity! I am loaded with personal and material questions. The separation, which has lasted too long, has made the tension grow excessively. I doubt whether we will be able to discuss everything properly here.

On April 20, Freud encourages the analytic work Ferenczi is doing with Toni, but is more reserved about the possibility that psychoanalysis could be granted recognition by government agencies. He is not caught up in Ferenczi's enthusiasm: "Restraint, we are not suited for any kind of official existence, we need our independence on all sides [...] We are and remain nonpartisan except for one thing: to investigate and to help." Freud wants to preserve, for each of them, the freedom to pursue his own research, but he also values the magic of the exchanges possible between men looking for the truth: "I will also miss the chance to see you. I have the same need for exchanging thoughts that you express, and for that reason I have hatched the plan that you should accompany Toni to Vienna." On March 21, 1919, the Hungarian Soviet Republic was proclaimed.

The letter Ferenczi wrote Freud on April 21 makes it clear that he did not adopt the restraint Freud had counselled:

Owing to the intervention of a friend, who has influence in such matters, we succeeded in having the decision go along very *favorable* lines. *Affairs of the university* are also stirring. *Dr. Radó* was appointed an assistant at the

Moravcsik Clinic, and Fräulein Dr. Révész became a regular trainee there
[…] I was offered a nice hospital section, which I will accept.

Ferenczi ends his letter on a more personal note: "My private affairs require a
special letter, which I won't be able to write until tomorrow." And he adds a post-
scriptum about Toni: "In reality, it has to do with a relapse of his illness!!" meaning his physical illness.

Transference in analysis and between collaborators

In an undated letter written in April 1919, Ferenczi the analyst speaks of his isolation
in the work of reflection required by the practice of analysis: "I can't tell you how
difficult it is to bear the intellectual separation from you, which grows increasingly
chronic." Moreover, he is spending time with Toni, whose health is deteriorating:

> I see him daily, but I content myself with listening to his complaints and
> providing distraction for him […] Actually we [Toni and I] are only coming
> closer these days; it is all the more painful for me to see how sad it is with him.

Ferenczi is afraid he will lose the like-mindedness he shares with Toni, just when
he is suffering from physical separation from Freud. Ferenczi emphasises that this
intellectual solitude which could deepen even more can in no way be eased by
the attention, the love and the help he receives from his remarkable wife, Gizella.
He adds: "A small remnant of neurosis still disrupts certain vital mechanisms of
pleasure. But she knows nothing of this." But Freud must know what Ferenczi is
referring to, since he analysed the author of the letter. On April 29, the news about
Toni's state is not good. At the same time, Ferenczi is surprised at his own good
health. The fact that he has just been named Professor "for Psychoanalysis" might
have something to do with it. On May 12, Freud wrote that he was saddened by
Toni's state, and he was afraid he wouldn't be able to see him. What he would
like to see, however, is the beneficial effect of analysis on Ferenczi, "How glad
I would be to have a glimpse of your new existence as husband and professor."
   The first part of Ferenczi's long letter dated May 23, 1919, is dedicated to Toni,
who has just undergone radiotherapy: "His internist is, to be sure, not giving up all
hope […] The radiologist has a different opinion – he is pessimistic." As for the
patient, he feels better: "[…] although he remains quite remote from his former
professional affairs, he does, however, occupy himself daily and with satisfaction
his newly chosen profession – the exercise of which I give him the opportunity."
Was Ferenczi sending Freund his first patients?

> He helps me with his factual knowledge, his reason, and his diplomacy in the
> confusion of these tumultuous days – is the only psychoanalyst around me,
> as it were, whom I can trust completely. We have become friendly, and I can
> absolutely *not comprehend* the idea that we could lose him.

Ferenczi wants to remain hopeful, and to believe that Freund, who had started, in a manner of speaking, his analysis with him before continuing it with Freud, would soon be able to travel to Vienna:

> As soon as contact with Vienna has been restored, the patient is supposed to go to you, not only for the sake of psychoanalysis and reassurance, but also so that the medical specialists there will give their views on the tumor and its therapy.
> Since the end of 1917, Ferenczi's relationship with Freud has changed considerably.

He no longer writes long letters to speak of his feelings and resentments, as he did immediately following the end of his third segment of analysis. But this progress in his relation to the father of psychoanalysis and to the analytic cause does not prevent him from examining the manner in which he overcame his transference onto the person of Freud. Although hesitant to "mention in the same breath" more personal matters that might seem petty "compared to the possibility of seeing such a valuable life end so tragically" – Toni's life – Ferenczi sets his embarrassment aside and dedicates the next part of the May 23 letter to these personal matters. It is not a neurotic indulgence, but a need: "But it has to be. I have afflicted you too long with dry, almost telegraphically stylized letters." He explains what has caused him to re-examine the trajectory of his personal analysis. Earlier in May, while moving to a new home, he says: "I had to lay hands on the big pile of detailed, amicably patient letters which you directed at me in the course of the last ten years." When he wrote this letter, over 800 letters had already been sent back and forth, between Budapest and Vienna. As he reread Freud's letters, one thing stood out first and foremost: "The entire new developmental history of the newer psychoanalysis has been put down in them." This obvious conclusion is followed immediately by the observation of their powerful transferential relation and its tensions: "But at the same time they are also documents attesting to the extent of the care, benevolence – indeed, I may say: love – with which you have pursued, led, shielded, my oh, so difficult development." Here, Ferenczi is referring to Freud's influence on his training path, which caused him to be an even more determined analyst than he had been before his personal analysis. This backward glance over the recent events of his analysis allowed him to make several discoveries, that were not so much a gaining of awareness, as a dazzling knowingness:

> On this occasion there arose in me like a gleam the insight that since the moment in which you advised me against Elma, I have had a resistance toward your own person which could not even be overcome by the attempt at a psychoanalytic cure, and which was responsible for all my sensitivities.

In this letter dated May 23, 1919, Ferenczi is placing the focus on the negative transference underlying transference resistance. He knows how active this resistance still is after the analysis, and that it is still there in him, in this present time when he is regaining his ability to love and to work. Behind the obvious positive transference which makes him express his gratitude to Freud, negative transference shows its grimacing countenance: "With an unconscious resentment in my heart, I, as a loyal 'son,' nevertheless followed all your suggestions, left Elma, again turned to my present wife, with whom I have stayed, despite countless temptations from other quarters." Ferenczi has learned to live with his double-faceted condition; although he can work and love, he cannot claim to be cured: "The marriage, sealed under such unusually tragic circumstances – did not at first bring about the hoped-for inner consolidation." Suspecting that these insights can only burden Freud and disturb his ideals – an "unbeing" experience – Ferenczi tries to be reassuring: "Yet the resistance seems to be gradually exhausting itself – and a letter such as the present one may show you that I am willing to resume – perhaps, actually – to begin the frank intercourse with you, free from petty sensitivity." This new beginning in their relationship is to be inscribed, in its turn, in the story of the "finished but not terminated" treatment, which will have to complete itself, between the analyst and the analysand turned analyst, by taking other paths than that of the couch, unprecedented paths that have yet to be invented.

Ferenczi is deeply moving when he strives to make Freud understand that even an analysis which is not conducted to its termination and leaves in its wake all kinds of transferential residues is still not a failure. Ferenczi is vaguely aware, with good reason, that he is trying to ensure a permanent, fundamental relation with Freud. His psychic well-being depends on it:

> It appears that I can be happy in life and content in work only when I can be and remain in good, indeed, in the best relations with you. The realization that in Frau G. I have the best that could befall me – with my constitution – is the first fruit of my inner reconciliation with you.

This plea arouses great emotion, at a deeper level than the promises of recognition of psychoanalysis made by government officials. For Ferenczi, what is at stake is the very future of his prospective path as an analyst: "I ask you, don't lose patience with me in the future, either. I hope to offer you less occasion for that than in the past." After this heartfelt plea, in the last part of his letter Ferenczi returns to the situation of psychoanalysis in the prevailing context in Hungary: "My fervent wish to legitimize psychoanalysis, and my didactic intentions at the university have been brought to fruition all too stormily [...] I hope I will succeed in keeping psychoanalysis free of all political tendencies at all times."

Although Toni's state is worsening, good news on other fronts abound:

> Next Sunday I will open the university psychoanalytic Society, which was founded by medical students, with a lecture. I will begin the course of lectures on psychoanalysis around June 4–5. It remains to be seen whether the sanatorium which was assigned to me can be transformed into a psychoanalytic

clinic. In any event, the rector and the dean have already "taken" the oath of office from me (as a full public professor of psychoanalysis!).

But Ferenczi must have known that these rosy prospects were uncertain. Given the unstable circumstances around him, he felt an ardent need to be reassured about the continuity of his dialogue with Freud. His letter ends with a bit of wit and self-mockery: "But you must forgive my talkativeness – it is like the opening of a sluice that was closed – almost rusted – for a long time." At the end of July, when he started to teach, Ferenczi's state of mind had not changed: On July 26 he wrote: "Aside from didactic things I can't report on any recent scientific activity. Perhaps the change of air will help [...] I long finally to talk things out with you." This need for the freedom provided by sincere dialogue between men passionately searching for the truth was all the more urgent since the political situation favourable to the transmission of psychoanalysis was fundamentally unstable. Very quickly, actual events confirmed Ferenczi's worries: the promising spring was followed by the cruellest upheaval. On July 31, 1919, the communists – the Hungarian Council Republic favourable to the teaching of psychoanalysis in university – were forced to resign and were replaced by the Social Democrats. On August 3 and 4, the Romanian army took Budapest. A counter-revolutionary government headed by Miklos Horthy overturned the Social Democrats. This was followed by massive executions and arbitrary arrests. Jews were accused of having collaborated with the communists, and were specifically targeted. In early August, Ferenczi had to leave his teaching post.

In less than a year, the prospects opened by Ferenczi's tireless work disappeared and hopes for psychoanalysis were lost. Budapest would not be the capital of psychoanalysis, Ferenczi would not have time to act as President of the IPA. Worse still, he was no longer in a position of strength that would have allowed him to put forth the analytic orientation centred on the "analyst's activity," which Freud thought should inspire future trends in psychoanalysis. Even more trying for Ferenczi was the fact that the heavy impact of political events on the analytic movement caused Freud to take charge of the affairs of the movement once again, at least for the moment. This allowed him to divest himself of the function of analyst in relation to Ferenczi, a role he had accepted reluctantly.

Relentless as usual, Ferenczi prepared to face this devastating situation that distanced him from the centre of analytic activity, which quickly moved to Berlin. Nevertheless, in his personal trajectory, he was able to advance from these losses to the pursuit of his own aspirations.

Chapter 6

From public consecration to personal aspirations (summer 1918–spring 1919)

An ominous future

In the only letter Ferenczi wrote to Freud in this dark month of August 1919, on August 28, he describes the catastrophic situation he faces in his country:

> after the unbearable 'Red terror,' which lay heavy on one's spirit like a nightmare, we now have the White one [...] the ruthless clerical – anti-Semitic spirit seems to have eked out a victory [...] we, Hungarian Jews are now facing a period of brutal persecution of Jews.

He expects the conditions of life to become difficult: "It will very soon become evident how one can live and work here. It is naturally the best thing for psychoanalysis to continue working in complete withdrawal and without noise." In these conditions, teaching psychoanalysis at the university has become impossible: "The blackest reaction prevails at the university. All Jewish assistants were fired, the Jewish students were thrown out and beaten."

This collision of the history of psychoanalysis with the history of mankind gives Ferenczi pause: "Personally, [I] will have to take this trauma as an occasion to abandon certain prejudices brought along from the nursery and to come to terms with the bitter truth of being, as a Jew, really without a country." Therefore, to think that such a government could offer refuge or a home to psychoanalysis would have been an illusion. Hope had to come from another source: "One must distribute the libido which becomes free [...] between the few friends whom one has rescued from this debacle, the only true soul that accompanies one through thick and thin [Gizella?], and science." But this love of science, while pursued alone, would have to be shared with a witness: "So you will have to excuse me if henceforth I seek the opportunity more often than before of communicating with you personally, or at least by letter." On September 5, Freud's reply is warm and full of concern:

> When I see you again in Vienna at the end of this month, a whole year will have passed, a year without personal intercourse, the first in the history of our

relations. Perhaps the most difficult year for you as well, as it was one of the most difficult for me [...]

Sensing his friend's distress, Freud goes on to say: "[...] a year which ends with a burning disappointment for you, one which has robbed you of a fatherland [...]" And that is the least of it, since Ferenczi loses not only his country, but also the political ideals he had adopted, hoping that the Republic of Councils would provide a favourable environment for the development and transmission of psychoanalysis.

Freud points out that despite the disappointments, the year had brought some rewards:

[...] and yet – you will have to be thankful to it, for it has brought you a wife, without whom you wouldn't be able to bear life today; [and] the teaching position which you have wished for so long, and which will, let us hope, continue to be yours [...]

Freud knows, just as Ferenczi does, that these accomplishments owe much to the trying work of personal analysis carried out in the years just past. Without the analysis, Ferenczi would never have taken the bold initiative of having the 1918 Breslau conference moved to Budapest. Not only was the Congress a great success, but it led to Ferenczi's two recent, though short-lived, nominations. In his letter, Freud lists yet another reason for which Ferenczi might feel doubly hopeful: "[...] and – if you didn't have it yet – also the certainty that our scientific movement, in which you are assuming a leading role, [can stand] up to all storms and perils." Thus, Freud asserts his faith in the strength of the analytic movement, and in the triumph of psychoanalysis; indeed, he sees it confirmed in Ferenczi's eminent position at the head of the analytic movement. The letter ends with a heartfelt wish: "The next year should begin beautifully with the joyful meeting of friends who haven't seen one another for a long time!"

In October, Ferenczi goes to Vienna. On October 12, Freud informs Eitingon about the decisions made during this visit:

Jones was here, Ferenczi and Freund are still here; alas, the latter is a man who is slowly dying, while displaying perfect lucidity and self-control. Our orientation towards the West has been accomplished, Ferenczi resigned the presidency in favour of Jones.

Thus, Ferenczi never exercised his functions as President of the IPA. A few weeks later, on November 20, 1919, he acknowledged that he was shaken, but spoke with courage and great determination: "After the beautiful days in Vienna – despite all the calamities I had to learn of there, they were still the most beautiful of the year gone by – I began compulsory service here on the day after our arrival." Aside from working on his own biological project (*Thalassa*) and preparing the yearly report of the Hungarian Psychoanalytic Association, he has been writing reviews of biological works. Heeding Freud's advice to believe, in those difficult times, only in the future victories of psychoanalysis, Ferenczi imparts a more confident tone to his writing: "I hope I have found the tone which expresses our superiority in the face of the new findings [...] approximately the way we came to an agreement about this at one of our nice Thursday meetings." Showing no change of heart or bad temper, Ferenczi pursues the work in the worst political climate: "[...] about the political conditions in Budapest [...] the anti-Semitic terror rages on indefatigably, they won't allow Jewish auditors into the university, harass Jews wherever possible." Ferenczi is able to focus all his energy on science and on his active participation in the analytic movement because his *desire* for analysis is now rooted in what is left of his working relationship and his direct connection with Freud through the spoken (written) word: "Coming back to the Vienna vacation (it is certainly the nicest thing to think of our scientific and amicable relations), I must affirm that they will remain unforgettable to me in many respects." Despite the progress achieved in his personal analysis, and despite its enduring deferred effects, Ferenczi remains dependent not so much on Freud personally – infantile position – as on the sphere of significance created and maintained on condition of his ongoing exchanges with the father of psychoanalysis. This need for a space of direct exchange, made possible by the presence of another, never left Ferenczi: "In the few hours that were at our disposal, we were able to exchange such a wealth of insights as perhaps never before [...] All this was able to compensate me fully for the loss of this year's summer vacation." Ferenczi softens reality a great deal when he reduces the hardships of the previous year to the mere loss of his vacation. After all, has he not seen, within a few months, any hopes of the well-deserved recognition of his hard work as an analyst vanish? Has not the promising future emerging on the horizon been swept away by the White terror reigning in Budapest and by the imminent death of Anton von Freud, his newfound friend? In order not to fall apart in such catastrophic circumstances, Ferenczi, like Freud, can shift his hopes to the future of science and psychoanalysis. But unlike Freud, he now needs another person to trust and to exchange with even more than before: "It will, to be sure, be difficult for me to renounce again for months this intimate contact, of which I have become so fond."

Fervent desire, mourning and renunciation

On November 28, 1919, Freund's condition is still alarming in Budapest: "Now we have become modest and want to rejoice over every moment that our friend still spends in our midst." But the prognosis is clear: "The doctors must fulfill his demand for euthanasia; he has complete justification for it." Ferenczi wishes to help Freund, who is perfectly lucid, to make arrangements for his legacy: "I would like to give him the satisfaction of securing his large endowment." On December 3, Freud expresses great concern about Freund's condition, but is also thinking about the survival of the analytic movement. On December 11, he worries about the fund Anton von Freund is bequeathing to psychoanalysis. The donation has been made but has not yet been notarised, and the transaction proves to be more difficult than expected. On December 17, Ferenczi reports on the negotiations, and on the fact that certain influential people, antagonistic to psychoanalysis, are attempting to direct the endowment towards a charitable organisation, or grant it to a child welfare organisation. He informs Freud of his plan, adding: "The matter is very urgent already with respect to the constantly fluctuating political conditions." Ferenczi would like to put forward the scientific foundations of psychoanalysis. In his answer dated December 18, Freud steps into the role of a general dispassionately giving orders to his commander-in-chief:

> In my view, the original plan of a great teaching and treatment institute can't be realized in Budapest for a long time to come. Our friend will take this beautiful hope with him. Let us give it up and salvage what can be salvaged.

He encourages Ferenczi to show himself, as Freud does, uncompromising:

> All plans which are based on working together with some agency or other are objectionable. We would always be pressed to the wall […] To accept no additional limitations, to demand that (half of) the amount be handed over directly; in the other instance, complete refusal on your part […]

Freud goes on to specify the use to which the endowment is to be put. He ends his letter with an order to Ferenczi not to back away from direct confrontation: "You ought to be able to replace the 'scientific' rejoinder with a harsh scolding addressed to Bôdy (the mayor of Budapest)," who would like to benefit from a portion of Freund's endowment. On December 26, Ferenczi, who continues to believe in the mediation process, summarises the difficulties encountered in the ongoing negotiations, which have not yet provided a solution.

In the first letter of the year 1920, like in his recent personal analysis, Ferenczi encounters Freud's unshakeable firmness, this time used to "scold" him at a particularly vulnerable time when, after having been there for Freund in Budapest as his condition deteriorated, he is now doing his best to carry out negotiations with various government agencies.

Change of tone

On January 1, 1920, Freud sends Ferenczi best wishes for the coming year, makes no mention of their friend Toni who is now in Vienna, adopts a more severe tone and, like an irate father, calls him to order: "I greatly regret the impression that you didn't get further with Bôdy; I consider him a cowardly and false beast, and I think one must approach him differently, in a more peremptory fashion." Freud sets out his view of the reasons for Ferenczi's hesitating approach: "You seem to place yourself before him like humble audience-seekers whose suggestions he has no time to address, whereas you could deal with him as a party with equal rights." After giving his analysis of the situation, Freud outlines his instructions in a threatening tone: "So I suggest that you no longer beg for a gracious audience with Bôdy, but rather have Béla Lévy [the lawyer] write him a formal letter in a resolute style with approximately the following content [...]" In addition, Freud repeatedly admonishes Ferenczi to leave off imposing his own convictions upon the city, and to speak "in the name of the founder," Freund. Freud recommends intransigence, and a tough attitude: "So much for the letter; it can be even rougher, under no circumstances milder. Refuse flat out any dissipations and requests for compromise. Ultimatum!" He realises that Toni's death is imminent and insists: "Rapid and energetic proceeding on your part seems to be called for."

Freud was speaking like a far-sighted, decisive leader capable of taking charge. The large endowment left by Toni Freund was crucial, if not for the future of psychoanalysis, at least for its inscription in social reality; the creation of a new journal and of the first training institute for psychoanalysts was now conceivable. Therefore, Freud displays exemplary firmness in his fight to preserve the chances offered psychoanalysis to make itself known throughout the world in the turbulent postwar era. Of this, there is no doubt. Still, we must remember that it was to Ferenczi that he first disclosed his determination.

Whether he knows it or not, whether he chooses to or not, is it not a fact that Freud is also addressing his former analysand? To be more precise, is he not taking advantage of Ferenczi's return to the political arena, in the interest of their common cause, to engage with the analysand Ferenczi was and must stop being, in Freud's view? Despite his firmness, Freud does not encourage his former analysand to identify with his own strong ego as an analyst and a man; rather, he focuses on his symptom, his deeply rooted need for agreement and appeasement, which he sees as the origin of Ferenczi's avoidance of conflict. While during the actual analysis Freud demanded that his analysand make a decision about his love life, he now asks him to step back and consider the ineffective emotional position he displayed in his recent errors as a strategist. He criticises, above all, Ferenczi's stance as one who seeks an audience, even "begs" for an audience, as Freud puts it. He goes even farther, pointing out that it is pitiful to have such a submissive attitude towards a scoundrel, "a coward and a false beast" who must be approached differently. But Ferenczi, faithful to his symptomatic inner convictions, wants to believe in the possibility of honest dialogue, regardless of the interlocutor, and even despite the latter's paranoia or perversity. As if sensing that Ferenczi does not have the internal resources needed to overcome his pathetic need for an audience, Freud admonishes him to set his convictions aside and to speak in the name of the founder, von Freund, who is creating the endowment. But is Freud himself not the figure of the founder, for Ferenczi? And was this visceral quest for an audience not manifestly at work in Ferenczi's transference onto Freud, in the analysis itself, as well as before and after it, in different ways? Therefore, the question arises whether Freud, acting in his position as commander-in-chief, has not become a militant analyst, blind to his countertransference, made deaf by his conviction that recovery is tied to the father.

Is it not possible that this cold firmness and exasperation, apparent in Freud's January 1, 1920, letter, could have been, above and beyond a suitable reaction to an urgent matter, a delayed reaction to Ferenczi's earlier, November 20 letter? In that euphoric letter, had Ferenczi not spoken of having "found the tone which expresses our superiority in the face of the new findings"? After the tensions generated by his analysis, was Ferenczi not expressing his joy at re-establishing renewed and "unforgettable" scientific and amicable relations with Freud? Was Ferenczi not confessing that exchanging "such a wealth of insights as perhaps never before" was compensating him for the hardships they were now facing? Was he not telling Freud that he can only continue on as a humble but happy audience-seeker, as someone who knows that henceforth he will not be able to give up for long what he most cherishes: "this intimate contact." We make the conjecture that on January 1, 1920, Freud is opposing this regressive dependent relationship when he admonishes Ferenczi – rightly or wrongly, since there are good and bad dependency relationships. While imaginary dependence on someone's supposed authority is always alienating, willing dependence on the symbolic order of language and speech guarantees freedom and subjective identity. Freud seems not to know this difference (dear to Jacques Lacan), but Ferenczi knows it only too well. It is the source of the constant awkwardness between them, which the analysis they undertook together did not dissipate.

In 1910, in Palermo, Freud had been irritated by Ferenczi's insistent desire for an amicable audience and shared work. He had seen it as infantile or feminine dependence. In 1912, Jung rebelled against the submissiveness that Freud imposed on his pupils, subjected to his wild interpretations. That same year, Ferenczi transformed his audience seeking into a desire for personal analysis with the only analyst he could trust. In 1920, although after the analysis this desire took another form, the yearning for an audience was still present in Ferenczi the man and the analyst, to Freud's great displeasure. This is why, as early as January 1 of that year, he takes a severe paternal tone. Because he relies on Oedipal logic to the exclusion of everything else – that is, subjection of the son to the law of prohibition of incest enforced by the father – Freud seems to overlook the aspect of Ferenczi's burdensome dependence that springs from a fundamental need for recognition and love. A primary need Freud himself had described and experienced at an earlier period. Many years before, when he was developing *A Project for a Scientific Psychology*, which would become the foundation of psychoanalysis, he had looked closely at the mechanism of satisfaction allowing the child to attain alterity. In fact, *A Project* (1895) described how a living organism becomes a human body, and how the infant becomes a subject by entering the field of language, where he gains access to speech. All those many years ago, Freud had shown that the human baby's incomplete development prevents him from discharging and quieting endogenous stimuli – originating in the cells of the body – creating needs that demand satisfaction. The infant can only achieve this satisfaction through the intervention of a helpful other attentive to his sensations and able to respond by taking "specific action." Having been heard, the savage cry becomes an appeal through this response. Aside from structuring the space into inner and outer, into organic and psychical, this fundamental primary response, Freud emphasises, acquires "an extremely important secondary function – viz., of bringing about an understanding with other people." This function, which establishes the relationship with another person and leads to the emergence of a subject, comes into play, just as primary identification does, before any object-choice at the Oedipal stage. The helpful other, like the proverbial fellow well-met, is not a paternal or maternal figure; Freud even calls it prehistoric. And it is clear that each person, whether he knows it or not, remains dependent on this fundamental relationship. It ensures the subject's continuity of being in the world in which he must emerge, even if later he may discover that the other who heard his appeal is not a perfect listener, because he too has suffered castration.

The fact that Freud did not make the distinction between good dependence on speech – always mutual between two interlocutors – and the dream of an imaginary total complicity maintained, between Vienna and Budapest, a misunderstanding that would deepen over time, especially since events were now moving quickly.

Death strikes, "la séance continue"

Before Ferenczi could answer Freud's first letter, another letter dated January 21, 1920, brings the sad news of Toni's death. Not inclined to emotional displays, Freud simply describes the actual events:

> Yesterday, Tuesday, January 20, 5:30 P.M., our good friend Toni died. I last saw him on Saturday; he was a painful sight. Lajos [the doctor] played the angel of death [...] the postmortem examination showed how much good was done to him with that. The immediate cause of death was a sepsis proceeding from the kidneys [...]

Freud then speaks of the tasks now awaiting them: "Now we have to protect his legacy, Vera [his daughter] and The foundation."

Ferenczi had not yet sent off his reply, started on January 17, in which he deplored the loss of a man he had "succeeded – (a rarity at my age) – in gaining [as] a friend in the most beautiful sense of the word," when he learned, from a newspaper, about the death of Sophie, Freud's daughter, carried off by the Spanish influenza on January 25, at the age of 26 and pregnant with her third child. On January 30, in an addendum to his letter, Ferenczi expresses his shock:

> Two days have already passed since I know this, and I still seem to myself to be dumb and paralyzed when I am supposed to write down even a word of consolation or sympathy. I treasured and loved your Sophie, often had an almost paternal affection for her [...]

Ferenczi asks only one thing: "Please [...] at least reassure me about the fact that your strength of spirit is also a match for this misfortune." On January

29, Freud sends some brief facts about Sophie's death, but not about his own feelings: "And with us? My wife is very shaken. I think: La séance continue." Still, he ends with an ironic understatement: "But it was a bit much for one week."

On February 4, Freud reveals something about himself: "Don't worry about me. I am the same except for somewhat more fatigue. The death, as painful as it is, does not overturn any attitude toward life." He exposes the inner world from which he draws sustenance: "Since I am profoundly unbelieving, I have no one to blame, and I know there is no place where one can lodge a complaint." Turning to literature, he finds support in Schiller's injunction: "Think only of the duty of the hour!" and in Goethe's "sweet habit of living." While determined to live up to his own honourable demand, Freud does admit that something else is lurking under the surface: "Very deep within I perceive the feeling of a deep, insurmountable narcissistic insult." Presumably to respect Freud's wish not to dwell on personal matters, the letters which follow are dedicated to information about the affairs of the analytic movement.

But on March 20, Ferenczi allows himself to refer to his dismal and exhausting situation in Budapest: "The material situation is almost unbearable […] my strength is beginning to fail." He concedes that the past year has taken a heavy toll on him: "But the worst thing is that I obviously don't possess that inexhaustible source of energy that I admire in you, so that in the evening I am completely exhausted and incapable of any intellectual work." This is not a psychical failing, but a profound body-and-soul weariness:

> I was absolutely unable to take care of the most pressing scientific tasks, to write the reviews, to conceive the paleo-biological paper, to realize two [moderately important projects] […] Not a word has yet been brought to paper about all that.

He worries about a somatic breakdown: "I can still [consider myself happy] if my health stands up to the overwork." Indeed, in 1920 Ferenczi only wrote a single article. To escape his unbearable situation, he is considering a radical solution – emigration to America: "Over there I would limit my work time and be able to dedicate myself much more to science." But he is held back by the unbearable thought of separating from Freud: "We would be terribly far apart from each other, but – haven't we for years been in the same predicament anyway? – and do we have hopes that this will change?"

The next letter Ferenczi received from Freud had been written on March 15. The situation in Vienna is as catastrophic as that in Budapest, and it affects Freud as well. He is sick and can't pursue his scientific work. He closes his letter with some good news, which must have secretly caused Ferenczi a twinge of sorrow, as he learned that his project had been accomplished elsewhere, without him: "The most gratifying thing at this time […] is the opening of the Berlin polyclinic […] (February 14)."

Nostalgia, nostalgia

Ferenczi is now a man whose recent past has brought many losses. He gave up Elma, he lost his professorship and the presidency of the IPA, his country has sunk into chaos, and his dream of a polyclinic housing a training institute was destroyed. Budapest would not become the centre of the analytic movement. Ferenczi would be unable to introduce into the psychoanalytic movement the new orientation focusing on "analytic activity" as it is carried out in daily practice. But other losses are even more painful for him. Not only will the Lamarck project with Freud be set aside, but Ferenczi has lost the valuable support he had found in Freund. He continues his correspondence with Freud, he is kept informed, the intellectual exchanges go on, but the passion is gone.

Returning from a trip to Vienna at the end of March 1920, Ferenczi makes a comment about "group psychology," a text Freud had discussed with him. On April 18, 1920, he comes back again to the question of ambivalence as presented by Freud – an important theoretical notion, but not devoid of certain transferential aspects. Behind the son's ambivalence towards the father, there is, in the transference – as both men well know – the ambivalence of the analysand towards the analyst. In his polite commentary, Ferenczi discretely refers Freud to an intuition he had been the first to formulate in 1909, in "Introjection and Transference" his first analytic article. In it, he was differentiating between a paternal act of hypnosis, through intimidation and fear, and a maternal act, producing hypnosis through tenderness and persuasion. In his letter to Freud in April 1920, Ferenczi goes back to his hypothesis, to further develop Freud's reflection on ambivalence:

> The hostile impulse toward the father is an attempt to realize the ideal of becoming a father; the subordinating impulse to obedience (that of suggestibility in the tendency on which "paternal hypnosis" is based), would be the more primitive (group) mode of reaction.

On April 22, Freud politely acknowledges receipt of Ferenczi's letter: "Thanks for your announcements of works; I will be mindful of your theoretical stimulation." But he did no such thing, only mentioning in passing, in the completed version of his text on groups, the notion of introjection introduced earlier by Ferenczi, who was duly named. But nothing was said about Ferenczi's distinction between paternal and maternal hypnosis. Freud's text only considered the relation to the figure of the father – that based on the Oedipal myth, and found in *Totem and Taboo*. For his part, Ferenczi did not set aside his intuition, formulated prior to his personal analysis; he chose to make it part of his clinical approach to transference.

Although he had already done so, after his personal experience with transference on Freud's couch in Vienna, he relied on this hypothesis even more. We believe this is what he is pointing out to his former analyst, who is also still a colleague. By discussing the distinction between the two types of hypnoses, he is pointing out to Freud that for the analysand negative transference is also a means of affirming his identity, a defence against the effects of potential paternal hypnosis. And, just as before, in conducting the analysis and overseeing the life of the movement, Freud does not hesitate to impose his own ideas and to use a threatening tone.

Freud seems not to pay attention to Ferenczi's theoretical comment, and not to notice its transferential aspect – which is nevertheless radical, given that it concerns the very nature of negative transference as it manifests itself repeatedly in the analytic process. This unintentional dismissal makes it obvious that the two men, whether they know it or not, are no longer on the same path, and each will have to follow his own road in the future. Thus, they will continue to advance, separately, on the two banks of the same river, psychoanalysis, whose development and transmission remains a priority for both of them. But after the analysis, their relationship cannot return to what it was before, despite the nostalgia each of them may feel.

The letters the two men exchange now are cordial, but somewhat limited to news about the movement and to the solitary work in which each one is engaged; their tone has changed. Ferenczi's letters have lost their old enthusiasm, and the passionate quest for personal analysis is no longer there. Freud, while happy to see what he considers a welcome liberation from transferential dependence in Ferenczi, is eager to renew work and friendship ties with the man who has finally become a worthy peer, Freud's most faithful companion. In fact, Freud, who used to be irritated with Ferenczi's analytic *furor* and the furnace of transference that went with it, now seems concerned, not to say regretful, that they have disappeared or lessened.

As for Ferenczi, deprived of what gave him solidity and nourished his vision, his task is more difficult. His personal quest will now have to shift and be pursued elsewhere and differently.

Loosening old ties

On May 14, 1920, Freud ends his letter dedicated to reporting on the affairs of the analytic circle, with a personal request: "I am eager also to hear personal things from you." The personal news that Ferenczi sends on May 30 is not very good. He has just been expelled from the Medical Society to which he belonged: "I reacted organically, as usual, with a transitory heart condition [...] It was [...] otherwise only thunderstorms and threatening clouds everywhere, whose description I would rather pass up."

Although Ferenczi no longer wants or is able to talk about himself in the excessively direct manner that once characterised him, he does so on June 4, by means of an interesting analytic situation in which he is involved: "I can discuss purely personal matters, which are nonetheless not uninteresting scientifically (to me); therewith I also accede to your request to write 'personal things' about myself." Therefore, in answer to Freud's request, Ferenczi's long letter describes the treatment of a difficult case we will examine more closely later. Ferenczi ends his letter without the least mention of his personal life. Not responding directly to Freud's wish is perhaps a way of placing the latter in the position of the seeker:

"Now I have written enough, at least in terms of quantity. But you have [summoned] the spirits!" Moreover, he assigns a new role to Freud, that of a potential supervisor: "Please, would you share with me your opinion about the questionable points, in not too long a time, if possible."

Ferenczi uses this strategy to admit to Freud indirectly that although he has regained his capacity to work and to love, he is nevertheless at the mercy of disputes which complicate relations between men and women, making even the happiest relationships imperfect.

The letter dated June 4 and June 5 reveals a remarkable subjective liberation on the part of Ferenczi, who no longer needs to expose himself completely, and only invites Freud – given his presumed knowledge – to confirm or refute the pertinence of the initiatives he is taking in a particular treatment. Thanks to the progress achieved in his own analysis, as well as thanks to the moments of impasse it encountered, Ferenczi learned from his experience of transference. This knowledge reinforces his convictions, whose validity he tests in his practice, which leans more and more towards the analyst's intervention – a new orientation Ferenczi no longer has the means of instilling in the policies of the analytic movement.

Freud answers this letter on June 17, gives some news, makes some harsh comments on the new case which Ferenczi implicitly submitted to supervision and, ignoring the admission made in the post-scriptum of Ferenczi's letter, he adds: "I am pleased about the favorable turn in your personal affairs and ask you to give your dear wife cordial greetings from me." The situation is clear, but delicate: Ferenczi no longer wants to indulge in the account of his love life and sex life; Freud no longer cares to hear this account, but still wants to have personal news. The time of the analysis is past for them both; this time has reshaped, more than they know, their old work relations and their friendship. Both of them regret it but can do nothing to change it.

On July 18, Ferenczi complains:

> Our correspondence, which is supposed to substitute for talking things out, is becoming more and more halting. In the end one has so much to say that one doesn't begin with it at all – all the more since what is essential can only be communicated orally.

This situation, where a special bond remains after its initial magic has dissipated, has another significant effect: "I feel morally and intellectually isolated, cut off from the psychoanalytic movement." In this respect too, after his analysis Ferenczi comes to admit that he must accept the solitude that will henceforth be his. In a letter written the same day, Freud appears to be in a similar state of mind: "Otherwise, I would have so much to tell you that it excludes communication by letter."

On October 11, after both men attended the Congress in The Hague, Freud wrote:

> In the Dutch tumult it was altogether impossible [for us] to talk intimately with each other. I also have no intention whatsoever of letting our private

correspondence dissipate in the circular writings of the Committee, no matter how purposeful the latter may prove to be.

Then he tries to maintain a work relationship of sorts, although it be at a distance: "Just read your paper on tic. It seems very ingenious to me, quite correct and thoroughgoing, also forward-looking, but an actual high point or punch is missing." In his reply on October 16, Ferenczi starts by referring to the profound changes in their relationship: "The private correspondence, freed of the ballast of official communications, can only gain in intimacy and caliber." He expresses his hopes regarding this correspondence: "Here we can report to each other – [in addition] to personal communications – about germinating ideas (scientific ones), as in the good old [days]." But he knows that he himself is now unable to sustain this mutuality in theorising: "To be sure, I can't be of service with such germinating ideas just today." The news of himself which follows includes the mention of "a pronounced heart palpitation" that he has had for several days.

In his letter dated October 31, Freud explains why he has not commented on Ferenczi's paper on tic: "I intentionally refrained from going more deeply into your tic, because, as on earlier occasions, I am striving not to put anything in the way of your independence." Given their subjective disparity, Freud remains true to his ideal of an independent Ferenczi, while the latter continues to seek the space of mutuality he needs to introduce and develop his burgeoning ideas. In his letter, after providing a rationalisation for his behaviour, Freud makes a remark which combines the voice of the analyst with that of the concerned friend, when he refers to somatisation, a symptom he knows only too well. "I consider your palpitations to be less tragic and am only in doubt as to which part I should ascribe to the Basedow and which to the motionless lifestyle." But he is mindful of his friend's well-being: "Don't you have any other things to be concerned about?"

Three weeks later, on November 20, Ferenczi sends Freud a brief note, to reassure him. He refers to an unspecified indisposition, "already mostly overcome," which prevented him from writing. On November 28, Freud writes that he feels reassured by the information he received from Ferenczi's physician. This said, he goes on to speak as Ferenczi's disconcerted analyst: "I see that it is the same as it was years ago, and I understand it just as little as I did then." Freud has become used to Ferenczi's long-standing and constant physical complaints: "No doubt that you are working it out hypochondriacally, [but] strong suspicion that you have some real nucleus or other." Freud is surely remembering that four years earlier, the last series of sessions and his refusal to continue analysing Ferenczi were followed by a four-month period of hospitalisation for the latter. As if to compensate for his admission that he fails to understand, Freud rationalises: "Your work and the conditions in your city certainly play a part in the causation."

Three weeks later, on December 21, 1920, Ferenczi can report to Freud that he has recovered, and that a second doctor he consulted eliminated any hypochondriacal foundation for his heart condition. The letter ends on a nostalgic note, with Ferenczi remarking:

> I will miss the opportunity once and for all to talk things out properly with you […] I think sadly about the times when I was able to be with you every few weeks and spend half of the summer with you.

In his own last letter of the year, dated December 25, Freud shares Ferenczi's nostalgia: "You give me the desired excuse for a Christmas letter by reminding me how different and how much more beautiful it was years ago." Indeed, both men have now seen that the altered mode of dialogue brought about by the personal analysis has ended their easy-going intellectual complicity, just as the end of the analysis, "finished but not terminated," had ended the intimate dialogue of their unconscious. From now on, simple, straightforward dialogue will not be possible: "Intercourse also requires a certain continuity, and when one sees one another only at great intervals, it works like [a long-distance] telephone conversation, where one also never knows what to say." After this, Freud refers to a remark Ferenczi made in a recent circular letter: "I find the passage in your last *Rundbrief* excellent, where you say that we are all doing badly, but our cause is doing well." And he adds: "It really is such that the cause is consuming us and that we are being dissolved in it, as it were."

Ten years after he embarked on his great adventure, Freud is surprised by the turn things have taken. Having once seen his passionate intellectual complicity with Fliess dissolve in self-analysis, for the benefit of the cause, he had hoped that he could spare his disciples this experience: "[…] we are being dissolved in [the cause]. And it is probably quite right that it is [so], only I would have wished for the younger, second analytic generation to be able to resist the [dis]solution for a while longer." Then Freud repeats his admission of what he doesn't understand: "I don't understand anything about your illness and satisfy myself with the constantly repeated confirmation that they don't mean anything serious or threatening." The analyst gives up, leaving his analysand to continue on his own, now that he is no longer on the couch. The latter is left to take elsewhere, and to deal otherwise with the love and the hate which, in transference, coloured and shaped a quest for knowledge addressed to Freud, the man.

The sequence of letters exchanged in 1920 makes it clear that, after the hard experience of analysis in which they were both involved, Ferenczi is no longer in total agreement with Freud on the subject of analysis, and that Freud has abandoned the wish to find an heir in him. Each one must pursue his own path alone. Freud, the rigorous theoretician, will continue to enrich the necessary theoretical body of knowledge. Ferenczi, the passionate practitioner, will ceaselessly examine the practice and the metapsychology of the psychic processes involved in the analyst's activity. Freud would continue to explore Oedipal phenomena and the paternal function, while Ferenczi would focus on the more primal level of the early relationship with the mother who cares for the infant. Freud believes that the relationship with the father – the witness to castration – is the key to recovery; Ferenczi relies on restoring a pre-traumatic relationship, to counteract the deadly influence of a harsh mother. Practised in the art of treating feminine hysteria, Freud avoids dealing with "crazy" women, while Ferenczi resolutely takes into treatment these women in whom love is close to a pathology and has the characteristics of erotomania.

Although Freud, like Ferenczi, was uncompromising in his resolve that psychoanalysis must not become medicalised, unlike his former analysand, Freud was always careful to preserve cohesion in the IPA; their respective advocacy of lay analysis was a case in point. Showing less diplomacy in his interactions and more daring in his experiments, Ferenczi maintained his singularity in his participation in the life of the analytic movement. Willing to be outrageous, he was going to point out the limited effectiveness and the pitfalls of what he called classical analysis, as practised by overly obedient and insufficiently inventive analysts. He would always prefer, instead of the teaching provided by the Berlin Institute, the training gained – or not – through personal analysis, reinforced by the deepening of the analyst's work in his practice.

This is the acquired wealth from which Ferenczi benefits at the end of the first stage of his adventure, whose structure and orientation were entirely determined – in our opinion – by his experience on Freud's couch. For Ferenczi, the fundamental impasse in his analysis consisted of its interruption, decided on by Freud.

This active intervention on Freud's part had beneficial effects: Ferenczi became a decisive and self-assured analyst. If fate had not intervened, he would have been at the helm of the analytic movement. Freud had cause to be pleased with his analysand's progress, now that he had become the combative colleague who could later be chosen as his successor. But this same firm positioning also had detrimental effects. Ferenczi was solidly entangled in inner complications that constituted impediments to harmonious sexual relations in his love life. Specifically, he remained blocked by a knot consisting, not of ambivalence, but of the turning against oneself of powerless rage that failed to become hatred turned outward. Indeed, Freud failed to see, in the somatic events strewn throughout Ferenczi's analysis, the infant's rage trying to emerge as hate in the present context of negative transference. Yet Ferenczi had posed a specific question when he made his request for analysis: "I don't know […] how much that is apparently organic is psychogenic. (I would like to be instructed by you about that.)" The analysis gave this theoretical question, so deeply rooted in the body, real form: the Basedow's syndrome and the many and various functional disorders about which Freud finally admitted that he understood nothing – an admission that the real left him baffled. The fact that in the fall of 1916 Freud cut off all possibility of continuing the treatment condemned this fundamental analytic question to remain unanswered, and the analysis itself to be left unfinished.

This shortcoming of the treatment contributed to separating the two men, but, as Freud maintained – and despite the cost – in the best possible manner. The element related to subject-formation processes, which was problematic in Ferenczi's life and was not worked through in his analysis, did not remain a crippling symptom. Although Freud neglected it in the analysis, Ferenczi rediscovered it in his new relation to his practice. It was up to him to become the analyst of what was left unanalysed in his history. This is what he wants Freud to know, and it is to that purpose that he describes how he has worked with the "craziness" of Eugénie Sokolnicka, who would become an analyst and whose analysis with Freud the latter had interrupted. The fact that the end of his own analysis was inadequate did not produce a crippling symptom in Ferenczi, but prompted the search for a way to continue on elsewhere and differently. Paradoxically, the worst produced the best, even if Ferenczi remained focused on the question of the end of analysis, which became the subject of his future investigations. While Freud formulated the first fundamental rule of psychoanalysis, Ferenczi formulated the second, the rule concerning in-depth analysis for future analysts.

Ferenczi understood that he had no choice but to become and to remain, as Lacan said in 1955, "the first-generation author who most relevantly raised the question of what is required of the analyst as a person, in particular as regards the end of the treatment." This is the task to which he would devote himself henceforth, with or without Freud. Does this mean that, as Lou Andreas-Salomé wished and predicted since 1913, Ferenczi's time has finally come? In any case, she still believes in him and in his ideas.

Lou Andreas-Salomé, unwavering

At the end of 1920, Lou Andreas-Salomé, now an analyst, has moved on from her position in 1913, when she thought that Ferenczi's time must come. But, ever faithful to her trust in the two thinkers she holds in high regard, she is optimistic. Remarkably, she even thinks that very soon Freud will be able to accept without difficulty certain Ferenczian concepts which would complete and enrich his own ideas. Indeed, the recent publication of *Beyond the Pleasure Principle* could provide the eagerly expected opportunity to finally engage in the contradictory debate on the "death drive." In a letter to Freud dated December 26, 1920, Lou Andreas-Salomé expresses her scepticism regarding the hypothesis of a death drive: "Of the thoughts of life and death, as they are set forth, I can say, strangely: I agree with you, just as I can say: in this, I disagree with you." This is her opportunity to plead Ferenczi's cause, as Emma Jung had once attempted to plead her husband's cause.

Once again, she draws Freud's attention to the transferential problem which interferes with Ferenczi's progression: "Ferenczi, the most philosophical of your 'sons,' has never dared to follow his impulse to explore the 'deep meaning'; as a result, many important things have never been written [...]" Lou makes a list of the occasions when Ferenczi was clearly held back by this problem detected seven years earlier, and she wants to believe that the publication of *Beyond the Pleasure Principle* could henceforth facilitate the dialogue between the two men. She pleads Ferenczi's cause: "[...] I am sure this essay must have made him happy, and perhaps he is working on those things [...] so much more now because he is the most deeply loyal and the most genuine of your 'sons.'" But Lou is wrong.

She seems to be unaware that the personal analysis has completely altered the transferential relation between the two men. This relation can no longer be seen as simply a conflict between a son on his way to finding his path to recognition, and his father's wish to protect his own achievements.

Ferenczi and Freud know this. The time for reconciliation is past, and that for necessary separation – which is not a breaking off – has come. Future events were to confirm this distinction.

Birth announcement or farewell letter? (May 1922)

In his particularly moving letter of May 15, 1922, Ferenczi describes his evolution since the disappointments of the trying year 1919, when the psychoanalytic hopes intended for Budapest were in effect realised in Berlin. Ferenczi is more frank with Freud than ever before, and scrutinises the changes the analysis has produced in their relationship. With some exaltation but without his usual complaints and self-criticism, he starts by saying: "I must wonder myself about the fact that I don't give in more often to the impulse to write to you." He is aware of the transferential aspect of this symptom crystallised by their long and complex analytic relation: "When I think about how great a space your person and the thoughts about common interests take up in my psyche, I am forced to seek more deep-seated reasons for this tardiness." This negligence contrasts with the excessive output of his letters in the past:

> There is no doubt that I also was unable to resist the temptation, as a recompense for everything that I have from you, to "bestow" on you the entire extent of overtender and oversensitive impulses of feeling which are appropriate only in relation to one's own father.

It is moving to hear Ferenczi express his indebtedness for the enormous knowledge he received from the inventor of psychoanalysis, while showing his embarrassment about the feelings that once characterised his massive transference.

But in the spring of 1922 he has reached a different stage: "The stage in which I now seem to find myself is the – badly belated! – weaning and the attempt to submit to my fate." Here, the missive becomes a farewell letter. Ferenczi knows that ethically he has no choice left but to pursue his own path, although he already knows that the road will be lonely:

> The fact that we now meet so seldom forces me, among other things, also to a kind of intellectual self-reliance. Earlier I was happy about an idea mostly as a favor to you. I could hardly wait for the moment when I could offer you the discovery.

The subsiding of the love for the man who seemed to open the doors of a new knowledge to him liberates his thinking and brings the research into focus:

"Gradually, I learned to renounce this pleasure and to occupy myself with science for its own sake, thus, in a more matter-of-fact way."

To devote himself to science, Ferenczi has to consent to renouncing his earlier transferential position, which brought both comfort and torment. He has things to say and he must be able to put them in writing, even if it means opposing Freud and disturbing his colleagues. He is pleased – and a little sad – to be able to say this: "If I am not greatly mistaken, I am, the way I am now, a much more comfortable collaborator than at that time in Palermo [...] In a word: I have – unfortunately – become older and more sensible." In fact, Ferenczi's age is now just about what Freud's age was when they met. This "farewell letter" brings to an end the subjective duration of an analytic relationship that lasted over ten years. Ferenczi is continuing forward with confidence, but also with some regret: "This matter-of-factness comes to the advantage of the sobriety of my views. But I admit that I think not without sadness about the time when I was that much [stormier], happy-unhappier."

After the expression of gratitude, the leave-taking and the admission of sadness, the letter looks to the future. Ferenczi informs Freud of the particular way in which he intends to participate in the development and transmission of psychoanalysis in the future: "To [...] speak about practical things: my intellectual constitution is not unfavorable for work. Now and then I have not bad ideas, but I feel more and more secure in psychoanalytic technique." This moving letter is also a warning to Freud, who should keep in mind that from now on Ferenczi will not be speaking as the President of the IPA, as a chair holder, or as Director of the Polyclinic, but as an experienced analyst. He has learned from his personal analysis and from his involvement in the analytic organisation. He expresses this clearly in his letter: "in general the tendency toward rounding off, enlarging old experiences and accomplishments, seems to predominate in me."

In this May 1922 letter, Ferenczi lets Freud see him as a man happy to have recovered his ability to love and to work, and especially an analyst confident that he has acquired, through difficult work in his own analysis, the emotional independence and the freedom to think and to write, which he lacked, despite his prolixity, when he felt himself to be under the scrutiny of the father of psychoanalysis. He declares that he is now ready to defend the singularity of his views on analytic matters, and to voice his opinions in the debates on doctrine which the analytic movement can no longer postpone. No doubt that when he read this declaration Freud must have been glad to surmise the part played in this happy turn of events by the personal analysis Ferenczi had forced him to conduct, and which in recent years had complicated their relationship.

An unparalleled nomination

A year later, as if echoing this declaration, Freud would praise, not so much Ferenczi himself, but his exemplary analytic journey. In the space of about 20 years, this journey turned a young neurologist and psychiatrist – who one day casually picked up *The Interpretation of Dreams* – into a convinced and even more convincing analyst. Indeed, Freud now calls Ferenczi "a master and teacher of psycho-analysis."

In 1923, Freud wrote the foreword for a special issue of the *Zeitschrift*, in which Ferenczi received tribute on the occasion of his 50th birthday. Freud points out the exemplary nature of this journey in which – according to our hypothesis – the personal analysis played the major and most decisive role: "These were the beginnings of Ferenczi, who has since himself become a master and teacher of psychoanalysis." From this point on, there are two masters in psychoanalysis: Freud, its inventor, and Ferenczi, who became a master through analysis. We should point out that Freud does not use the terms "didactic analysis" or "training analyst," although they had been in use since the recent foundation of the Berlin Institute.

This designation Freud bestows on Ferenczi alone presents the latter as an analyst more capable than the others to transmit psychoanalysis to his young colleagues. Such a nomination goes beyond the esteem he earned following the success of the Budapest Congress in 1918, an occasion on which Freud recognised him as one who would set new directions in psychoanalytic therapy, and would occupy a central place in the activities of the movement. In 1923, receiving this distinction grants Ferenczi renewed legitimacy not on the basis of his qualifications – which others possess as well – but thanks to the exceptional fact that he underwent personal analysis, which produced a more clear-sighted and self-assured analyst: "Ferenczi, who, as a middle child in a large family, had to struggle with a powerful brother complex [has] under the influence of analysis [!] become an irreproachable elder brother, a kindly teacher and promoter of young talent."

In our view, in 1923, Freud praised an analyst with determined vision and unshakeable faith in the benefits of in-depth personal analysis for the training of analysts. But in Budapest there was still no training institute. Under unfavourable political conditions, Ferenczi promotes the transmission of psychoanalysis relying neither on the theoretical teaching of Freudism, nor on didactic analysis as it has recently been introduced in Berlin. In contrast to what is done in Berlin, he teaches unaided, and conducts long and difficult analyses whose value – or lack of value – as didactic analyses remains to be determined later, based on their deferred effects. Freud is understandable happy with developments in Berlin, but he is just as pleased with the vitality of the Hungarian Freudian circle: "As for the local group he founded in 1913, it overcame all obstacles and became, under his direction, a centre of intense and productive work." Freud went on to praise Ferenczi's numerous outstanding talents and contributions. And yet [...]

Troubled or untroubled?

In the last paragraph of his homage to Ferenczi, after listing his major contributions, Freud addresses Ferenczi one last compliment. The greatest contribution of this master and teacher is not to be found in his 138 scientific publications, but in his work yet to come: "Ferenczi has held back even more than he has made up his mind to communicate." Is it the case that Freud, like Lou Andreas-Salomé ten years earlier, thinks that Ferenczi's time is yet to come? Yes and no. Freud knows that Ferenczi will pursue the path he proudly claims as uniquely his. But Freud worries, because he also knows that what Ferenczi will "[make] up his mind to communicate" will be presented in his own style: lively, forceful, sometimes provocative, adventurous and unconventional. This is the slight shadow in Freud's praise. A remark made in passing in the first paragraph might be revealing as well: "Starting with this first visit (1908) we enjoyed a long, intimate and hitherto untroubled friendship [...]" Why did Freud need to say "hitherto untroubled," if not because he is beset by a double fear? Freud, the father of psychoanalysis, senses that Ferenczi's proclaimed desire to "round off" and, above all, to "enlarge old experiences and accomplishments" will upset the analytic community. In addition, Freud the analyst knows that his former analysand has reservations about the way in which his tumultuous analysis was conducted. Freud is right on both counts. Indeed, at the dawn of the 1930s heavy clouds threaten to dampen his relations with Ferenczi. In 1932, the weather is stormy.

Chapter 7

Personal analysis and analytic trajectory

Finished analysis? Endless path?

My dear friend,

Thank you for your thoughts, always so dearly welcomed.

You are one of the very rare people whose approval helps me to work and to advance.

Till next time, with all my heart, your René Char.

My dear René,

[...]

What a great and profound thing it is to turn away, little by little, from all things and all people that deserve nothing, and to recognize little by little over the years and across borders a family of like minds. How numerous we suddenly feel when we find a few others [...]

You faithful brother, Albert Camus.

(*Correspondence* 1946–1959, Gallimard, 2013)

Ferenczi's analysis and its sad epilogue

Troubled times (1930–1932)

The storm clouds threatening Freud and Ferenczi's relation through the years finally burst at the start of 1930, under the pressure of disagreements about the practice and the theory of psychoanalysis, and more importantly still, about institutional policy.

In a letter dated December 25, 1929, Ferenczi summarises the lessons learned in the space of the past dozen years that led him from experimentation with Freud's "active technique" (1918–1926) to the application of the "relaxation and neo-catharsis principle," which led to occasional experimenting with "mutual analysis," that Ferenczi never developed into a technique. He resumes what he learned in two compact, strongly-worded statements. First, Freudian analysis ignores "the traumatic-hysterical basis for illness," and second, this is due to an "overestimation of fantasy – and the underestimation of traumatic reality in pathogenesis." This is a radical pronouncement, given that Freud and his disciples have made turning away from traumatic origin, to focus instead on the sphere of fantasy, the springboard of psychoanalysis.

On January 11, 1930, despite Ferenczi's insistence, Freud does not reconsider the issue raised by the latter; he is content to express regret about the increasing distance between them. In his reply on January 17, Ferenczi, deeply wounded, drives his point home even more forcefully. For the first time, he addresses two reproaches not to psychoanalysis, but to Freud the analyst, the one who, in his words, "did not permit carrying out my analysis to completion," and "did not comprehend and bring to abreaction in the analysis the [...] negative feelings and fantasies."

For Freud, who is 74 and suffering from cancer, this is a severe blow. He does not enter into a discussion and responds without conviction, on September 16, in a few short lines, to Ferenczi's radical propositions: "The new views about the traumatic fragmentation of mental life that you indicated seem to me to be very ingenious and have something of the great [quality] of the Theory of Genitality." But Ferenczi's acute sensitivity perceives what lies behind the apparent compliment: "I was pleased to hear that you find my new views 'very ingenious,'" he writes, adding: "I would have been much more pleased if you had declared them to be correct, probable, or even plausible." He forcefully rejects Freud's comparison between his current work and his old theories: "The 'theory of genitality' was the product of pure speculation at a time when, far removed from any practice, I totally gave way to contemplation (military service)." After his personal analysis, how could Ferenczi accept seeing his recent work reduced to the level of his old Freudian concerns? He insists: "The newer views [...] originate from the practice itself, were brought to the surface by it, extended and modified daily; they proved to be not only theoretically but also practically valuable, that is to say, usable." The misunderstanding is obvious, and will continue to deepen. A year later, on September 18, 1931, Freud answers Ferenczi, but not as the latter hoped. Freud is angry and he accuses: "[...] you are trying to press forward in all kinds of directions which to me seem to lead to no desirable end." On December 5, deeply affected by Freud's renewed refusal to comment clearly on his hypothesis regarding the overestimation of fantasy and subsequent setting aside of traumatic reality in pathogenesis, Ferenczi remains steadfast: "But honesty obliges me to say that, up to now, I don't feel called upon to change anything essential." A letter from Vienna dated December 13, 1931, delivers the final verdict: "[...] you have not embarked upon any fruitful path [...]"

But there is still worse: there is what Ferenczi truly cannot bear. In addition to the condemnation of the theoretical orientation of his work, his practice itself is subjected to criticism; what Freud rejects is not his practice as Ferenczi discreetly describes it, but as rumours in Vienna depict it, making a caricature of it. Taking on the tone of the severe father, Freud rejects what he reduces to a syrupy "maternal tenderness technique" that was unable to stop "before the kiss." This is a cruel blow for Ferenczi, whose work takes the risk of enacting not "his most spiritual experience," as Lou Andreas-Salomé had said years earlier, but what he considered his most highly analytic experience. His desire as an analyst is crushed by the man whom he has placed in the position of ultimate Other. It is in this context of confusion of tongues between the two men that, in 1932, Ferenczi chooses to set down his observations and develop his ideas in his *Clinical Diary*, and no longer in the *Correspondence*.

Ferenczi's notes in the *Clinical Diary*, which might not have been intended to be published in that form, and whose author was dispirited, even shattered, by the recent condemnation of his work, and therefore of the desire that supported him in his work as an analyst, paint a harsh portrait of Freud, the analyst. While in 1922 we saw Ferenczi express confidence in the future analytic path of the "master and teacher of psychoanalysis" that he had become, in 1932 we discover a tragically broken and desperate man, whose passion for analysis is nevertheless stronger than ever.

While in the past he tended to engage in endless analytical self-criticism of his troubled relations with women and his ambivalent relation to Freud, now he brings into question not only Freud's own desire, but the desire of the father of psychoanalysis.

Freud, an unanalysed analyst? (1932)

As we read the *Clinical Diary*, we sense how tense the relation between the two men has become. On March 17, Ferenczi observes:

> My own analysis could not be pursued deeply enough because my analyst (by his own admission of a narcissistic nature), with a strong determination to be healthy, and his antipathy towards any weaknesses or abnormalities, could not follow me down into those depths and introduced the 'educational' stage too soon.

On May 1, 1932, Ferenczi refers to certain recent remarks made by Freud: "Patients are riffraff. Patients only serve to provide us with a livelihood and material to learn from." And he added: "We certainly cannot help them." Ferenczi protests: "This is therapeutic nihilism," but concedes that despite this, if the analyst hides his doubts and if hope is awakened in him, he gains the patient's trust. Ferenczi finds this situation painful, and he remains opposed to it. He has been driven to solitude since the cooling off of his warm dialogue with Freud, who places the search for truth above the process of healing, which he considers secondary. This view causes him to maintain that analytic training should be reserved for "normal" people, not too neurotic and good at dreaming. Ferenczi only gave up talking with Freud after a long period of renewed attempts. On January 15, 1928, he had already written to Freud, who agreed with the position taken by the Berlin Institute analysts: "The analyst's properly being analyzed is the same thing that you call 'normality.'" In the *Clinical Diary* he even goes so far as to say that the best analyst is a cured patient. Similarly, in 1930 when Freud was saying that he was "fed up," tired of analysis "as a therapy," Ferenczi's reply on January 17 was:

> I, too, often felt 'fed up' with [the process], but I overcame this impulse and can report to you with joy that precisely here a whole series of questions is apparently moved into a different, sharper light, perhaps even the problem of repression!

Ferenczi was trying to make his ideas heard, but Freud's analytic interests were elsewhere.

On August 4, 1932, Ferenczi – like Emma Jung before him – reproached Freud for his ambiguous toying with the figure of the respected father, which he embodied so well:

> Contrary to all his technical rules, [Freud] adopted Dr. F[erenczi] almost like his son. As he himself told me, he regarded him as the most perfect heir of his ideas. Thereby, he became proclaimed crown prince, with the prospect of making his solemn entrance in America.

On several occasions, Ferenczi suggested that he could take Freud into analysis, perhaps in hopes of freeing him from his symptomatic relation to the figure of the son. Ferenczi knew that although Freud had successfully conducted a very demanding and rigorous self-analysis, he remained, nevertheless, unanalysed. Indeed, Ferenczi explains how his own symptom was intertwined with Freud's unanalysed symptom: "My enthusiasm, my depression when I was neglected even for one day; my inhibition about speaking in his presence, and my burning desire to win his approval, all this reveals me to have been a blindly dependent son." Remembering his earlier experience, Ferenczi supposes that Freud, contrary to his stated preference – that of having independent colleagues – may not be able to welcome an analyst who gained his independence in the course of personal analysis. He knows that Freud remains uninterested in the research he (Ferenczi) now dedicates entirely to the technique conducting the analysis, and to its therapeutic goals. Ferenczi considers analysis to have a traumatolytic goal – the only form of analytic healing constituting the true end of analysis – the type of analysis which produces a trained analyst. Partly misinterpreted, Freud's indifference to his ultimate contribution to the psychoanalytic edifice devastated Ferenczi.

The unwelcome analyst and his death-instinct

Still on August 4, 1932, Ferenczi desperately looks for the cause of Freud's deafness: "[…] the idea, perhaps very strong in the unconscious, that the father must die when the son grows up, explains [Freud's] fear of allowing one of his sons to become independent." He remembers having borne the consequences of Freud's symptom quite early:

> The [aggressivity aiming at mutual castration], which in the unconscious is probably crassly aggressive, is overlaid by [Freud's] the need – which should be called homosexual – for a harmonious father-son relationship. In any case he could, for example, tolerate my being a son only until the moment when I contradicted him for the first time. (Palermo).

Over 20 years later, on October 2, 1932, in a final note Ferenczi describes the internal devastation to which he is subjected by Freud's condemnation:

> Further regression to being dead. (Not yet being born is the danger [...]) In my case the blood-crisis arose when I realized that not only can I not rely on the protection of a "higher power" but on the contrary I shall be trampled under foot by this indifferent power as soon as I go my own way and not his.

Suffering from pernicious anaemia that is becoming more and more severe, six months before the end of his life Ferenczi formulates an implacable summary of the unconscious underpinnings of his brilliant career as an analyst: "Scientific achievements, marriage, battles with formidable colleagues – all this was possible only under the protection of the idea that in all circumstances I can count on the father-surrogate (Freud)."

He reproaches Freud with exploiting this pivotal dependence, instead of subjecting it to analysis. Hate and revolt, hiding behind the transference and its early signs of ambivalence that Freud did not know what to do with, were not "abreacted" and worked through. As a result, the child in Ferenczi stayed at the stage of "powerless rage" that cannot be converted into hate. Ferenczi even turned this dependence into a form of identification with his analyst, not identification with the presumed strong ego of the analyst, but with the aggressor as experienced by the hypnotised subject:

> Are the "identification" with the higher power [Freud], the most sudden "formation of the superego," the support that once preserved me from final disintegration? Is the only possibility for my continued existence the renunciation of the largest part of one's own self, in order to carry out the will of that higher power to the end?

The questioning now takes a tragic tone:

> And now, just as I must build new red corpuscles, must I (if I can) create a new basis for my personality, if I have to abandon as false and untrustworthy the one I have had up to now? Is the choice here one between dying and "rearranging myself" – and this at the age of fifty-nine? On the other hand, is it worth it always to live the life (will) of another person – is such a life not almost death?

Clearly, Ferenczi deplores Freud's manner of practising analysis, and the humiliating effects it had on him, but more than this, he continues to question the nature of Freud's desire as the father of psychoanalysis.

Did Freud believe in the unconscious?

For instance, on May 1, 1932, overlooking Freud's reproaches, Ferenczi questions and, in truth, interprets the close relation between Freud the man and psychoanalytic practice. He asks himself if Freud truly believes in his own analytic theory, or clings to it too desperately in order to protect himself from his self-analysis, that is, from his own doubts. Ferenczi goes on to say that although Freud initially followed Breuer with enthusiasm, he is now emotionally detached from psycho-analysis, which he approaches on a purely intellectual level. As a result, he only analyses others and not himself, giving rise to projection. Ferenczi's hypothesis is that at first Freud "occupied himself passionately and devotedly with helping neurotic patients (lying on the floor for hours when necessary next to a person in a hysterical crisis)." Thus, it appears that when he started out, Freud, like Ferenczi, was extremely passionate about analysis, believing strongly in the power of speaking and listening. Ferenczi goes on:

> [...] but he must have been first shaken, then sobered by certain experiences [...] and [by] the problem of countertransference which suddenly opened up before Breuer like an abyss. In Freud's case this corresponds to the discovery of the mendacity of hysterics.

It is moving to see that Ferenczi is eager to find a space of mutuality between himself and Freud, not noticing that their respective passion for analysis lies in different spheres. While for Ferenczi the difficulties encountered in conducting an analysis constitute opportunities for technical experiments leading to a renewed questioning of the theory and the practice, Freud turns away from these difficulties and constructs the theoretical framework of psychoanalysis quite differently. Here, Ferenczi touches upon a characteristic trait of Freud's relation to psychoanalysis.

This trait, which sheds light on Freud's long-ago abandonment of the hypoth-esis of the traumatic aetiology of neurotic suffering is related to a radical disap-pointment he describes in his 1913 technical text "On Beginning the Treatment." In it, he describes how much, and in what way, he believed that eliminating the repression related to trauma caused by early sexual abuse would suffice to free the hysterical patient from her obsessive fear. But he found that "the certain expecta-tion of [...] bringing the neurosis and the treatment to a rapid end" was illusory:

> It was a severe disappointment when the expected success was not forthcom-ing. How could it be that the patient, who now knew about his traumatic experience, nevertheless still behaved as if he knew no more about it then before? Indeed, telling and describing his repressed trauma to him did not even result in any recollection of it coming into his mind.

This admission made in 1913 was something Freud had already confessed to his long-ago friend Wilhelm Fliess in the 1890s. In the famous letter dated September 21, 1897, Freud confides "the great secret that has been slowly dawning on [him] in the last few months." He no longer believes in his *neurotica* (his theory of the traumatic sexual aetiology of neurosis). He gives Fliess the main reasons for this:

> The continual disappointment in my [attempts] to bring a single analysis to [a true end; patients who abandon the treatment, although for a time their

engagement was the strongest;] the absence of the complete successes on which I had counted; the possibility of explaining to myself the partial successes in other ways, in the usual fashion [the overestimation of the hold of fantasy] – this was the first group [of reasons].

Thirty years later, when Ferenczi looks once again at the role of the traumatic in psychic life, he does more than simply return to Freud's old theory of a traumatic aetiology, as the latter supposes. As early as the 1920s, and in his active technique, he has taken notice of the possible misuses of free association, and of the limits of interpretation, aware of the secret jouissance underlying them. More importantly still, and contrary to Freud's method, he does not insist on the elimination of repression and on remembering, but focuses on repetition. What Freud saw as an inevitable stumbling block in analysis, Ferenczi welcomes as a process serving to repeat the trauma in the context of transference. He works with what Freud considered an impossible to analyse failure of transference – which he later called negative therapeutic reaction – seeing it as an opportunity to relive in the transference the violation that caused splitting or worse still, atomisation. As Ferenczi has already commented to Freud, the difficult moments in any analysis require taking into account, in addition to the psychic economy of repression, the economy of splitting, which completes it. This is only possible provided that the analyst does not give in to the dread that can take hold of him when he stands before the "abyss of countertransference."

Is Ferenczi not entitled to wonder about the role played by Freud's countertransference in his personal analysis, like in other analyses? Hasn't Freud always avoided the "furnace of transference" and any *furor sanandi*? In 1895, when he still believed in the sexual aetiology of neuroses, did he not write, in his preface to *Studies on Hysteria*: "Hysteria, like the neuroses, has its deeper causes; and it is those deeper causes that set limits, which are often very appreciable, to the success of our treatment"? On April 16, 1900, in a letter to Fliess, Freud refers to a five-year analysis that has just been ended by the analysand: "E. at last concluded his career as a patient by coming to dinner at my house. His enigma is almost completely solved; he is in excellent shape, his personality entirely changed. At present a remnant of the symptoms is left." Freud seems concerned with this remnant of the symptoms, before making a double confession: "I am beginning to understand that the apparent endlessness of the treatment is something that occurs regularly and is connected with the transference." Ferenczi would say that the "endless" character of analysis is indissociably, and just as much, connected with countertransference. Freud's next statement in his letter seems to confirm this: "I could have continued the treatment, but I had the feeling that such a prolongation is a compromise between illness and health that patients themselves desire, and the physician must therefore not accede to it." He goes on to clarify his position: "The asymptotic conclusion of the treatment basically makes no difference to me, but is yet one more disappointment to outsiders."

Ferenczi, who was convinced of the curative effects of analysis, was made to suffer, before, during and after his analysis, by Freud's ambiguous relation to the end of analysis. He had been personally affected by Freud's relative indifference to what had been a regrettable incompletion, rather than an impossible conclusion. But in his case, disappointment expressed itself in two stages of contrasting nature. In the first stage (1922), it was constructive, while in the second (1932), it was devastating.

Can we try to solve the enigma of the strange timeframe of this disappointment differently than Ferenczi and Freud did? Both of them speak of this analysis as if it was a private affair between two people, in the privacy of the analyst's office, while in fact it took place in a turbulent analytic milieu and in an analytic community still awaiting the institutionalisation of regulations serving to govern the practices and politics of psychoanalysis. The first of its kind – in terms of what it had to teach and what paths it opened – this analysis, we must remember, took place at a time when analysis of the future analyst, and its end, had not been subjected to any discussion about doctrine. In that pioneering era, today's concept of supervision did not yet exist.

Some others and the analytic community

In his writings of the 1930s, Ferenczi did not take the measure, any more than Freud did in his 1937 essay, of the role played by the particularly close relationship in which Ferenczi was engaged in 1920 and 1921 with two other people, a woman and a man. These two extremely different people had one thing in common: their marginal position in the analytic community. Eugénie Sokolnicka was a "difficult" analysand whose analysis Freud had cut short a few years earlier, just as he cut short Ferenczi's analysis. Georg Groddeck was a practitioner of medicine and psychotherapy who, despite Freud's wishes, refused to join "the savage horde" of analysts. Ferenczi met them when he was still suffering the deferred effects of the definitive end of his analytic sessions, and was trying to leave behind, displace or transform what was left of his dependence on Freud. In May 1922, he presented himself to Freud as a qualified analyst, not only on the authority of his practice, of his detailed knowledge of Freud's texts, or of his merit in earning victories for the cause, but now also on the basis of the knowledge gained from his experience with personal analysis, which had affected him profoundly. In short, we can agree with Lacan that Ferenczi had become an analyst on his own authority, and was proclaiming it.

But although he can make this claim thanks to the progress, as well as the obstacles, encountered in his analysis, he is also bolstered by two decisive encounters with "some others." We believe that it is thanks to what he discovered in the analysis he conducted with Eugénie, and while observing the healing practised by Groddeck, that Ferenczi became able to make do with what was missing in his analysis. With these two others, he was able to compensate Freud's shortcomings in his role as analyst. It is also in their company that he found, outside of analysis, without Freud and outside the analytic circle, the personal sustenance which allowed him to transform the impediment in his analysis into an opening. What had remained left out in his incomplete analysis is now no longer an obstacle, but rather a new world to explore. Bolstered by this perspective found outside the institution, Ferenczi can finally claim and explore more fully and without fear the analytic intuitions he had for so long kept to himself. Certain that he could finally let his voice be heard and present his new ideas, he feels no need to reproach Freud with its failings as an analyst. With Eugénie and Georg, he begins to see how he can benefit from these failings, without elevating them, as he would do in 1932, to the status of a failure on the part of the father of psychoanalysis.

If it be the case that in 1922 the absence of any radical blame assigned to Freud is due, as we suppose, to the encounters discussed above, can we speculate that the subsequent emergence of grievances and of the reproach regarding Freud's unanalysed desire may be related to the undermining of the role played by these "others" in the process of becoming and remaining an analyst? Indeed, what, in fact, did Ferenczi gain from his relationship with Groddeck and from the analysis of Eugénie Sokolnicka?

With Georg Groddeck (1921)

Through Freud, Ferenczi had discovered the work of Groddeck in 1917, well before meeting him in the summer of 1921. Although at first Ferenczi was more reticent than Freud about Groddeck's unorthodox practices, surprisingly, he was soon won over. In a letter to Freud dated June 14, 1918, he expresses surprise at the therapeutic achievements of a practitioner who claims to treat physical ills with psychoanalytically oriented psychotherapy. Ferenczi thinks he has uncovered the secret of Groddeck's art of healing:

> The enclosed letter from the crazy Swedish woman provides us with interesting insights into Dr. Groddeck's method of treatment [...] It strikes me altogether as more and more probable that Groddeck is not curing at all *with analysis*, but rather that with the aid of the transference he puts the plastic power of hysteria into the service of the organic tendency to heal. Precisely because he doesn't analyze but rather displaces the tendencies as a block, he is able to perform such feats.

Ferenczi senses that Groddeck could provide an answer to the question that accompanied his request for analysis – the question related to the intervention between the psychic and the organic in pathological states. But, even more importantly, we think, when reading Groddeck, Ferenczi recognises an outside source that clearly echoes his own secret reflections. It is, in fact, he, Ferenczi, who after his recent analysis thinks, as yet vaguely, that classical Freudian analysis does not cure if it limits itself to the application of the usual technical rules. It is he who, going beyond Freud, truly believes in the unsuspected power of the virtues of transference, in which love places itself in the service of the organic tendency to heal. A year later, Ferenczi implicitly relies on Groddeck's ideas when he writes "The

Phenomena of Hysterical Materialization" (1919). He was to do this again much later, in May 1931, when he attributed a second function to dreams. To Freud's dream function, the fulfilment of forbidden wishes, Ferenczi adds a second, "traumatolytic" function of the dream: the elimination of day-residues and life-residues containing psychic impression of trauma. On September 5, 1921, Ferenczi meets Groddeck for the first time in Baden-Baden, where he would vacation several times after that. That year, on Christmas Day, he writes to this stranger who stays away from psychoanalysts. In his letter, he points out the main characteristic of his recent analysis: "I could never be completely [frank] with him, there was too much of this 'fearful respect'; he was too large for me, too much the father."

Even more surprisingly, like in his letter requesting analysis, Ferenczi describes his inhibition to put his most personal analytic intuitions in writing. He associates this reaction to the painful memory of the 1910 Palermo incident. For the first time, he reveals what he experienced as the most violent aspect of the incident: the request that he take down the notes Freud wanted to dictate to him. This was not how they were intended to collaborate. Ferenczi jumped up and refused. In his letter to Groddeck, he associates the traumatic impact of this incident with some still vivid humiliating memories. For instance, his mother's cold disapproval when, as a little boy, he tested his phallic ability as a burgeoning writer by making a list of all the swear words he knew, and proudly showed it to this mother, this busy woman he describes as indifferent to his need for tenderness and recognition. It is safe to guess that all this was discussed and worked through in the sessions, with no effect on the symptom.

But in this letter, and precisely thanks to the analytic work accomplished, Ferenczi goes a step further – a major step forward in our opinion. After describing in detail the various organic and functional ills that prevent him from writing, he speaks of the redeeming power of writing, which held such an important place in his life, just as it did in Freud's. "Had I your writerly talents I would write – as I began to do above – straight from the heart about my physical and mental ailments." At this point in his associations, as if he just heard what he has been saying, he makes another revelation that brings back another memory. Now, it is as if we are in the middle of a session, when suddenly Ferenczi inserts a *nota bene* in parentheses after what he has just said: "(Stop: I am dishonest! I believe that I do have writerly talents; I recall how much a disparaging judgment on a piece of work, or before that a poem, hurt me.)" The poem in question was a love poem he had written as a young man to his mother, who made fun of him. We suppose that at this juncture Ferenczi is aware of the dishonest component of his harrowing complaint, as well as of the reality of the symptom, recognised as the depository of an unspeakable jouissance: "The evil part of this is that my erotic self is apparently not satisfied with these revelations. I, my 'Id,' doesn't want analytic insights, it wants something real; a young woman, a child!" He wants the impossible, the very thing which he gradually consented to give up. Ferenczi ends his long letter as he started it, with a comment made in the new tone he has adopted with this new friend, who is not "too much the father": "It was, as I said, no small matter, either, for me to [set aside] my scholarly [pride] and present myself not as the superior one, the competitor, but rather as naïve, childish – what comes to mind is the word 'humble.'"

What Ferenczi discovers thanks to this intermittent, accessory transference to Groddeck is that he is not condemned to everlasting inhibition, and that he is a talented writer and can show it if he can relinquish the jouissance that maintains the symptom. This recovered freedom to think and to write is particularly valuable now that, with Groddeck, Ferenczi has given his research a new orientation, which a few months later he would defiantly present to Freud, invoking the need to "structure and complete the old experiences and know-how."

With Eugénie Sokolnicka (1920)

In *The Correspondence* with Ferenczi, Freud first mentions this name on January 19, 1918: "Sokolnicka [1884–1934] appears to be founding a psychoanalytic society in Warsaw." Ferenczi probably knows that she is Polish, that she studied at the Sorbonne before beginning her training at the Burghölzli Hospital in Zurich, and was then analysed by Freud (1913–1914) before becoming a member of the Vienna Psychoanalytic Society. Ferenczi is sure to know that Freud dislikes her. On February 10, 1920, he informs Freud that Frau Sokolnicka has been in Budapest for six weeks, "completing her analysis […] with me." On March 20, he reveals the interest he takes in her training: "Frau Dr. Sokolnicka is attending our sessions, which are being held in German for her sake [I had her write down a short but quite pretty observation of hers.] It is enclosed with this letter."

But it is not until June 4, 1920, that the difficult case of this analysand takes on a peculiar and unique role in the correspondence between the two men. When Freud expresses concern about not receiving any personal news from Ferenczi and asks to be informed, the latter responds in a strange way. Roughly, it is as if he were saying: "I will tell you about myself by talking about a difficult patient." But his actual response is more subtle: "I can [now tell you about certain] purely personal matters, which are nonetheless not uninteresting scientifically (to me); therewith I also accede to your request to write 'personal things' about myself." From now on, he would speak of himself no longer in tones of neurotic complaint, but through the description of an analysis that Freud had refused to pursue to its conclusion: "Point of departure [of personal things] is the analysis of Frau Dr. Sokolnicka, which I would now like to summarize in more detail." We leave it to the reader to enjoy the rest of this account in the letter. Before coming back to it, let us look at Freud's answer on June 17, in which he paints an unflattering picture of his former analysand: "Don't let yourself resolve to take Sokolnicka along on vacation. She has always been repugnant to me, despite undeniable talent." And he goes on:

> [The conduct of her analysis] seems quite excellent to me; the therapeutic prospects should be good, for you know that she always held onto her men, not out of love but rather out of unsatisfied anger, and you gave her the possibility of finally getting this affect out.

Freud admits that Ferenczi is conducting the analysis well, but he thinks it is a lost cause:

> But she also won't let go of you so soon. I don't consider her a paranoia but a basically disgusting person; she doesn't want to see now that she has already become an old woman. In that there is little to be done, and the development of quite crazy [*meschuggener*] traits can hardly be impeded.

There is nothing to add.

Sometime after this second analysis on his couch, Ferenczi helped Eugénie establish herself in Paris. Not being a physician, it was hard for her to be accepted into the French psychiatric milieu, but she was welcomed into the literary milieu, where those associated with the Nouvelle Revue Française gave her an enthusiastic welcome. A pioneer in child psychoanalysis, she was also the analyst of André Gide and a few distinguished figures of the Paris Psychoanalytic Society (PPS): Sophie Morgenstern, René Laforgue and Édouard Pichon. In 1926, she was co-founder and vice-president of the PPS. In 1934, marginalised within her institution, she committed suicide by turning on the gas in her apartment. She was 50 years old.

To understand how Eugénie came to belong to the ranks of those "few others" in Ferenczi's circle, let us go back to the analysis through which Ferenczi wanted to communicate to Freud certain personal things of great scientific importance. By reporting on this analysis, Ferenczi is letting Freud know that his method of interrupting certain analyses before their completion is unjustified, and that other techniques have to be devised. But, in our opinion, what is most valuable for Ferenczi in this situation is something else. With this difficult patient, an analyst who wishes to deepen and complete the analysis left unfinished by Freud, Ferenczi glimpses the new form mutuality can take in the transference. As early as 1920, with Eugénie he responds to the first request for mutual analysis; ten years later he would consent to mutual analysis with other difficult patients – women psychotherapists wanting to receive psychoanalytic training.

Eugénie and the disturbing strangeness of mutuality (1920)

The character trait that distorts Eugénie's relation to men and to women is clearly identified by Ferenczi: "In a word: she exaggerated her femininity in order to conceal her virility [Her rage to please] (and a kind of erotomanic conceit about her feminine powers of seduction) expressed itself from the very beginning." This tendency was repeatedly enacted in the course of the analysis:

> She also claimed, [for instance, that I too] had been somewhat in love with her in Vienna and she [supported this claim by referring to] the way in which I once asked her in a coffeehouse to tell me where else [we] could meet in Vienna.

The analysis continues in this tempestuous climate, with crises occurring from time to time; Eugénie does not want to be seen by the patient whose session follows hers, whom she met at a congress (Budapest?), for fear of being taken for a neurotic. To avoid this, she asks for a different time for her sessions. But Ferenczi stands his ground: "I hastened not to comply with her wish to change the hour, whereby I provoked an outburst of rage in her that lasted a few days." Then his attitude softens: "Finally, I accommodated her and wanted to analyze the entire event once and for all, *i.e.*, interpret it as a repetition of earlier (at the time perhaps suppressed) rage fantasies. That also went on for a while." But this concession to the request for changing the time of the sessions, and the recourse to interpretation, did not produce the expected effect:

> But soon she began to find fault with my indulgence; in every hour she found fault with something else in my technique (which she praised earlier as especially fine), but this time I remained steadfast, *i.e.*, continued to be indulgent, let her do everything herself (which she also did gladly, without being asked), but this indulgence increased her anger even more.

Let us remember what Ferenczi had emphasised in his letter to Freud requesting analysis, on December 26, 1912, concerning the impossibility for rage to be externalised as hate, and as a result turning into an explosive and deathly attack in the living organism. Ferenczi supposes that, in Eugénie's case, it is such deep-seated rage which repeats itself in a hallucinatory fashion in the trance-like state in which the analyst embodies this other who personified absolute seduction, the other who invited her desire only to reject it and refuse the love offered in response to his invitation. But Ferenczi observes that in the transference the rage which can become murderous in true erotomania takes another form, expressing itself in words of despair: "[…] finally there came words like 'idiot,' 'ass,' 'washcloth,' 'characterless,' but not as associations, but as her ironclad conviction. I did not yield […] until finally, today, after some weeping, she hesitatingly resumed work (which she evidently wanted to interrupt)." With the return of tears, a threshold is crossed: Eugénie reveals some of her pain, kept silent until then under her outbursts.

Armed with this new strength, she dares to go from insults to criticism of the analyst:

> Lately (since the feeling of her psychoanalytic superiority […] with respect to me has solidified), she turned [things] around, began to analyze me, called me a severe neurotic [who paralyzed the keenness of his own perception], counted out my analytic sins to me, my inability to work out my ideas, etc. In spite of this I remained steadfast and hope that, [for the time being,] we will be able to continue working.

Ferenczi ends the presentation of this singular analysis by asking Freud a question: should he or should he not let his patient come along to the place where he will be vacationing, to pursue her analysis. He is worried about the volatile dynamics of the treatment:

> Naturally, the case does not appear easier because of this! Her suicide threats, which appear in a [worrisome] light [after] an attempt at poisoning herself (in Poland) and [...] the infantile suicide known to you (jumping into hot water), command me not to give up the case. She is a very valuable personality.

But Ferenczi's reservations are easy to understand: "This prospect is certainly very unpleasant to me. It costs me no slight mastery to remain philosophical with her bickering; but I want to have peace and quiet in the summer." The analysand, in a hurry to finish her analysis, is making this demand of continuing the work over the summer. Rather than comply with this request for accelerating the analysis in order to end it sooner, Ferenczi adopts a position contrary to that Freud took with him in the fall of 1916: he advised continuing the analysis in the fall:

> Unfortunately, I did not protest immediately, out of an excess of caution; she was just then at her unhappiest. I told her only that I can't give her any date, and admitted that the analysis can only continue in the fall.

A fierce defender of the analysis, Ferenczi overlooks nothing: "That is unbearable to her; she feels abandoned here, her means, as mentioned, have become smaller, she can't earn money here (as I told her) because of the language difficulties." He remains firm, despite her objections: "So I got to talking about whether (if she has no trust in me) she doesn't want to go to you again; but she is (you will say: thank God) much too insulted by you." In order to stay on course and ensure that the analysis can continue, Ferenczi counts on her desire: "I [...] offered myself in further assistance, as befits my tactic of being mild with her." But he reminds Freud, who is reluctant to work with Eugénie again: "[...] she recognizes only one single analyst; you are he. She feels herself to be superior to the others, without exception. Despite her real talent, I see herein [typical megalomania.]"

Eugénie. Analysand, analyst or supervisor?

In the second part of this long letter dated June 4, 1920, after the detailed description of this problematic portion of an analysis of great interest for the emerging science that psychoanalysis was at the time, Ferenczi discusses his personal affairs more directly: "That is how matters now stand. Now, where is the personal in all this, you will ask. The answer is that the patient has this time diagnosed something correct in the doctor." The patient would have seen in her analyst something that the latter's analyst was unable to see. This accurate perception, which does not come from academic knowledge but springs, rather, from a different source, allows her to perceive a symptom persisting in her analyst:

> With her observation sharpened by the neurosis she has guessed that my 'laziness' in working cannot be explained by the (justified, by the way) tiredness. There is something else neurotic behind it. – Naturally, I must report to you once more about my married life.

At this stage, Ferenczi no longer reports to Freud the ups and downs of his love life. Here, he refers to it again as a way of reminding Freud that the marriage to which he wholeheartedly consented did not solve the problems he experiences in relationships with women. In fact, he refers to the last 12 months as "the unconscious year of mourning." He is expressing his gratitude not to Freud, but to this woman who has heard the distress of the unwelcome child he once was:

> Despite my analytic mildness, the patient seems to have guessed that scolding and bickering out of the mouth of a woman affects me as extremely unpleasant. That has to do with the most painful and effective traumas of my childhood, the relationship with my strict mother.

There it is: because she is a woman, because she is crazy and not crazy at all, this woman could hear, in her analyst and his passion for therapy, the traumatised child, the child petrified by the terrorism of suffering that a mother can inflict on a child she could not welcome. Because she herself was going through a painful time in her analysis, Eugénie was able to hear in her analyst, and precisely in his excessive solicitude, the child in the power of maternal hypnosis. It is this maternal hypnosis Ferenczi had tried in vain to bring to Freud's attention. Invited to her analyst's table, just as Ferenczi had been to Freud's, Eugénie went even further in her analytic interpretations:

> Right! The patient also tries to project her grandiosity onto me; she claims I want to undo [you]; that's why I am so slavishly subservient to you. The idea is good, but not new to me. What do you think, is this complex still active in me?

"Please would you share with me your opinion about the questionable points, in not too long a time, if possible." We already know that on June 17 Freud advised Ferenczi not to give in to his patient's demands.

What, then, did Ferenczi gain from his analysis of Eugénie Sokolnicka? We believe he gained a conviction which confirmed what he had glimpsed with Groddeck: when classical Freudian analysis – free association, evenly-suspended attention and interpretation of unconscious formations or of resistances – does not heal, does another approach to the furnace of transference or of madness make it possible to bring about a cure? With Eugénie – that darned woman – Ferenczi discovers that analysis can be continued beyond what Freud considers the bedrock of transference, particularly in the analysis of women like Eugénie, who do not present the characteristics of likeable hysterics.

In the company of these "few others," Ferenczi no longer needs to make bitter reproaches; he is now happy to see new research path open before him. He forges ahead, determined and optimistic. This is what makes us ask: what happened to explain that ten years later Ferenczi has become a broken man? Our hypothesis is that after he presented himself to Freud as an accomplished analyst in May 1922, Ferenczi failed to find, among the analysts of the Secret Committee, "a few others" whose approval could have provided continued support.

An analytic community between a group and a collective?

As we were asking: what happened between 1922 and 1932? How did Ferenczi, a determined and enthusiastic analyst in the time of the "few others," come to be a broken man in the end? In *Impardonnable Ferenczi, malaise dans la transmission* (*Unforgivable Ferenczi: Unease in Transmission*),[1] we recounted the often solitary and laborious struggle he had to wage in order to pursue the revision of "the old know-how," a revision for which he was not forgiven. The first step in this work was "A Historical Critical Retrospect," his richest contribution to *The Development of Psychoanalysis* (1924), written with Otto Rank, which did not meet with the reception it deserved. On this occasion, Ferenczi discovered the extent of the destructive effect his intermittent association with Rank – encouraged by Freud – had exerted on him. Rank, who had Freud's favour, was not part of the "few others" mentioned earlier. The combat Ferenczi later led in the United States in favour of lay analysis resulted in the hostility of American analysts. Upon his return, although at that point Freud considered him his only reliable ally, he also criticised his passion for analysis as endangering the International Psychoanalytic Association by disagreeing with the 1920 principles of analytic training established in Berlin. Thus, several times, the presidency of the IPA, which Freud thinks should rightly be his by virtue of his analytic rigour, is denied him for different reasons. As a result, Ferenczi concentrates more and more on his analytic practice and his pupils. This isolation torments him. He is unable to accept the fact that Freud agrees with his new ideas, but criticises the political danger created by his analytic opinions which, in fact, threaten the cohesion needed by the analytic movement. Exasperated, Freud refuses to listen to him. This is devastating to Ferenczi, who for a long time wanted to see Freud as the most valuable of his "few others"; but this role could not be played by Freud, the father of psychoanalysis, nor by Freud, Ferenczi's analyst.

Ferenczi sadly admits this on October 2, 1932, in his *Clinical Diary*:

> (I have just received a few personally friendly lines from Jones. He has sent roses, suggested a circular letter). Can not deny that I was pleasantly touched even by this. I did indeed also feel abandoned by colleagues (Rado, etc.) who are all too afraid of Freud to behave objectively or even sympathetically toward me, in the case of a dispute between Freud and me.

Where he was expecting to find a collective favourable to mutual exchange of ideas and open debate, he runs into political considerations and group phenomena: "A more restrained circulation of letters between Freud, Jones and Eitingon has certainly been going on for a long time. I am treated like a sick person who must be spared." Ferenczi knows his future is being decided. Although he does not yet know what dire treatment Freud and his friends are preparing for him, he is not mistaken. After his death in 1933, in addition to speculations of paranoia concerning him, there were those who opposed the publication of "Confusion of the Tongues between the Adults and the Child," the paper he presented at the Wiesbaden Congress, and who wanted his last writings to remain unknown, in order to protect his memory.

In the same note of the *Diary*, Ferenczi is clear about what gives him the strength to go on at this time when Freud and those close to him – although not excluding him entirely – give him no support: "My students' confidence in me could give me reassurance […]" Indeed, it is in the circle of his students that he finds a collective which *appreciates* his contributions and his style of analysis, always on the brink of crucial questions, and in this circle he finds "a few others." Thus, he grants a special place to a particular person who, in our opinion, enabled him to continue his work in those dark times. The *Diary* speaks of having "in particular the confidence of a person who is both student and teacher." This person is, clearly, Elisabeth Severn, designated as R.N. in *The Clinical Diary*. This American woman was already a psychotherapist and author of two books on psychotherapy. Like Eugénie, she had a strong character, was a particularly difficult case, and wanted to become an analyst. Elisabeth forced Ferenczi to put into practice the "mutual analysis" to which Eugénie had initiated him.

From Eugénie Sokolnicka to Elisabeth Severn (1920–1932)

In 1920, Eugénie's analysis is taken beyond the point where Freud abandoned it: an incompleteness he rationalised based on the principles he advanced in 1915 in "Observations on Transference-Love." Just as he would later advise Ferenczi to be wary of Eugénie, Freud was already advising analysts to "withdraw" from "women of elemental passionateness […] who refuse to accept the psychical in place of the material." With such women, he wrote, "one has the choice between returning their love or else bringing down upon oneself the full enmity of a woman scorned. In neither case can one safeguard the interests of the treatment." Was Freud thinking of his analysis of Eugénie when he wrote these lines? With Eugénie, Ferenczi discovered that there may be a way out of this impasse. This is what he was trying, in vain, to tell Freud, without laying blame or complaining.

In 1932, Ferenczi does more than continue Elisabeth's analysis, which started at the end of 1924. In the last years of this analysis, he finally consents to the patient's request that he recognise his deafness and ambiguity during analytic listening, given the reality of his human condition, and specifically the reality of his maleness. He therefore sometimes lies down on his own couch, letting the patient sit in the analyst's chair. Ferenczi is no longer misled by the inconsistency he attributes to Freud on August 4, 1932, referring to the ease with which Freud sacrifices the interests of women in favor of male patients. This is consistent with the unilaterally androphile orientation of his theory of sexuality. In this he was followed by nearly all his pupils, myself not excluded.

Not only is Ferenczi ready to accept responsibility, but he takes up a therapeutic challenge he is the first to criticise and recognise as impossible to put into practice. But even in this extravagant situation he remains true to his desire as an analyst, to review and revise the established know-how. It is for this reason that he is willing to insist on his demand for personal analysis, and a cure that must involve the repetition of the trauma in transference, so that a pre-traumatic link can be restored. On this daring journey, Ferenczi makes many discoveries: post-traumatic narcissistic splitting, identification with the aggressor, alien transplants, etc. – which cannot be discussed here.

In 1932, when Ferenczi's exclusion becomes obvious, it is made even more painful by his admission of his personal failure. His personal analysis was left unfinished. No matter what he gained along the way, he cannot claim to have completed his project. And although mutual analysis had much to teach him, it ultimately led to an impasse as well.

He admits this with great lucidity in a moving note dated June 3, 1932, bearing the eloquent heading: "No special didactic analysis!," which we suppose could constitute his analytic testament. In this note, he objects to the "training analysis" intended for future analysts, as well as to the "therapeutic analysis" conducted with patients. His conclusion is clear: all this results in analysts less well analysed than their patients. If a long analysis lasting several years is not possible, this must be corrected, he says, by "continuous complementary analysis." Although he openly criticises the training and teaching dispensed in Berlin, he also condemns mutual analysis, seeing it as "only a last resort." In this future, he says, "an authentic analysis by a stranger, without any obligation, would be better." His criticism of training analysis reserved for preselected candidates, not too neurotic and preferably physicians, leads to a firm conclusion: "The best analyst is a cured patient. Otherwise the student must first be made ill, then cured and made aware."

This criticism of "didactic analysis" is accompanied by a re-questioning of *supervision analyses*, standardised since 1920. Ferenczi always remained on the margins of the training and teaching models of the Berlin institution. He admitted seeking an alternative – yet to be devised – to a genuine and much-needed supervision in uncertain, "last-resort" situations. This was also a recognition and admission of his own difficulties and weaknesses. In his *Diary*, he noted: "Strictly supervised by the patients! No attempts [should be made] to defend oneself."

A few months before his death, Ferenczi confesses that when Eugénie introduced him to "mutual analysis," and when Elisabeth later forced him to conduct it, they were wildly but legitimately seeking to submit his practice to supervision, and to obtain what he himself could not obtain from Freud: the questioning of the desire that sustained his work as an analyst. The analytic aspect of "supervision" had now been defined.

This "last will" note expresses Ferenczi's sustained belief in analysis and in its future: "[…] a small group of men could be thoroughly analyzed – whose ambition is to know more than the patients they analyse." The strength of this desire authorises us to conclude that Ferenczi's personal analysis, so dearly paid and considered failed, was, after all, a success.

Note

1 Lugrin, Y., *Impardonnable Ferenczi, malaise dans la transmission*, Paris, Campagne-Première, 2012.

Conclusion
Possibilities for the future

Ferenczi's personal analysis experience with, and despite, Freud, with its achievements and limitations, with the promise it offered in 1922, as well as the stumbling blocks that seemed to mark its failure in 1932, confirmed Ferenczi in a belief he never abandoned. Indeed, despite the inequities to which he was subjected in the course of his lengthy and active participation in the life of the analytic movement and of its institutions, he never stopped believing in the possibility of creating, one day, "a small group of men [who] could be thoroughly analyzed." This is what we consider the essential success of this analysis, unique in its time. This belief, which resisted all adversity, is inscribed in an exemplary analytic path.

As early as 1910, in the text accompanying his proposal to create an international association, despite his lucidity concerning the inevitable group phenomena which constitute "the pathology of associations," Ferenczi expressed his hope for an association where the atmosphere is one of "mutual openness, and recognition of each member's abilities." He supposes that in such a climate "mutual surveillance will control narcissistic affects." Despite the awkward formulation, this concern with truth is noteworthy.

In 1925, when the question of lay analysis gained great interest in North America, Ferenczi denounced the difference made with no analytic basis between physicians who become analysts and lay persons who also become analysts. Instead of focusing on this arbitrary distinction which brings with it a danger of undue medicalisation in psychoanalysis, Ferenczi draws attention to "a more pertinent difference between analyzed lay analysts and untrained analysts." In this turbulent climate, he plans to create an association for "The Friends of Psychoanalysis," offering support to duly trained lay analysts. But he gains no allies for his project.

On April 22, 1928, Freud is disappointed by the virtual rejection of lay analysis. He writes: "Actually, I am only sure about you that you share my point of view without reservation." Despite this implicit support, Ferenczi was forced to relinquish his desire for the presidency of the IPA. On April 29 he describes to Freud what the orientation of his presidency would have been: "To be sure, my politics would have been less compromise-prone than his [Eitingon]; in place of that, a small crowd would have grouped around me, which, unconcerned by other interests, would do pure psychoanalysis."

In February 1929, the problem of lay analysis is still unresolved and Ferenczi makes a new proposal: "My first impression was that one has to undertake something radical in order to get free rein, e.g., resigning from the Association (under your leadership) and founding a new, small society [composed of trustworthy] adherents [...]" On June 10, more diplomatically and less aggressively, Freud advises caution: "If you don't want to destroy the IPA, you had better be careful." He also offers reassurance: "The first one who would resign from the IPA in the event that you should give in to the Americans [on] the question of lay analysis would be I, the author of 'The Question of Lay Analysis' (1926)." Freud knows that it is painful for Ferenczi to renounce the presidency of the IPA, in order to appease the Americans, who are annoyed by his analytic rigour and firmness. On December 13, 1929, Freud observes that his "paladin and secret Grand Vizier" has been distancing himself from him. He has the fleeting thought that this may signal "a step toward the creation of a new oppositional analysis."

> What I thought to myself, instead of such [blasphemy], was that you were holding it against me – or us – that we didn't give you the position that was due you of being the head of the IPA, which, in fact, did not occur in consideration of the nasty politics, the danger of increased enmity from Jones and of the disintegration of the Association.

On January 17, 1930, Ferenczi wrote Freud a long letter of clarification, since the latter continued to reproach him with the growing distance between them, instead of engaging in the discussion on doctrine Ferenczi was attempting to open. This letter lays out for the first time Ferenczi's reproaches and complaints regarding Freud's conduct of his personal analysis, but also discusses the "importance of the matters of the Association." Although he is no longer involved, Ferenczi knows what is at stake: "I appreciate the results that the Berlin Institute has to show, which can serve as a model for us all." Faithful to the analytic mission – to complete the existing know-how – a mission he assumed very early, Ferenczi ventures to make an unprecedented proposition: "To be sure, [I have thought of an addition to] the plan of organization through the creation of several new forms of [training.]"

This proposition made on January 17, 1930, is remarkably modern. Ferenczi suggests that the existing classification of analysts be expanded to include two new levels.

First, each local analytic association should make it possible for other professionals, who do not wish to become analysts, to acquire a psychoanalytic perspective on their activities: "The work of enlightenment (Univ. Extension) also belongs on the agendas of the Association [...]"

Second, the proposal of another type of affiliation – a surprisingly avant-garde suggestion: "Membership in the master school (guild) (academy) would have as a prerequisite a personal analysis, albeit one requiring years, which, however, encompasses the knowledge and mastery of the total personality." And he adds: "that which I call 'termination of the analysis.'"

On June 3, 1932, in his note under the heading "No special training analysis!," he is still saying the same thing. Clearly, he is still convinced – although he is alone in this – that the recruitment of analysts should be conditioned on the belief in the unconscious, for which he had paid so dearly in his personal analysis. In fact, we might ask ourselves if it was not the persistence, firmness, rigour and clairvoyance of this belief that caused Jacques Lacan to describe him in 1955 as "the first-generation author who most relevantly raised the question of what is required of the analyst as a person, in particular as regards the end of the treatment."

What, then, are our other reasons for considering this tormenting analysis a success?

First, because it was the very first in-depth analysis of an analyst. Second, because it involved two exceptional analysts who dared to embark on an unprecedented adventure which has not yet been examined analytically in complete detail. Indeed, the difficulties and stumbling blocks encountered in this process led Ferenczi to be the first analyst to consider the end of analysis closely, and to elevate the question of the analyst's training to the level of a debate on doctrine, never before undertaken. This analysis is also exemplary for its uncompromising quality, to which both Freud and Ferenczi consented, at the risk of losing what they most valued: their friendship and the collaboration that can only exist between two passionate men.

Bibliography

Brabant, E., Falzeder, E. and Giampieri-Deutsch, P. (Eds.) (1993–2000). *The Correspondence of Sigmund Freud and Sandor Ferenczi*, Harvard University Press, 1993: Vol. 1, 1996: Vol. 2, 2000: Vol. 3.

Ferenczi, S. (1909). Introjection and Transference, in *First Contributions to Psycho-Analysis,* Routledge, 2018.

Ferenczi, S. (1911). On the Organization of the Psycho-Analytic Movement, in *Final Contributions to the Problems and Methods of Psychoanalysis*, Routledge, 1994.

Ferenczi, S. (1913). Belief, Disbelief and Conviction, in *Further Contributions to the Theory and Technique of Psychoanalysis*, Karnac, 1994.

Ferenczi, S. (1916). On Influencing the Patient in Psycho-Analysis, in *Further Contributions to the Theory and Technique of Psychoanalysis*, Karnac, 1994.

Ferenczi, S. (1919). Technical Difficulties in the Analysis of a Case of Hysteria, in *Further Contributions to the Theory and Technique of Psychoanalysis*, Karnac, 1994.

Ferenczi, S. (1921). Psycho-Analytical Observations on Tic, in *Further Contributions to the Theory and Technique of Psychoanalysis*, Karnac, 1994.

Ferenczi, S. (1925). Stages in the Development of the Sense of Reality, in *First Contributions to Psycho-Analysis,* Routledge, 2018.

Ferenczi, S. (1926). The Phenomena of hysterical materialization, *in Further Contributions to the Theory and Technique of Psychoanalysis*, Karnac, 1994.

Ferenczi, S. (1928). The Elasticity of Psycho-Analytic Technique, in *Final Contributions to the Problems and Methods of Psychoanalysis*, Routledge, 1994.

Ferenczi, S. (1929). The Unwelcome Child and His Death Instinct, in *Final Contributions to the Problems and Methods of Psychoanalysis*, Routledge, 1994.

Ferenczi, S. (1949). Confusion of the Tongues between Adults and the Child, *The International Journal of Psychoanalysis*, 30: 225–230.

Ferenczi, S. (1988). *The Clinical Diary of Sándor Ferenczi*, Harvard University Press.

Ferenczi, S. and Rank, O. (2012) *The Development of Psycho-Analysis*, Martino Fine Books.

Fortune, C. (Ed.), *The Sandor Ferenczi – Georg Groddeck Correspondence, 1921–1933*, Open Gate Press, 2002.

Freud, S. and Breuer, J. (1895). *Studies on Hysteria*, S.E. 2: 1–321, Hogarth.

Freud, S. (1901). *On Dreams*, S.E. 5, Hogarth.

Freud, S. (1911). Formulations on the Two principles of Psychic Functioning, S.E. 12, Hogarth.

Freud, S. (1912). Recommendations to Physicians Practising Psychoanalysis, S.E. 12, Hogarth.

Freud, S. (1913). *Totem and Taboo*, S.E. 13, Hogarth.

Freud, S. (1913). On Beginning the Treatment, S.E. 12, Hogarth.

Freud, S. (1914). On Narcissism: An Introduction, S.E. 14, Hogarth.

Freud, S. (1914). On the History of the Psycho-Analytic Movement, S.E. 14, Hogarth.

Freud, S. (1915). Observations on Transference-Love, S.E 12, Hogarth.

Freud, S. (1915). A Project for a Scientific Psychology, S.E. 1, Hogarth.

Freud, S. (1917). Metapsychological Supplement to the Theory of Dreams, S.E. 14, Hogarth.

Freud, S. (1917). Mourning and Melancholia, S.E 14, Hogarth.

Freud, S. (1919). On the Teaching of Psycho-Analysis in Universities, S.E. 17, Hogarth.

Freud, S. (1920). *Beyond the Pleasure Principle*, S.E. 18, Hogarth.

Freud, S. (1921). *Group Psychology and the Analysis of the Ego*, S.E. 18, Hogarth.

Freud, S. (1926). *The Question of Lay Analysis*, S.E. 20, Hogarth.

Freud, S. (1937). Analysis Terminable and Interminable, S.E. 23, Hogarth.

Index

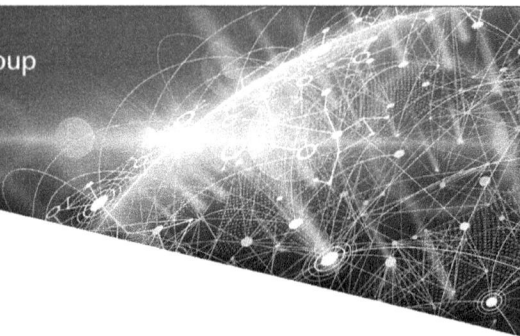

For Product Safety Concerns and Information please contact our EU
representative GPSR@taylorandfrancis.com
Taylor & Francis Verlag GmbH, Kaufingerstraße 24, 80331 München, Germany

9 780367 444990